International and Development Education

The *International and Development Education Series* focuses on the complementary areas of comparative, international, and development education. Books emphasize a number of topics ranging from key international education issues, trends, and reforms to examinations of national education systems, social theories, and development education initiatives. Local, national, regional, and global volumes (single authored and edited collections) constitute the breadth of the series and offer potential contributors a great deal of latitude based on interests and cutting-edge research. The series is supported by a strong network of international scholars and development professionals who serve on the International and Development Education Advisory Board and participate in the selection and review process for manuscript development.

Titles:

Higher Education in Asia/Pacific: Quality and the Public Good
Edited by Terance W. Bigalke and Deane E. Neubauer

Affirmative Action in China and the U.S.: A Dialogue on Inequality and Minority Education
Edited by Minglang Zhou and Ann Maxwell Hill

Critical Approaches to Comparative Education: Vertical Case Studies from Africa, Europe, the Middle East, and the Americas
Edited by Frances Vavrus and Lesley Bartlett

Curriculum Studies in South Africa: Intellectual Histories & Present Circumstances
Edited by William F. Pinar

Higher Education, Policy, and the Global Competition Phenomenon
Edited by Laura M. Portnoi, Val D. Rust, and Sylvia S. Bagley

The Search for New Governance of Higher Education in Asia
Edited by Ka-Ho Mok

International Students and Global Mobility in Higher Education: National Trends and New Directions
Edited by Rajika Bhandari and Peggy Blumenthal

Curriculum Studies in Brazil: Intellectual Histories, Present Circumstances
Edited by William F. Pinar

Access, Equity, and Capacity in Asia Pacific Higher Education
Edited by Deane Neubauer and Yoshiro Tanaka

Policy Debates in Comparative, International, and Development Education
Edited by John N. Hawkins and W. James Jacob

Forthcoming titles:

Curriculum Studies in Mexico: Intellectual Histories, Present Circumstances
Edited by William F. Pinar

Taiwan Education at the Crossroad: When Globalization Meets Localization
Chuing Prudence Chou and Gregory Ching

Increasing Effectiveness of the Community College Financial Model: A Global Perspective for the Global Economy
Edited by Stewart E. Sutin, Daniel Derrico, Rosalind Latiner Raby, and Edward J. Valeau

POLICY DEBATES IN COMPARATIVE, INTERNATIONAL, AND DEVELOPMENT EDUCATION

EDITED BY
JOHN N. HAWKINS
AND
W. JAMES JACOB

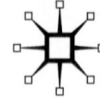

POLICY DEBATES IN COMPARATIVE, INTERNATIONAL, AND DEVELOPMENT EDUCATION
Copyright © John N. Hawkins and W. James Jacob, 2011.

First published in 2011 by
PALGRAVE MACMILLAN®
in the United States—a division of St. Martin's Press LLC,
175 Fifth Avenue, New York, NY 10010.

Where this book is distributed in the UK, Europe and the rest of the world,
this is by Palgrave Macmillan, a division of Macmillan Publishers Limited,
registered in England, company number 785998, of Houndmills,
Basingstoke, Hampshire RG21 6XS.

Palgrave Macmillan is the global academic imprint of the above companies
and has companies and representatives throughout the world.

Palgrave® and Macmillan® are registered trademarks in the United States,
the United Kingdom, Europe and other countries.

ISBN: 978–0–230–62067–4

Library of Congress Cataloging-in-Publication Data

   Policy debates in comparative, international, and development
education / edited by John N. Hawkins, W. James Jacob.
      p. cm.—(International & development education)
      ISBN-13: 978–0–230–62067–4 (hardback)
      ISBN-10: 0–230–62067–1
      1. Education and globalization—Government policy. 2. Education and
state. 3. Comparative education. I. Hawkins, John N. II. Jacob, W. James.

LC71.P567 2011
379—dc22   2010049029

A catalogue record of the book is available from the British Library.

Design by Newgen Imaging Systems (P) Ltd., Chennai, India.

First edition: September 2011

10 9 8 7 6 5 4 3 2 1

Printed and bound in Great Britain by
CPI Antony Rowe, Chippenham and Eastbourne

Contents

Figures

Tables

Series Editors Introduction

We are pleased to introduce this new series by Palgrave Macmillan, focused on International and Development Education. In conceptualizing this series we took into account the extraordinary increase in the scope and depth of research on education in a global and international context. The range of topics and issues being addressed by scholars worldwide is enormous and clearly reflects the growing expansion and quality of research being conducted on international and development education. Our goal is to cast a wide net for the most innovative and novel manuscripts, both single-authored and edited volumes, without constraints as to the level of education, geographical region, or methodology (whether disciplinary or interdisciplinary). In the process, we have also developed two subseries as part of the main series: one is cosponsored by the East West Center in Honolulu, Hawaii, drawing from their distinguished program, the International Forum on Education 2020 (IFE 2020) Asia Pacific; and the other is a publication partnership with the Higher Education Special Interest Group of the Comparative and International Education Society that highlights trends and themes on international higher education.

The issues that will be highlighted in this series are those focused on capacity, access, and equity, three interrelated topics that are central to educational transformation as it appears today around the world. There are many paradoxes and asymmetries surrounding these issues, which include problems of both excess capacity and deficits, wide access to facilities as well as severe restrictions, and all the complexities that are included in the equity debate. Closely related to this critical triumvirate is the overarching concern with quality assurance, accountability, and assessment. As educational systems have expanded, so have the needs and demands for quality assessment, with implications for accreditation and accountability. Intergroup relations, multiculturalism, and gender issues comprise another cluster of concerns facing most educational systems in differential ways when one looks at the change in educational systems in an international context. Diversified notions of the structure of knowledge and curriculum development occupy another important niche in educational change at both the precollegiate and collegiate levels. Finally, how systems are managed and governed are key policy issues for educational policymakers worldwide. These and other key elements of the education and social change environment have guided this series and have been reflected in the books that have already appeared and those that will appear in the future. We welcome proposals on these and other topics from as wide a range of scholars and practitioners as possible. We believe that the world of educational change is dynamic, and our goal is to reflect the very best work being done in these and other areas.

The current volume serves as a broad introduction to the series, and we have identified several key policy areas that form the foundation for the series. Policy debates are at the core of many issues on education, and they often swing like a pendulum, depending on which political party holds power or which perspective is widely accepted by scientific communities. The contributing authors of this volume introduce policy debates from dialectical perspectives. They begin by providing a background and global overview of each topic of debate, which is followed by case study examples from one or more countries, offering readers a local and critical perspective on the topic. Social justice issues of gender, indigenousness, access, and equity are at the forefront of education policy debates. Most contributors include social justice themes either as the primary focus or as a subtheme of their overall topic. As an incubator of knowledge for so many centuries, higher education institutions often take the lead in research and development, innovation, and progressive education policies and practices. Institutional reform and progressivism is portrayed in the several chapters with a higher education focus. Whereas most education policies evolve naturally from within nation-states, some policies are imposed by external sources. Foreign aid programs form the policy debate topics introduced in the final section of this volume. Contributors offer case study examples from different regions and countries to show how education policies are influenced, for good for bad, through external aid agencies and governments.

Policy debates in general, and education policy debates in particular, are relative to so many hinging factors and are often cloaked behind shifting values, norms, and education methodologies. The policy issues introduced in this volume are central and active topics of debate in comparative, international, and development education (CIDE). An overarching goal of this volume is to paint a landscape depicting the delicate nature of key policy debate issues in CIDE. Regardless of which side of the debate you find yourself, we hope that the chapters in this volume will help bridge the gaps, sometimes very wide ones, between education policy and social justice by overcoming misunderstandings and ensuring correct practice.

JOHN N. HAWKINS
University of California, Los Angeles

W. JAMES JACOB
University of Pittsburgh

Acknowledgments

The editors would like to thank all the contributing authors to this volume. Without their unique contributions to policy debates in comparative, international, and development education, this book could not have been written.

We thank Palgrave Macmillan's Burke Gerstenschlager and Kaylan Connally for their support of this research compilation endeavor. Heejin Park provided editorial support throughout the review process and in direct correspondence with contributors.

We are also grateful to the UCLA-based Tomomi Takagi Memorial Fund for providing support as research for this volume was conducted.

Abbreviations and Acronyms

ACC	Accreditation Committee of Cambodia
ADB	Asian Development Bank
ADCSC	Academic Degrees Committee of the State Council (China)
ADEA	Association for the Development of Education in Africa
AIDS	Acquired immunodeficiency syndrome
ALBA	Lebanese Academy for Fine Arts
AUB	American University of Beirut (Lebanon)
AusAID	Australian Government's Overseas Aid Program
AVU	African Virtual University
BAU	Beirut Arab University (Lebanon)
BNS	Baltic News Service
CAP	Concepts about Print
CCP	Chinese Communist Party
CCPCC	Chinese Communist Party Central Committee
CE	*Comparative Education*
CER	*Comparative Education Review*
CERN	China Education and Research Network
CFCRS	Chinese-Foreign Cooperation in Running Schools
CGS	Centre for Governance Studies (Bangladesh)
CIDA	Canadian International Development Agency
CIDE	Comparative, international, and development education
CMOE	China Ministry of Education
DAC	Development Assistance Committee
DFID	Department for International Development (UK)
DLE	Digital learning environment
DPs	Development Partners
DPE	Directorate of Primary Education (Bangladesh)
DPEO	District Primary Education Office (Bangladesh)
DRC	Democratic Republic of the Congo
DSE	Deutsche Stiftung fur Internationale Entwicklung
EC	European Commission

ECP	Enhanced Cooperation Program
EDN	Educator's Development Network
EFA	Education for All
EGRA	Early Grade Reading Assessments
ELATE	E-learning and Teacher Education Project (Uganda)
EMIS	Education Management Information System
ESP	Education Strategic Plan
ESTEEM	Effective School for Enhanced Education Management *Project (Bangladesh)*
EQUIP2	Education Quality Improvement Program 2
EU	European Union
FAS	Femmes Africa Solidarité
FCUBE	Free Compulsory Universal Basic Education Programme (Ghana)
FedEx	Federal Express
FMRP	Finance and Management Reform *Project* (Bangladesh)
FMU	Financial Management Unit (Bangladesh)
FPE	Free Primary Education (Malawi)
FTI	Fast Track Initiative
FY	Fiscal Year
GABLE	Girls' Attainment in Basic Literacy and Education Programme (Malawi)
GAD	Gender and development
GATE	Global Alliance for Transnational Education
GATS	General Agreement on Trade in Services
GDP	Gross domestic product
GER	Gross enrollment rate
GIS	Global information system
GM	Gender mainstreaming
GOB	Government of Bangladesh
GOU	Government of Uganda
GUNI–AP	Global University Network for Innovation–Asia and the Pacific
HEC	Higher Education Commission (Pakistan)
HEEACT	Higher Education Evaluation and Accreditation Council (Taiwan)
HEI	Higher education institution
HIV	Human immunodeficiency virus
HR	Human resource/s
HRD	Human resource development
HRDM	Human resources development and management

ICT	Information and communication technology
IJED	*International Journal of Education Development*
ILO	International Labour Organization
IMHE	Programme on Institutional Management in Higher Education
INQAAHE	International Network of Quality Assurance Agencies in Higher Education
IRA	International Reading Association (USA)
IRR	Inter-rater reliability
ISO	International Organization for Standards
IT	Information technology
JICA	Japan International Cooperation Agency
JUAA	Japan University Accreditation Association
KESSP	Kenya Education Sector Support Programme
KYU	Kyambogo University (Uganda)
LAU	Lebanese American University
LGED	Local Government Engineering Department (Bangladesh)
LIEP	Language-in-education policies
LPR	Leave Prior to Retirement
LU	Lebanese University
MaTVE	Ministry of Technical and Vocational Education (Lebanon)
MDG/s	Millennium Development Goal/s
MEHE	Ministry of Education and Higher Education (Lebanon)
MEXT	Ministry of Education, Culture, Sports, Science, and Technology (Japan)
MFPED	Ministry of Finance, Planning, and Economic Development (Uganda)
MIS	Management information system
MIT	Massachusetts Institute of Technology
MLA	Monitoring Learning Achievement
MOE	Ministry of Education
MOEC	Ministry of Education and Culture (Tanzania)
MOES	Ministry of Education and Sports (Uganda)
MOESS	Ministry of Education, Science and Sports (Ghana)
MOEST	Ministry of Education, Science and Technology (Kenya)
MOF	Ministry of Finance
MOI	Medium of instruction
MOPME	Ministry of Primary and Mass Education (Bangladesh)
MoYS	Ministry of Youth and Sports (Lebanon)

MNEaFA	Ministry of National Education and Fine Arts (Lebanon)
MPO	Monthly pay order
MSN	Microsoft Network
MT	Mother tongue
MTDS	Medium Term Development Strategy
MTEF	Medium-Term Expenditure Framework
MTN	Mobile Telephone Networks
MTR	Mid-Term Review
MUK	Makerere University (Uganda)
MUST	Mbarara University of Science and Technology (Uganda)
MWHC	Ministry of Works, Housing and Communications (Uganda)
NAAC	National Assessment and Accreditation Council (India)
NAEYC	National Association for the Education of Young Children (USA)
NAPE	National Assessment Progress in Education (Uganda)
NARC	National Rainbow Coalition (Kenya)
NATO	North Atlantic Treaty Organization
NCLB	No Child Left Behind
NDEA	National Defense Education Act (USA)
NEIDGE	National Evaluation Institute for Degree Granting Education
NGO	Nongovernmental organization
NIAD-UE	National Institute of Academic Degrees and University Evaluation (Japan)
NPR	National Public Radio (USA)
NTU	Nanyang Technical University (Singapore)
NUS	National University of Singapore
NZAID	New Zealand's International Aid and Development Agency
OECD	Organization for Economic Co-operation and Development
OLRs	Open learning resources
PEC	Primary Education Cadre
PEDP II	Second Primary Education Development Programme (Bangladesh)
PETS	Public Expenditure Tracking Survey
PGDE	Post Graduate Diploma in Education
PIRLS	Progress in International Ready Literacy Study
PISA	Programme for International Student Assessment
PNG	Papua New Guinea

PPC	Program Progression Chart
PRAESA	Project for the Study of Alternative Education in South Africa
PRC	People's Republic of China
PRSP	Poverty Reduction Strategy Paper
PTA	Parent Teacher Association
QA	Quality assurance
QECs	Quality Enhancement Cells
RIHE	Research Institute for Higher Education (Japan)
RMB	*Renminbi* or People's Currency (China)
ROC	Republic of China (Taiwan)
SACMEQ	Southern Africa Consortium for Monitoring Educational Quality
SEC	State Education Commission (China)
SFAI	School Fee Abolition Initiative
SLIP	School Level Improvement Plan
SMRS	Systematic Method for Reading Success
SMC	School Management Committees
SSA	Sub-Saharan Africa
SWAp	Sector Wide Approach
SWC	Simon Wiesenthal Center
TIB	Transparency International Bangladesh
TIMMS	Trends in International Mathematics and Science Study
TNCs	Transnational corporations
TWAEA	Taiwan Assessment and Evaluation Association
UCLA	University of California, Los Angeles
UDSM	University of Dar es Salaam (Tanzania)
UEO	Upazila Education Office (Bangladesh)
UGC	University Grants Commission (India)
UMU	Uganda Martyrs University
UN	United Nations
UNAIDS	Joint United Nations Programme on HIV/AIDS
UNDP	United Nations Development Programme
UNEB	Uganda National Examinations Board
UNESCO	United Nations Educational, Scientific and Cultural Organization
UNICEF	United Nations Children's Fund
UPE	Universal Primary Education
UPS	United Postal Service
USAID	United States Agency for International Development
USJ	University of St. Joseph (Lebanon)
USSR	Union of Soviet Socialist Republics

WBI   World Bank Institute
WHO   World Health Organization
WID   Women in Development
wpm   words per minute
WTO   World Trade Organization
Y2K   Year 2000

Part 1

Overview of Key International Education Policy Debates

Chapter 1

Setting the Global Education Policy Stage: Shifts, Trends, and Perspectives

W. James Jacob and John N. Hawkins

Introduction

The field of comparative, international, and development education (CIDE) has a long and distinguished history, and it now occupies a prominent place in the pantheon of knowledge in most universities worldwide. Numerous societies exist in as many countries, and a World Congress of Comparative Education Societies represents a sort of umbrella organization. Professional peer-refereed journals abound in the field, and a variety of methodologies, principally drawn from the social sciences, are utilized in the conduct of CIDE research (Jacob and Cheng 2005). Indeed, the field has matured over the years, and as a result some enduring policy issues have risen to the surface and dominate the discussion today. This volume surveys some of the more critical of these policy issues.

When perusing the pages of *Comparative Education* and *Comparative Education Review,* as well as other journals in the field, it becomes evident that the authors represent a considerable variety of intellectual and methodological traditions, which form the foundation of the policy issues that comprise the chapters of this book (Hawkins and Rust 2001; some portions of this section are from the article by Hawkins and Rust). While the emphasis on a few perspectives has changed over time, three principal policy perspectives tend to be represented in most contemporary articles published in the top journals in the field. For purposes of simplicity we might refer to these policy perspectives as follows: perspectives based on area studies; perspectives based on the social science discipline, or interdisciplinary fields; and those based on development/planning studies (with considerable overlap between perspectives in some cases). These perspectives are also reflected in the academy in the broad area of international studies, where they have in recent years been in considerable conflict with each other for legitimacy, power, and funding (Hawkins et al. 1998).

Area studies approaches to international studies have a long tradition in Western scholarship, and in the United States have been best represented by post–World War II legislation for area and language studies programs and centers (*National Defense Education Act* Title VI—NDEA VI). In a general way, area studies approaches can be defined as a perspective that utilizes a holistic analysis of a specific place and culture to build understanding and knowledge. These approaches typically combine disciplinary training with language and area knowledge. Scholars from this tradition typically will have expertise in language and area knowledge, extensive field experience, and either social science or humanities backgrounds (Bennett 1951).

Scholars identifying with a social science disciplinary base tend to give allegiance to their discipline and to the pursuit of knowledge that is not contextualized. That is, they seek to explain and predict phenomena in terms of context-independent elements that have been abstracted and dislodged from the everyday world. For disciplinary studies, the national setting or region is not the primary unit of analysis, but it serves as an appropriate setting where problems and issues, and theory and methods, can be examined. Scholars in this tradition often do not have extensive language and cultural preparation, and extensive field experience in a particular setting is rare (Hawkins et al. 1998).

Development studies can be seen as a complex mixture of area studies and discipline studies. A subset of development studies is educational planning, which is focused on identifying optimal national investments in education as a means of stimulating and even optimizing economic expansion. Development/planning scholars often use a transdisciplinary approach and comparative applications of the social sciences. However, they also utilize a holistic approach, common to area studies, to understand social, economic, and political change. As is the case with the social science disciplines, practitioners of development studies often do not focus on a region or area, and most do not have fluent language skills or extensive field experience in a particular setting.

In the two decades following World War II, all three of these perspectives were represented in comparative education. By the 1960s the field had clearly identified itself with the social sciences. In the process, the concept of theory underwent a dramatic shift. In the social sciences, theory referred to the lens through which social scientists viewed the subject of study, rather than the object of research itself. Specialists concentrating on making comparative education a more "scientific" enterprise complained that comparative education had been linked too closely with "comparative philosophy of foreign education," and they wished to shift it toward an "empirical approach of the social sciences" (Eckstein and Noah 1969).

Prior to the 1970s, area studies perspectives had also thrived in comparative education research, and centers and programs in universities were well supported. As the cold war wound down, so did support for these programs; combined with new hiring practices for educational research, there was a decline in political and financial support as well. The emphasis began to shift toward problem areas, and discipline-focused research began to reassert itself. Consequently, support for language and cultural studies declined in recent years, and scholars with vast area knowledge have not been seen at the forefront of research. Thus, one of the principal contradictions is that just at a time when global relations are being redefined, new nations are being formed, ethnic tensions are at an all-time high, and deep knowledge of the contexts in which change is occurring sheds light on the change process, the intellectual ground has shifted away from the viability of the area studies model.

The area studies model had assumed that with linguistic competence came a form of ethnographic transparency that allowed the area specialists to legitimize their work and the representative claims that came with it. Linguistic competence was not enough, however, for area studies. It needed to be conjoined with grounding in the social sciences, and it was this conjunction that completed the area scholar's training and research.

It was also during the 1960s that the development/planning perspective became a visible part of the field. This was achieved particularly through the establishment of a center for the study of development education at Stanford University. The University of Chicago had already begun efforts toward development activities through the work of scholars such as C. Arnold Anderson, Philip Foster, and Mary Jean Bowman. The planning perspective also grew tremendously as a field because of its use by the developing nations with the support of international and national agencies such as UNESCO, the World Bank, and the Institute for International Education. In the case of the World Bank, planning became a prerequisite for the receipt of assistance (Farrell 1997).

Within the context of these policy perspectives, a variety of policy issues have emerged in the field. Policy often precedes practice in most formal education contexts worldwide. While education policy is at the forefront of education movements globally, many scholars argue that the education sector is a laggard among social government sectors because it does not keep pace with major changes in the global economy, technology, and the job market. This often translates into outdated and irrelevant curricula for many millions of students, teachers, and administrators at all levels.

Significant and timely policy shifts are often difficult to formalize, as it takes many years of debate in parliaments and other governing bodies. By the time education policies are finally implemented, some policy items are already outdated and need to be revisited by policymakers. Some of the key education policy debates include issues relating to social justice, curriculum content, teacher preparation (both preservice and in-service teaching), administration, infrastructure development, quality, and governance. This volume seeks to focus on an analysis of major educational policy issues and also contribute to the complementary fields of comparative, international, and development education.

The volume is structured around current education policy trends at the global, regional, national, and local levels, and the chapters are lodged within one or more of the three policy perspectives outlined earlier. The broad themes contained in the 13 chapters of this volume include:

- How comparative education research has evolved over the years
- Transnational higher education
- Education and the knowledge industry
- Higher education and quality assurance
- Strategic planning in higher education
- Curriculum reform in higher education
- Gender, equality, equity, and excellence in education
- The debate on "reading" in educational reform
- Emerging democratic accountability
- The challenge of development and aid in education
- The challenge of universal primary education
- "Time and learning" in school

Contributing authors to this volume include a mix of leading CIDE scholars and practitioners. Virtually every major region in the world is represented in this volume, with case study examples from Africa, Middle East, Asia, North America, Latin America, and Oceania.

In Part I, a brief overview of key international education policy debates is introduced. Chapter 2 begins, appropriately enough, with a historical survey of the field by Val Rust and Xuehong Liao. Their focus is on the cognitive structure of the field as revealed through methodology. They look at the evolution of research strategies in comparative education since the time it became an academic field of study. Research strategies in all fields of study are closely connected with the terms "method" and "methodology." These terms have been so intertwined that it is difficult to sort them out in a meaningful way. The terms are inextricably associated with intentions of academic fields to be scientific, and in this chapter the authors clarify the nature not only of methods and methodology but also of the epistemology of the field. This exposition helps set the agenda for the subsequent sections and chapters.

Part II of the book focuses on policy debates as they relate specifically to the higher education subsector. Ka Ho Mok and Xiaozhou Xu's chapter 3 on transnational higher education in Zhejiang, China, provides a critical analysis of China's educational emergence and puts this phenomenon in the historical context of the economic transition that began in the 1970s. One of the features of this opening up of China was the establishment of transnational higher educational institutions. A number of students from Zhejiang province were enrolled in these institutions, and the authors place this experience in the context of globalization, marketization, and the public-private debate. The experience has raised for Chinese policy-makers several issues of quality assurance, public-private boundaries, and the nature of the regulatory regime for higher education in China in a general sense.

In chapter 4, the policy debate shifts to the notion of the knowledge society. Dean Neubauer examines five aspects of contemporary processes of social change and develops the basis for what Neubauer hopes will be a continuing dialogue on the implications of these phenomena for educational policy and how education is done in the coming decade. Neubauer concludes that education in its root sense is a knowledge enterprise and that the logics that are impelling change among more readily recognizable parts of the industry are affecting it as well. He identifies five phenomena that, though they are familiar to many, have not been examined in a systematic manner. In the order of their discussion, these phenomena are: (1) the increasing boundarylessness of our globalized world; (2) the continued emergence of networks in society and of a networked society; (3) re- and de-statusing as they take place within organizations migrating from industrial to Information Technology (IT) network models and practices; (4) the revaluing of information within the new economics of digitalization as represented by the Long Tail; and (5) *search* and its implications for how we do information and how it does us.

The focus in chapter 5 is on the ubiquitous phenomenon of quality assurance and how this has become a major policy issue worldwide. Hawkins notes that the policy context in which the heightened interest in quality assurance occurs in Asia is particularly interesting. Just as we watched the happy anarchy of higher education change in the United States in the 1970s and 1980s, universities in Asia are also experiencing a somewhat different shift in emphasis between themselves and their host societies. While decentralization of higher education is occurring on the one hand, a contradictory central (i.e., Ministry of Education [MOE] or other state body) obsession with quality assurance is occurring on the other, resulting in what some scholars refer to as centralized decentralization. In this chapter, some illustrative national examples of quality assurance trends and issues are presented, along with a brief outline of the policy context in which this is occurring. Throughout the region, a number of factors influence the quality assurance movement. Higher education has become more diverse and international, it is more available but there is less money to go around, the private sector has expanded, and governance of higher education has undergone dramatic changes, all of which has resulted in more competition. The net consequence has been a demand for more accountability. Quality assurance has in some instances replaced external controls by the state, yet the state remains very much involved in the quality assurance process.

Chapter 6 focuses on the critical issue of strategic planning and uses Lebanon as a case study. Hana El-Ghali, John L. Yeager, and Zeinab Zein note that the 140-year development of Lebanon's higher education subsector has resulted in the current system consisting of the national Lebanese University and several private institutions. The authors note that Lebanon has been characterized by significant internal disruption that has contributed to a damaged infrastructure, loss of life, increased population displacement, poverty, and social inequalities. These disruptions have contributed to a difficult policy environment. As a result, several national reforms, including a strategic plan, have been initiated by the Ministry of Education and Higher Education (MEHE) to assist in the future development of the higher education sector.

The final chapter of Part II (chapter 7) introduces policy shifts in information and communications technology (ICT) and media in developing countries. With the decline of government/public funding to the higher education subsector, Christopher B. Mugimu and Connie Ssebbunga Masembe note that institutions have to learn how to do more with less so as to prepare graduates to become innovative, creative, and entrepreneurial for the private and public sectors. It therefore becomes a government strategy to reform and improve curricula and instruction in priority disciplines to enhance quality and relevance of higher education particularly to meet the national development needs of a diverse clientele. The realities in paradigm shifts in pedagogy, delivery of instruction, and teaching in higher education are not clear. The government has played important roles in shaping ICT policies in higher education and encouraging these institutions to utilize new technologies to transform teaching, learning, and technology research and development. This chapter describes various case studies implementing ICT policies and curriculum reform, challenges, and lessons learnt that could be utilized by other tertiary institutions in the policy formation process to improve their capacity in resource-poor contexts.

In Part III the focus shifts to those policy debates that have an enduring impact on educational systems. In chapter 8, Maureen Porter examines both the historical and current concepts and definitions of gender equality in education from case studies of multiple countries. The findings are based on public policy consequences of the changing trends of gender participation at all levels of the education sector. Investment in education, for both boys and girls, with a gender-based framework has been acknowledged consistently as the single and most powerful vehicle of self-advancement and fulfillment of developmental outcomes for present and future generations; and it is also the most important determinant of national development, with positive implications for all other measures of progress. While many policies have been established in theory, the actual implementation of these policies seems to fall behind in many countries, which has particularly rendered females at a disadvantage with respect to many educational opportunities. This chapter highlights several of the primary causes that work against gender equity in a global context.

Luis Crouch and Amber K. Gove follow with chapter 9, which is focused on education policy and quality for students in the context of a developing world. One of the key problems facing nations in attempting to develop an educational policy for access and quality assurance is the dilemma of scale and timeliness. The authors of this innovative chapter argue that policymakers are able, by focusing on the subject of reading in the early grades, to identify a useful "entry-point into quality," one that is easily measurable and upon which the various stakeholders can more easily agree. They discuss in detail the development of a useful tool in this endeavor, the Early Grades Reading Assessment instrument, and show how it can be applied in the context of a developing nation, all with valuable implications for quality assurance.

In chapter 10, Doyle Stevick provides an interesting discussion of how Estonia responded to forms of international pressure as part of the European Union (EU). In addition to the influence of globalization, broadly understood, education systems in European Union countries are bound by transnational regulatory regimes. The educational prescriptions developed by long-term members of the EU are not always welcome in the countries of the former Soviet bloc. Some, in fact, face overwhelming domestic opposition. National governments—not the EU—face the consequences of unpopular policies in the voting booth. Governments have a strong incentive to pursue policies that placate conflicting majority groups in a democracy. Perhaps no case is a better exemplar than Holocaust education. Western Europe and the United States hold Nazi Germany as one of the greatest evils in human history; however, those that endured Soviet dominion disagree. Estonia, under NATO and EU pressure, adopted a Holocaust education day policy to satisfy foreign demands, but it included a voluntary provision and noncommittal implementation to avoid domestic recriminations. This resulted in a non-policy, a shell that finesses conflicting pressures.

In chapter 11, Elizabeth Cassity discusses Australian aid and education policy in Papua New Guinea (PNG). Donor coordination, harmonization, aid effectiveness, participation, good governance, and sustainable growth are familiar keywords in policy documents generated by bilateral and multilateral agencies. This chapter examines the role of bilateral aid agencies in shaping education policy reforms globally, and the role of the Australian Government Overseas Aid Program (AusAID) in the current global development environment, with a particular focus on PNG. Since 1975, Australia has been the most significant aid donor in PNG, both in terms of volume and impact on policy formation. AusAID currently accounts for 70 percent of PNG's foreign aid budget; yet, PNG's development indicators are some of the lowest worldwide. This raises some serious concerns about aid effectiveness. The Australian Government's *Port Moresby Declaration*, signed in March 2008, reaffirmed Australia's policy commitment to working with Pacific nations and the international community. This chapter explores the ways AusAID has been reframing its engagement with the PNG Government through a sector-wide approach in an attempt to improve educational quality and equity.

Mikiko Nishimura and Albert Byamugisha shift the focus to Sub-Saharan Africa (SSA) in chapter 12. Universal Primary Education (UPE) Policy in the form of fee abolition has become popular in many countries in SSA as they seek to achieve Education for All (EFA). Recent uniformity of the educational policies in SSA in general, and UPE policy in particular, suggests that there should be studies to examine how these seemingly similar policies are responding to the capacity and needs of each country. This chapter attempts to analyze how UPE policies have been formed, implemented, and evaluated in the region, and what kinds of policy challenges have been raised from comparative perspectives.

Finally, in chapter 13, Audrey-Marie Schuh Moore, Joseph DeStefano, and Elizabeth Adelman tackle the elusive policy issue of the relationship between instructional time and student achievement, with a focus on issues of length, type, and focus of time. They draw on data from case studies of four countries: Ethiopia, Guatemala, Honduras, and Nepal. The loss of time due to inappropriate nonacademic activities in the classroom is just one of the many interesting findings of relevance to policymakers. This loss of valuable academic time on nonacademic tasks is accentuated in the four nations investigated, and the authors offer a variety of innovative suggestions for improving this critical educational relationship.

The 13 chapters of this volume cover a wide territory geographically as well as methodologically. Together they present the complexity of the policy issues facing the field of comparative and development education and at the same time illustrate the range of policy responses that have been offered by governments, NGOs, and a wide range of educational agencies, as well as specific higher education agencies. It is our hope that these studies will be useful for students, teachers, and policymakers alike.

References

Bennett, Wendell C. 1951. *Area Studies in American Universities*. New York: Social Science Research Council.

Eckstein, Max, and Harold Noah. 1969. *Toward a Science of Comparative Education*. London: Collier-Macmillan.

Farrell, Joseph P. 1997. "A Retrospective on Educational Planning in Comparative Education." *Comparative Education Review* 41 (3): 277–313.

Hawkins, John N. and Val D. Rust. 2001. "Shifting Perspectives in Comparative Education." *Compare* 37 (4): 501–506.

Hawkins, John N., et al. 1998. *International Education in the New Global Era*. Los Angeles: UCLA.

Jacob, W. James, and Sheng Yao Cheng. 2005. "Mapping Theories in Comparative, International, and Development Education (CIDE) Research." In *Global Trends in Educational Policy*, ed. David P. Baker and Alexander W. Wiseman, 221–258. New York: Elsevier Science, Ltd.

Chapter 2

The Evolving Nature of Comparative Education Research

Val D. Rust and Xuehong Liao

Introduction

Methods and methodology are fundamental to the cognitive structure of any field of study (Wells 1981). Their nature and role have generated a great deal of debate, both within the field of comparative education and, more generally, within the academic community. The purpose of this chapter is to describe how research strategies have evolved since comparative education became an academic field of study.

Method, Methodology, and Epistemology

The terms "method" and "methodology," and, from a philosophical perspective, "epistemology," are intrinsic to research strategies in all fields of study. But the terms have been so intertwined that it is difficult to sort them out in a meaningful way. Yet, it is important to explore the different emphases they represent, in order that researchers may be guided in the overall design of their studies and readers may more critically assess research results. Thus, in this section, we try to disentangle these intertwined terms.

Method

A research method usually refers to a technique or a way of gathering evidence (Harding 1987). Harding talks about three basic categories of evidence-gathering techniques: listening to (or interrogating) informants (e.g., interviews and survey questionnaires), observing behavior (e.g., participant observation), and examining historical traces and records (e.g., collecting documents). These techniques are all forms of data collection. Phillips points to another level of research method, data analysis. When deciding on a method of data collection, one has to decide about what kind of information should be sought, from what sources, and under what circumstances (Phillips 1976). When one decides on methods of data analysis, one has to decide about how to make sense out of the data that has been collected. This process of deciding on an appropriate research method moves the researcher into the realm of methodology and epistemology.

Research Methodology

Whereas "method" refers to a specific research technique, methodology identifies a general approach to studying research topics (Willig 2008). In other words, research methodology points to the larger context for the methods being applied. Various methodologies usually have varying theoretical implications, and they make differing theoretical assumptions of how research does, or should, proceed (Harding 1987). Thus, methodological issues involve the relationship between the researcher and the object of research, and they also involve questions about the selection of research methods (that is, methods of data collection and data analysis) based on theoretical grounds. In a sense, methodology is a form of justification of the choice of particular research methods.

The first academic scholars of comparative education, such as Isaac Kandel (1930), Nicholas Hans (1955), and Friedrich Schneider (1961), argued that education can only be understood within the context of a country's broad economic, political, cultural, and social forces. Such assumptions demanded that they not only describe educational systems in detail but also explore the meaning of educational phenomena by interpreting the economic, political, cultural, and social conditions within which an educational system is found. Thus, their theoretical assumptions defined what kinds of data to collect and how to interpret the collected data.

Epistemological Issues

Epistemology is the branch of philosophy that deals with the study of knowledge, how we know what is real or true. The term epistemology comes from the Greek word *epistēmē*, meaning knowledge. We all hold assumptions about the world and how we can best understand it. We have an epistemological perspective. People taking different philosophical positions will have different answers to epistemological questions. For example, those who believe in "naturalism" claim that knowledge is gained by identifying natural causes and effects, and by testing explanations of cause/effect links to see if the explanation holds true. But the neorealist sees a dualistic reality, and truth exists when what is in the mind is identical to what is "out there."

Methodology is also concerned with how we know, but in a concrete sense. It involves the practice of research, while epistemology involves broad philosophical assumptions about *how* we know.

These concepts of epistemology, methodology, and method can be organized hierarchically, with epistemology as the broadest and most inclusive concept, followed by methodology, and then methods. Not everyone would agree with this organization. Thus, in some approaches, methodology is considered as higher than epistemology in the hierarchical relationship. Helen Longino, for example, advocates a *methodological approach* involving communicative rationality (advocated by Habermas) to resolve difficulties between epistemologies (Longino 2002; Habermas 1984–1989). However, methods can almost always be seen as following the epistemology/methodology nexus.

Methodological Debates in Comparative Education

Comparative education has a long methodological tradition. That is, research design has been concerned not only with methods of data collection and data analysis but also with how such choices are justifiable based on a theoretical background. The theoretical orientation of early scholars in the field, such as Kandel, Hans, and Schneider, drove them to go beyond description of education systems, to look at the political, cultural, and social context in order to interpret the meaning of educational phenomena.

As the field of education sought to become more *scientific*, methodological debates shifted their focus to issues of the more conventional social sciences: sociology, economics, and political science. Brian Holmes (1977, 1984) and George Bereday (1964) argued whether research should proceed inductively or deductively. Earlier comparative education scholars took for granted that the process was inductive. Educational systems were first described, and then these systems were interpreted from the broader economic, political, cultural, and social context. Bereday's *comparative methodology* was inductive in that it began with descriptions of two or more countries whose systems were interpreted from that broader context. Then the data for the countries was juxtaposed. Finally this data was compared. Clearly, this methodology was inductive in nature. Brian Holmes challenged this tradition, relying on John Dewey (1910), Karl Popper (1963), and others to expound on what is called *hypothetico-deductive approach* to research. He criticized his colleagues for the tendency to begin the research process with descriptions of educational phenomena, arriving at theory only at a later stage in the process. This discussion has not yet ceased and continues as a methodological issue in, for instance, debate over what is called *grounded theory* (Strauss and Glasser 1967).

The methodological debates that characterized comparative education in the 1960s and 1970s have not been sustained. There is almost no contemporary discussion of the basic issue of inductive versus deductive research, quantitative versus qualitative research, or analysis versus synthesis, and, in fact, since 1985, studies published in journals of comparative education make almost no reference to the issues so vital to earlier scholars (Rust 1999).

Research Strategies in Comparative Education

Comparative education researchers publish primarily, though not exclusively, in journals devoted to the field. We conducted a study at the University of California, Los Angeles, that sought to document the various research strategies in the field. We analyzed three data sets drawn from the *Comparative Education Review* (*CER*), *Comparative Education* (*CE*), and the *International Journal of Education Development* (*IJED*) (Rust 1999), comprising a total of 427 studies appearing in these journals in 1985, 1987, 1989, 1991, 1993, and 1995. To gain some historical sense, we created a second data set consisting of 112 studies drawn from every issue of the *CER* and *CE* for the 1964–1966 period.[1] The unit of analysis was the individual journal article, the data set being the research strategies for data collection and analysis in each article.

Of the 112 studies for the 1964–1966 period, there were a total of 158 data collection strategies; certain studies used more than one strategy. We found a narrow band of data collection strategies. Studies rarely included data from existing data sets, such as census data, UNESCO data, and so on. Nor did they indicate involvement in conventional field work, requiring some combination of participation/observation, formal interview, and questionnaire. Comparative educators have long insisted that "being there" is essential not only to collect data but to interpret data, and also to write articles and books (Geertz 1988). However, from 1964 to 1966, most of the early comparative education articles were written as if they were literature reviews of available materials concerning educational conditions in the countries that were being studied; and the authors of most of these articles failed to provide any indication of the contribution "being there" made to the manuscript. Finally, studies did not include what we judged to be project evaluations or content analysis of textbooks and other texts. If these findings reflect the field at large during the first half of the 1960s, we must conclude that those publishing in the field relied heavily on contemporary and historical literature. Thus, these studies may be described as interpretive; rarely were any other data collection strategies adopted.

In contrast, in 1985, 1987, 1989, 1991, 1993, and 1995, examples of data collection found in articles published in *CER*, *CE*, and *IJED*, relied on social science research strategies of the day. There is one glaring omission: experimental studies, using control groups, pretesting and posttesting, and single-variable manipulation, were not a part of the field's tradition. There are clearly many studies that assess intervention strategies, but none of the studies reviewed attempted to situate their intervention strategies in an experimental form where the only difference between the experimental group and the control group is a single or a minimum number of research variables. Many specialists make reference to what is called "natural experiments," which, it is asserted, have great potential for theory development, because societies show variation and their consequences are explored (Lonner and Berry 1986; Glaser 1986). Some comparative education studies are opportunistic, usually after the fact has been established, and only quasi-experimental, but they fail to satisfy strict criteria for experimental studies.

With this exception, between 1985 and 1995, comparative education research studies have reflected the strategies of the general social sciences. Of the 427 research articles for this period that were reviewed, content analysis resulted in a count of 834 research strategies; the average number per article was 1.95. Researchers engaging in field research, for example, usually rely on some combination of interview, participation/observation, and questionnaires.

Between 1985 and 1995, the most common research strategy, by far, remained that of literature review. Almost one-quarter (24.3 percent) of the articles relied exclusively on literature review, or included literature review with some other strategy. Nevertheless, in spite of its continued importance, literature reviews decreased significantly compared with the mid-sixties when they accounted for 48.1 percent. The next most popular research strategy, 38.4 percent, was any type of field research (participation/observation, interviews, or questionnaire). There was a dramatic and substantial increase in this method from the mid-sixties (when field research accounted for only 5 percent). The third most common strategy was comparative research (30.9 percent). The fourth strategy, 22.5 percent, tapped into large survey research data bases.[2]

Only a small number of journal articles (10.5 percent) relied on historiography, project evaluation (12.2 percent), and content analysis (11.0 percent). Historical research decreased significantly since the 1960s while project evaluations and content analysis, essentially missing from the earlier period, became standard data collection strategies.

Content analysis of articles published in CER between 2001 and 2009 show new developments. Of special significance is the dramatic shift that has occurred in comparative analysis. As recently as the 1980s and 1990s, the field was characterized mainly by single-country studies. Of course, single-country studies are potentially comparative in nature, as they may be used for testing general theories. But we were concerned that too many studies focused on a single country and made no attempt to extend findings beyond that country. For the period 1985 to 1995, applying a criterion that defines a study as comparative only if it is concerned with more than one country, region, continent, or, indeed, the world, 30 percent of the studies satisfied this condition (Rust 1999).

However, a content analysis of 155 research articles appearing in the CER from 2001 to 2009 revealed that 71 articles (46 percent) were concerned with making comparisons across countries, regions, or across the globe. This is a notable increase, and we attribute a major cause of this shift to the focus on globalization.

Toward Social Science Disciplines in Comparative Education

Comparative Education has recently been considered a subfield of various social studies disciplines, such as history, sociology, and political science. Each of these disciplines has its own characteristic theoretical and methodological approaches. In addition, each discipline has traditions that define what problems warrant study, what constitutes knowledge, and what are appropriate theories. The contributions of these various disciplines have created the variegation that defines the nature of the comparative education community, including its theoretical orientations and research biases.

In the early stages of comparative education, its founders had come from a small number of disciplines. Even though its founders had been trained in fields other than comparative education, they were united regarding the theoretical and methodological nature of the new field. In large part, their own academic backgrounds were similar, and they interacted actively with each other in defining the emerging nature of the new field.

These scholars shared historical and humanistic inclinations, and included historians Isaac Kandel, Friedrich Schneider, Nicholas Hans, Robert Ulich, and Franz Hilker. They all would have agreed with Kandel's comment: that "the methodology of comparative education is determined by the purpose that the study is to fulfill" (Kandel 1933). However, in reality, their approach to data collection and interpretation was remarkably narrow and uniform. They began a research project by describing conventional aspects of national education systems, such as the curriculum, the educational preparation of teachers, the administrative structure, and the various levels of the school system, school finance, and so on. They then set out to interpret this information in the context of national "forces and factors," "driving forces," or "conditions and factors" that might be explanatory (Kandel 1933; Hans 1955; Schneider 1931/1932). In doing this, they relied almost entirely on secondary literature sources.

As a new corps of academics joined these early pioneers, historians continued to be heavily represented, including scholars such as Andreas Kazamias, Claude A. Eggertsen, and William W. Brickman. They were joined by the so-called humanistic scholars, who relied on what Robert Cowen calls "the culturalist motif"; these included British scholars such as Joseph Lauwerys, W. D. Halls, Vernon Mallinson, and Edmund King (Cowen 1980). A few of the good early comparative education scholars could be identified with the more conventional disciplines within the social sciences, and they included C. Arnold Anderson in sociology, Philip Foster in sociology/economics, and Harold Noah in economics. Since that time, comparative education has broadened to the point that the discipline of history has lost its hold on studies appearing in its journals, in favor of the more conventional social sciences.

We sent a questionnaire to as many of the 427 authors, as could be found from our 1999 study of research strategies published between the years 1985 and 1995. Approximately 200 authors responded to the survey that had a number of questions with a five-point Likert scale indicating the degree to which various academic disciplines and professional orientations were reflected in their articles. The authors were free to select all, any, or no disciplines and list each of them on a separate scale (Henrickson, Faison, and Val 2003). Combined responses allowed for the "weighting" of each discipline.

We found that 3.4 percent of the authors indicated a single-discipline orientation; 27 percent indicated two; 35.6 percent, three; and 27.5 percent, four. In other words, they tended to identify their work as multidisciplinary or interdisciplinary. We invited authors to indicate the degree to which each discipline was reflected in their research article. More than 80 percent of the authors indicated some reliance on sociology, almost 70 percent indicated some reliance on political science, and almost 63 percent reported drawing on history, while approximately 50 percent relied to some degree on economics.

Thus, in these journals, the more conventional social science disciplines, particularly sociology, political science, and economics, had come to dominate comparative education. Psychology was barely represented. And, outside the social sciences, even professional education was not well represented. With the social sciences as disciplinary bases, it is not surprising that the specific theories reflected in the journals can be identified generally with sociology, political science, history, and economics.

Geographic Orientation of the Field

Besides the broadening theoretical and methodological focus of comparative education, researchers have also been broadening their geographic scope.[3] In the 1960s, studies were largely focused on the developed world. Of the 112 studies surveyed, 68 (60.7 percent) were of highly developed countries and another 19 (17.0 percent) were either not country-specific or focused on global concerns (for a total of 77.7 percent of all studies). In comparison, contemporary comparative educators attend to countries at all levels of human development, though the attention given to countries reflecting low human development appears to be less than that given to medium and high development countries. Only 16 percent of all studies focused on countries reflecting low human development, and included countries such as Afghanistan, Algeria, Angola, Bangladesh, Benin, Bhutan, and so on; while 28 percent of the studies focused on countries reflecting high human development, and included Denmark, Dominica, Finland, France, Germany, and so on. More recently, among the studies published from 2001 to 2009 in the *CER*, 20 percent of the 83 articles focused on countries reflecting low human development.[4] Even though our more recent observations are based on a single journal, they suggest that the focus of the field is increasingly diverse. Such a finding is consistent with claims that globalization intends to penetrate every corner of the globe.

There is additional evidence of the impact of globalization: according to recent reports of the Comparative and International Education Society, an increasing number of publications in the *Comparative Education Review* are authored or coauthored by scholars from the developing world (*CER* Editorial Office 2003).

Role of Qualitative *vs.* Quantitative Research in the Field

A final issue that we wish to address has to do with data analysis. While a central issue of any research investigation is the means of data collection, data must also be dealt with in some systematic and thoughtful manner. Data analysis typically closely follows the data collection strategy, but an analytic distinction must be drawn between the two. Two major paradigms have emerged in social science research. On the one hand, a tradition has emerged that is mainly positivist, experimental, and empirical in nature. This is known generally as "quantitative research." On the other hand, a second tradition exists that is constructivist, interpretive, and naturalistic, known generally as "qualitative research," and more recently as "postmodernism," in that it represents a countermovement to the positivist tradition. According to Creswell (1994), there are a number of philosophical assumptions behind the two paradigms. Ontologically, quantitative researchers tend to see reality as being objective and singular, existing apart from the researcher, while qualitative researchers tend to see "reality" as being subjective and multiple. Epistemologically, quantitative researchers tend to claim that they are outside the sphere of their research, while qualitative researchers tend to believe they are continually interacting with the subject matter being researched. Axiologically, quantitative researchers usually claim that they are operating in a value-free and unbiased fashion, while qualitative researchers usually believe their values and biases come into play in their research activities.

While Creswell provides a useful distinction, these paradigms are only incommensurable when referring to the extremes of qualitative and quantitative analysis. There are several levels of stratification along a qualitative/

quantitative continuum that scholars relate to in their quest for and explication of knowledge. There are (1) studies involving direct, concrete, and subjective experience with reality; (2) nominalistic studies based on specific times, proper names, and places; (3) studies deriving descriptive and historical generalizations; (4) nomothetic studies using common language; (5) studies based on mathematical models or theories; and (6) studies involving transcendental or cosmic conceptions. Even these levels may overlap immensely. For example, a physicist may formulate a certain set of mathematical symbols that are used to predict experimental tests, but in discussing this work with non-physicists the physicist may express these symbolic representations in more common language. However, positivist Bertrand Russell reminds us that "ordinary language is totally unsuited for expressing what physics really asserts, since the words of everyday life are not sufficiently abstract. Only mathematics and mathematical logic can say as little as the physicist means to say" (Russell 1931). This is rarely the case in studies of comparative education, and so we find great overlap in qualitative and quantitative analysis. Even so, a distinction between the two orientations is valuable. On the one hand, analysis using common language lends itself well to the explication of everyday experiences and emotional states, to the richness of cultural life, but those in the natural sciences have long recognized that sense experience is difficult to retain with what might be called scientific-mindedness, because the concepts and their relations may be almost as numerous as the experiences themselves. Logical unity is usually achieved by reducing experience to a limited number of concepts and relations. Some claim that scientific progress is achieved mainly by moving to higher and higher levels of abstraction (Lauden 1977), though a price is paid. The higher the stratification process, the fewer the contact points our analytical constructs have with sense-experience and social reality. Comparativists are faced with a tough balancing act as they attempt to remain connected with social reality while also becoming more scientific.

Turning again to the UCLA review of research appearing in the *CER*, *CE*, and *IJED* between 1985 and 1995, studies were generally judged to be qualitative in nature, regardless of the journal in question. Of the 427 articles reviewed, 304 (71.2 percent) were judged to be qualitative. And 82 percent of all articles relied, at least in part, on qualitative research strategies. Only 74 articles (17.3 percent) were found to rely mainly on quantitative analysis, though another 46 (10.8 percent) used a combination of quantitative and qualitative analysis. *IJED* published a greater number of quantitative studies than the other two journals. While there is a pervasive tendency in comparative education to rely on qualitative analysis, interestingly, from the mid-sixties there was also an increase in quantitative studies. In this period, 94 (83.9 percent) of 112 studies were judged to be qualitative; another 12 studies (7.3 percent) also included quantitative data. Only 5 studies (4.5 percent) relied heavily on quantitative analysis. This increase in studies that used quantitative methods, from a total of 11.8 percent in the 1960s, to 28.1 percent between 1985 and 1995, continued in the recent 10 years. Of the 155 articles published from 2001 to 2009 in *CER*, 105 (67.7 percent) used a qualitative approach, while 37 (23.9 percent) used quantitative analysis and another 13 (8.4 percent) used a mixed approach, making a total of 32.3 percent.

While there were some quantitative strategies in most studies, we found that most of these dealt with existing data sets and questionnaires. Qualitative strategies typically consisted of conceptual studies, literature reviews, historical studies, comparative research, project evaluations, content analysis, participation/observation, and interviews. There were, of course, some quantitative data in some studies judged to be qualitative, but this was strictly descriptive, such as numbers of teachers, curriculum tables, and so on, and do not lend themselves to statistical computation and analysis. Thus, while use of quantitative techniques are on the increase, the pervasive analytic research orientation of the field of comparative education remains qualitative, thus suggesting that scholars in comparative education tend to rely on similar philosophical assumptions.

Concluding Remarks

We have relied on the major journals in the field of comparative education to flesh out how research strategies in the field have changed. Our analysis shows that the data collection strategies used by researchers have evolved from a narrow band of methods (e.g., contemporary and historical literature) to a wide range used in the general social sciences (e.g., participation/observation, interviews, questionnaires, etc.). In addition, we found that the discipline orientation of the field has also expanded from historical and humanistic to include the social science disciplines, particularly sociology, political science, and economics. As to the geographic focus, increasing attention is being given to countries reflecting low levels of human development. A qualitative approach to data analysis continues to dominate the field, but there is a slight increase in the number of articles that rely on quantitative methods.

Some of the changes can be attributed to the fuller development of comparative education as an academic field and shifts in the training of comparative education researchers. We have also observed the influence of globalization. Comparative education has begun to move away from a focus on understanding a single foreign country's educational system in relation to other countries, and toward a field that has begun to tackle educational issues from a global perspective.

Notes

1. Because *IJED* began publication only in 1981, we were not able to include articles from that journal.
2. We do not include statistical analysis here. The interested reader can go to the original publication for such analysis (see Rust 1999).
3. In the United Nations Human Development Indicators, 53 countries are designated as having (1) high human development, 44 countries are designated as having (2) medium human development, and 53 countries are designated as having (3) low human development.
4. We used the Human Development Indicators in 2003 to differentiate higher human development, medium human development, and low human development.

References

Bereday, George Z. F. 1964. *Comparative Method in Education.* New York: Holt, Rinehart and Winston.

CER Editorial Office. 2003. *Annual Report of the Comparative Education Review.* New Orleans: Comparative and International Education Society.

Cowen, Robert. 1980. "Comparative Education in Europe: A Note." *Comparative Education Review* 24 (1): 98–108.

Creswell, John W. 1994. *Research Design: Qualitative and Quantitative Approaches.* Thousand Oaks, CA: Sage Publications.

Dewey, John. 1910. *How We Think.* Boston: D. C. Heath.

Geertz, Clifford. 1988. *Works and Lives: The Anthropologist as Author.* Palo Alto, CA: Stanford University Press.

Glaser, Myron. 1986. "Field Work in a Hostile Environment." *Comparative Education Review* 10 (2): 367–376.

Habermas, Juergen. 1984–1989. *The Theory of Communicative Action.* Translated by T. McCarthy. Cambridge, MA: MIT Press.

Hans, Nicholas. 1955. *Comparative Education: A Study of Educational Factors and Traditions.* London: Routledge and Kegan Paul.

Harding, Sandra. 1987. *Feminism and Methodology.* Bloomington, IN: Indiana University Press.

Henrickson, Leslie, Steve Faison, and Val D. Rust. 2003. "Theory in Comparative Education." *World Studies in Education* 4 (1): 5–28.

Holmes, Brian. 1977. "The Positivist Debate in Comparative Education: An Anglo-Saxon Perspective." *Comparative Education* 13 (2): 115–132.

———. 1984. "Paradigm Shifts in Comparative Education." *Comparative Education Review* 28 (4): 584–604.

Kandel, Isaac. 1930. *Essays in Comparative Education*. New York: Teachers College, Columbia University.

———. 1933. *Comparative Education*. Boston: Houghton Mifflin.

Lauden, L. 1977. *Progress and Its Problems: Towards a Theory of Scientific Growth*. Berkeley: University of California Press.

Longino, Helen. 2002. *The Fate of Knowledge*. Princeton, NJ: Princeton University Press.

Lonner, Walter J. and John W. Berry. 1986. *Field Methods in Cross-Cultural Research*. Beverly Hills, CA: Sage Publications.

Phillips, Bernard S. 1976. *Social Research: Strategy and Tactics*. New York: Macmillan Publishing Co.

Popper, Karl. 1963. *Conjectures and Refutations: The Growth of Scientific Knowledge*. New York: Harper and Row.

Russell, Bertrand. 1931. *The Scientific Outlook*. New York: W. W. Norton.

Rust, Val D., Aminata Soumaré, Octavio Pescador, and Megumi Shibuya. 1999. "Research Strategies in Comparative Education." *Comparative Education Review* 43 (1): 86–109.

Schneider, Friedrich. 1931/32. "Internationale Paedagogik, Auslands Paedagogik, Vergleichende Erziehungswissenschaft: Geschichte, Wesen, Methoden, Aufgaben und Ergebnisse." *Internationale Zeitschrift fuer Erziehungswissenschaft* 1.

———. 1961. *Vergleichende Erziehungswissenschaft*. Heidelberg: Quelle und Meyer.

Strauss, Barney G. and Anselm L. Glasser. 1967. *The Discovery of Grounded Theory: Strategies for Qualitative Research*. Chicago: Aldine.

Wells, Richard H. and J. Steven Picou. 1981. *American Sociology: Theoretical and Methodological Structure*. Washington, DC: University Press of America.

Part 2

Policy Debates in International
Higher Education

Chapter 3

When China Opens to the World: A Study of Transnational Higher Education in Zhejiang, China[1]

Ka-Ho Mok and Xiaozhou Xu

Introduction

The economic transition in China since the late 1970s has led to not only drastic social transformations but also rapid advancements in science and technology, as well as the revolution in information and communications technology. In order to enhance the global competence of the Chinese population in coping with the challenges of the knowledge-based economy, the higher education sector has been going through restructuring along the lines of marketization, privatization, and decentralization. Responding to the globalization challenges, the Chinese government has opened up the education market by allowing private/*minban* higher education institutions and even overseas universities to offer academic programs in the mainland. Hence, we have witnessed the proliferation of education providers, the diversification of education financing, and the increase in private–public partnership in education provision since the policy of educational decentralization was introduced in the mid-1980s. After China's accession to the World Trade Organization (WTO), the Chinese government has allowed overseas universities in collaboration with local universities to co-launch higher education programs. In this policy context, we set out in this chapter to examine the current developments of transnational higher education in China. More specifically, we focus on how students in Zhejiang province enrolling in these overseas programs evaluate their learning experiences. We also identify and discuss major issues arising from the onset of transnational education in China.

Responses to Globalization: Marketizing and Privatizing Higher Education

China's Transitional Economy and New Education Strategies

Since the late 1970s, the modernization drive, China's reform and opening up to the outside world, has transformed the highly centralized planning economy into a market-oriented and more dynamic one. In the new market economy context, the old way of "centralized governance" in education is rendered inappropriate (Yang 2002). Acknowledging that over-centralization and stringent rules would kill the initiatives and enthusiasm of local educational institutions, the Chinese Communist Party (CCP) called for resolute steps to streamline administration and devolve powers to units at lower levels so as to allow them more flexibility to run education. The *Outline for Reform and Development of Education in China* issued by the Communist Party of China in 1993 identified the reduction of centralization and government control in general as the long-term goals of reform (CCPCC 1993). The government began to play the role of "macro-management through legislation, allocation of funding, planning, information service, policy guidance and essential administration," so that "universities can independently provide education geared to the needs of society under the leadership of the government." As Min (2004) has rightly suggested, higher education has experienced structural reforms ranging from curriculum design, financing, promotion of the private/*minban* sectors in higher education provision, to adopting strategies to quest for "world-class universities" (2004). Reshuffling the monopolistic role of the state in educational provision, reform in educational structure started in the mid-1980s and has manifested a mix of private and public consumption (Cheng 1995). Proliferation of education providers and diversification of education finance has become increasingly popular (Chen 2002; Ngok and Kwong 2003). Thereafter, we have witnessed a large-scale development of higher education institutions in the 1990s, and different types of tertiary institutions have evolved in mainland China, including both national (public) and private/*minban* higher education (Chan and Mok 2001; Mok 2006b).

With intention to improve the higher education level of the population, the Chinese government has endorsed a policy of massification in higher education. In the past decade, the number of undergraduate and postgraduate students has increased significantly, up to 20 million students enrolled in Chinese universities in 2004 (Min 2004; Ngok 2006). Dependence on local institutions alone cannot meet the pressing demands for higher education; with intentions to identify and learn the good practices from foreign universities, the Chinese government has allowed overseas universities, in collaboration with local institutions, to jointly develop academic programs in the mainland. Transnational higher education has become increasingly popular especially after China joining the World Trade Organization (WTO) and its agreement signed with the GATS (Huang 2005a).

China Joining WTO and Transnational Education

Since the 1990s, there have been a few major legislations governing transnational education in China. The most important national legislation influencing the emergence of transnational education in China is the *Education Act of the People's Republic of China* issued in 1995, encouraging exchange or cooperative education with foreign partners (Huang 2005b). Based on this Act, two documents concerning transnational education were promulgated and implemented, namely, the *Interim Provisions for Chinese-Foreign Cooperation in Running Schools* issued by the State Education Commission (SEC, renamed as the Ministry of Education [CMOE] in 1998) in 1995, and the *Regulations of the People's Republic of China on Chinese-Foreign Cooperation in Running Schools*. According to the first legal document, transnational education was introduced as *Zhongwai Hezuo Banxue*, in Chinese meaning that overseas higher education providers can only provide academic programs in collaboration with local institutions in China and not solely by themselves.

In addition, the 1995 document also restricts levels and forms of academic programs. The document stipulates that "Chinese and foreign parties may run educational institutions of various forms at varying levels, excluding China's compulsory education and those forms of education and training under special provisions by the state" (SEC 1995, Chapter 1, Article 4). Most important of all, the document also makes it explicit that running academic programs by overseas institutions should not have any profit pursuit. According to the document:

> Chinese-foreign cooperation in education shall abide by Chinese law and decrees, implement China's guideline for education, conform to China's need for educational development and requirement for the training of talents and ensure teaching quality, and shall not seek profits as the objective and/or damage the state and public interests. (SEC 1995, Chapter 1, Article 5)

Apparently, the notion of "profit making" by transnational education in China is very different from the experiences of other overseas institutions in Australia, the United States, and the United Kingdom, since most of these institutions had set up offshore academic programs to generate additional incomes for home institutions. Before China joining the WTO and its consent given to GATS, the government had adopted "transnational education" as a policy tool to help create additional learning opportunities in higher education for local high school graduates, and not establishing "transnational education" as a "trade." In 1997, the Academic Degrees Committee of the State Council (ADCSC) issued another legal document entitled "Notice on Strengthening the Management of Degree-granting in Chinese-Foreign Cooperation in Running Schools" as an important supplement to the 1995 document, further emphasizing that all Chinese-Foreign cooperation in running schools should be governed by the legal framework in China. Nonetheless, the Chinese administration experienced difficulties in implementing the newly enacted laws when confronting an increased number of these overseas programs.

After China joining the WTO, the Chinese government started revising its legislations to allow overseas institutions to offer programs in the mainland, in line with the WTO regulations. In September 2003, the State Council started implementing the "Regulations of the People's Republic of China on Chinese-Foreign Cooperation in Running Schools"; this newly enacted legal document provided further details regarding the nature, policy and principle, concrete request and procedure of applying, leadership and organization, teaching process, financial management, supervised mechanism and legal liability, and so on. Unlike the 1995 document that attaches importance to vocational education, the 2003 document encourages transnational higher education. More specifically, the 2003 document encourages local universities to cooperate with renowned overseas higher education institutions in launching new academic programs in order to improve the quality of teaching and learning and to introduce excellent overseas educational resources to local institutions (State Council 2003, Chapter 1, Article 3). More importantly, the 2003 legal document does not forbid overseas institutions of higher learning from making profit for running courses in China. According to Futao Huang (2006b, 25), the fundamental changes in the 2003 document has shown that transnational education has gone through "a transfer from the informal, incidental and Laissez-Faire phase prior to the more structured, systematic and well regulated phase after 1995." We should also note that, unlike other states practicing ideas of neoliberalism in education policy to facilitate an "education market" to evolve, the education market in mainland China is heavily regulated by the state, which is a "governed market" or "state-guided market" in China's transition economy (Lin et al. 2005; Mok 2006a, 2006b). According to GATE, there are various forms of transnational education, including branch campuses, franchises, articulation, twinning, corporate programs, online learning and distance education programs, and study abroad (GATE 1999). In this chapter, we focus only on one major aspect, namely, the joint venture between overseas and local universities in offering higher education programs for Chinese citizens. At present, there are two major types of transnational higher education programs, one type comprises nondegree-conferring programs and the other comprises degree programs leading to awards issued by foreign universities or universities based in Hong Kong, a special administrative region of China (D. Yang 2002; Huang 2006b). The present research was set out in the policy context briefly outlined above to examine the learning experiences of students who have enrolled in transnational higher education programs in Hangzhou city of Zhejiang province in China. More specifically, this research aims at examining how students enrolling in transnational higher education programs in Hangzhou city have evaluated the quality of these programs.

Transnational Higher Education in China: A Brief National Survey

Since the promulgation of the 1995 legal document, foreign degree programs have had remarkable growth and development in China. In 1995, there were only two joint programs that could offer a foreign degree. However, by June 2004 the number of joint programs provided in Chinese institutions in collaboration with overseas partners increased to 745, while joint programs that were qualified to award overseas or Hong Kong degrees went up to 169 (CMOE 2004). As to the country of origin of these overseas academic partners, most of them were from countries and regions with developed economies and advanced technology. With the biggest shares in the export of educational service, almost half of the cooperative universities across the world are from the United States (26 percent) and Australia (28 percent), while a number of universities from the European countries are also approved by ADCSC to grant their degrees to students under the Chinese-Foreign Cooperation in Running Schools (CFCRS) (CMOE 2006).

These degree programs approved by ADCSC are taught in some famous universities in China, such as Peking University, Tsinghua University, Zhejiang University and so on in collaboration with over 100 foreign universities or colleges. However, among these foreign higher education institutions, most are not ranked as "world class" universities in terms of research and teaching. For example, among 40 approved CFCRS American degree programs, most are provided by state universities or second-class universities in the US-based university league. Such a situation has indicated the gap in the policy goals in promoting international collaboration between top universities in China and renowned universities abroad.

Levels, Fields, and Locations of CFCRS Degree Programs

As mentioned earlier, the Chinese government is the approving authority on these overseas degree programs. According to the list of CFCRS degree programs publicized by the ADCSC of the State Council, there are altogether 103 degree programs, about 31.7 percent are bachelor degrees and the rest are higher degrees, including doctoral degrees or high-level professional diplomas. In June 2004, for instance, the Chinese government recognized only 164 foreign degrees out of the total number run by foreign institutions in cooperation in China. In regard to the field of studies, most were programs or courses related to business, commerce, and management (57 percent); engineering (22 percent); education (8 percent); medicine, nursing, and optometry (5 percent); law (2 percent); social sciences (1 percent); literature (1 percent). All the other fields of study constituted only 4 percent of the total CFCRS programs (CMOE 2006).

On a close scrutiny of where these overseas programs are run, we can easily find that most are run by institutions concentrated in the eastern coastal areas, the most economically prosperous region in China. In 2004, most of these programs were concentrated in the following provinces: Shanghai (111), Beijing (108), Shandong (78), Jiangsu (61), Liaoning (34), Zhejiang (33), Tianjing (31), Shanxi (29), Guangdong (27), Hubei (23).

Most of these areas are close to the eastern coast of China.[2] The above brief survey has provided us general background information about the recent development of transnational higher education in mainland China. We will be able to make better sense of the development of transnational higher education in Zhejiang province if we can analyze the present case study in relation to the national development.

Transnational Higher Education in Zhejiang Province: Students' Perspectives

In order to understand how students enrolling in these joint programs evaluate their learning experiences, we conducted a study based upon an opinion survey in Zhejiang province. The province of Zhejiang was selected for our case studies because this is one of the provinces in China with the fastest economic growth. The institutions that we selected for the study are located in Hangzhou area, one of the most economically prosperous cities in China. In the past few years, the annual GDP growth rates of Hangzhou and Zhejiang have been ranked among the top three in the country, while people in Hangzhou have also taken the lead in salary increase when compared with other places in China. Of course, we have no intention of claiming that the present case study can represents the whole of China, but the examination of this area of rapid economic transition will considerably enable us to understand how economic dynamism has affected people's quest for higher quality education (Wen 2005).

More specifically, the major objectives of the present research are to, first, examine how students evaluate their learning experiences and then to assess students' overall satisfaction level with CFCRS institutions and programs. In addition, the survey examines how students assess the educational quality of CFCRS and their confidence in the diploma/award offered by these joint programs. The participants in the survey are students recruited by CFCRS institutions and those in programs run in Zhejiang province. Zhejiang province was chosen for our case studies because it is one of the richest provinces and has a comparatively longer history of having joint-degree programs in collaboration with overseas academic partners in China. The sampling frame for the present survey research is based on the purposive sampling method. Since we had already developed contacts with relevant/targeted institutions in Hangzhou area, we interviewed students from three academic institutions that had joint academic programs with overseas partners. The questionnaires were delivered to Hangzhou Teachers College because this local institution has cooperated with the University of Canberra, Australia, for launching a joint master's degree program in Educational Leadership; to the International College of Zhejiang Forestry University for its joint program of a bachelor's degree in business administration and trade with the University of Sydney from Australia; and to Zhejiang Normal University, which jointly runs a master's degree program in Education Administration with Edith Cowan University from Australia. We sent out a total of 200 questionnaires, and 143 of these were returned as valid responses, with a response rate of 72 percent. After carefully checking the returned questionnaires, the validated data were entered into our data set; analysis of this data with the SPSS 11.5 software package was conducted afterward. In addition to the survey research, we also conducted some focus group discussion with selected students to learn more about their own evaluations of their learning experiences. We fully acknowledge the limitations of such a research design, since the present study cannot represent the total population in China mainland. Nonetheless, the selection of respondents from Hangzhou, one of the most economically dynamic areas in China, would considerably reflect how people living in an economically prosperous region in China evaluate joint academic programs in China.

Findings

Student Evaluation of Course Arrangement

When asked how they evaluated the program/course arrangement by the CFCRS institutions, more than half the students (58 percent) considered the existing course arrangements relatively appropriate and that the course delivery could meet their needs in study and work; 27 percent of the respondents chose the response of "it is just all right." Among all the respondents, only 8 percent considered the current course arrangements as highly suitable and also that these joint programs could meet the needs of their study and work. Nonetheless, about 7 percent of the respondents considered the course arrangements inappropriate, and they somehow found that such courses did not meet the needs of their study and work.

When examining how the respondents evaluate the appropriateness of the proportion between foreign and Chinese courses, 63.3 percent considered the proportion "appropriate," while 16.1 percent considered it to be "not too appropriate" and believed that more foreign courses could be included. Among them, about 12.6 percent believed that the proportion was "not too appropriate" and wanted more Chinese courses to be added. The proportions of those who responded with "very appropriate" and "not appropriate" took up 5.6 percent and 2.1 percent, respectively, both of which comprise a small proportion. Putting the above data into perspective, although the students of the CFCRS institutions are generally happy about the course arrangements, they still consider that there is room for improvement, and they have especially proposed changes to the proportion between foreign and Chinese courses.

When asked for comments on the compilation of teaching contents, 46.2 percent (66 students) of the respondents stated that they were "relatively satisfied," 11.2 percent stated they were "very satisfied," while about 7.7 percent of the respondents showed their disapproving attitude ("not too satisfied"), and one individual respondent even gave the remark "not satisfied at all." As the above data show, the respondents enrolling in these joint programs are generally happy with the teaching contents adopted by the CFCRS institutions.

Student Evaluation of Educational System and Class Time Arrangement

When examining about student satisfaction with the educational system and class time arrangement, 39.2 percent of the respondents considered this to be "just about right," 51 students (35.7 percent) were "relatively satisfied" with the arrangement, and 17 students (11.9 percent) expressed dissatisfaction. Whereas 15 students (10.5 percent) were "very satisfied" with the arrangements, some were not at all happy with the arrangements made. Looking closely into these responses, we can easily find that the majority of the respondents were not happy with the arrangements and there is certainly room for improvement in this particular aspect.

Student Evaluation of Teaching Methods

As for the teaching methods and teaching strategies, the opinions of the respondents are as follows: 61 students considered the teaching methods "appropriate" (around 41.3 percent); 20 (14 percent) of them ranked the teaching methods as "very good"; only three students (2.1 percent) expressed dissatisfaction in the teaching methods used. In this regard, most of the respondents in the study were found to be generally happy with the teaching methods that the CFCRS institutions have selected. Nonetheless, some respondents also pointed out a few areas for further improvement. For example, a number of respondents considered students' ability in using foreign language to communicate with overseas teachers as one major aspect needing improvement. This view is generally supported by 93 percent of the respondents, since they have recognized their deficiency in using foreign languages during the teaching and learning processes and are not happy about their competence in communicating with the foreign teachers.

Student Evaluation of Examination Methods

Another aspect of student evaluation is related to the assessment methods. In our survey, 65 respondents (45.5 percent) considered the examination method "just about right" and 54 students (37.8 percent) ranked the assessment methods as "appropriate." Among them, 18 students (12.6 percent) rated the assessment methods "very good," but 6 students (4.2 percent) showed their disapproving attitude to the assessment methods.

Which are the kinds of assessment methods that are more appropriate? Who should be the one conducting the examination/test? According to our survey, we have learned that nearly half of the respondents (46.2 percent) thought that the test for the CFCRS students should be carried out by the overseas partners; 50 students (35 percent) believed it should be carried out by the Chinese side; 27 students (18.9 percent) felt it should be carried out by the foreign side. Assessment is an important part of the teaching process. It is not only for the verification of the quantum of knowledge and technical ability that students have imbibed but also for assuring academic quality. The results of the study show that students are generally satisfied with the assessment methods. But when they were asked to recommend alternate assessment methods, we can easily find the differences in the responses between postgraduate and undergraduate students. It seems that not many students are happy about the test/examination carried out by the foreign side (as reflected by the responses of 81.1 percent of the respondents, who do not want foreign institutions to control the assessment methods).

Student Evaluation of Tuition Fees

According to the "2003 Regulations," the criteria of tuition fees of a CFCRS institution are decided according to the related price policy issued by the government. The cooperative institutions cannot add new items or elevate criteria for tuition fees without prior permission of the government. When asked to assess the tuition fees criteria of CFCRS programs, most of the respondents considered the tuition fees "relatively high." Among the respondents, 86 students (60.1 percent) rated the tuition fees as "a little bit high"; 28 students (19.6 percent) considered the tuition fees to be "very high"; 29 students (20.3 percent) regarded the tuition fees to be "about right." None of the respondents considered the tuition fees to be "low or very low."

What is the reasonable level of tuition fees? When asked to opine about the appropriate level of tuition fee, the majority of respondents in Hangzhou Teachers College and Zhejiang Forestry University (81 students, accounting for 78.6 percent of the population) thought that the reasonable tuition fee level should pitch between 25,000 and 30,000 RMB, while 15 students (14.6 percent) considered the reasonable level to be between 30,000 and 35,000 RMB. Only four students believed that the reasonable tuition fee level should be set between 35,000 and 40,000 RMB; and only three students proposed setting the level between 40,000 and 45,000 RMB.

As the above data show, although the tuition fee of CFCRS is much lower than the fee required for studying abroad, the students who had enrolled in the joint programs still considered the tuition fee to be high. As these joint programs are now a service offered by the overseas institutions as trade, it is inevitable that the foreign institutions of CFCRS aim at profit making. In the case of the domestic students in China, most are still unable to pay for programs charging such "high fees." Therefore, setting the right level for tuition fee has become a major issue for these overseas partner institutions, and it is imperative that they consider the affordability of courses to students when deciding the fee level.

Evaluation of Teaching Facilities

One major dimension regarding student satisfaction about educational programs is related to facilities offered by these joint programs. In our study, 35.7 percent of the students considered that the facilities in their institutions are "all right"; 35.7 percent rated the facilities "not bad"; and about 19.6 percent (28 students) rated their institutions' facilities as "very good." Not surprisingly, some of the respondents were not happy with the facilities. Among them, 8.4 percent (12 students) ranked their institutions' facilities as "bad," and one individual rated the facilities as "very bad."

Student Evaluation of Faculty

The competence of the academic staff involved in the joint programs directly affects students' learning experiences. According to the "2003

Regulations," "foreign teachers and administrators in the institutions of CFCRS should have at least bachelor degree and certification accordingly, and need more than two years' experience of teaching." When examining the "quality" of the teaching staff for these joint programs, 78 students (54 percent) regarded the qualifications of their teachers as "good," 37 students (26 percent) gave the rating, "this is all right," but 19 percent rated highly the qualifications of the teaching staff. Combining these data, we find that 99.3 percent of the respondents are satisfied with the qualifications of the faculty involved in these joint programs.

Major Issues and Challenges for Transnational Higher Education in China

Quality Assurance of Transnational Higher Education

Our above study has pointed out that a major issue/challenge that confronts transnational education programs in China is "quality assurance." According to the "2003 Regulations," both the central government and local government have to take full legal responsibilities for approving or chartering the establishment of transnational education programs in line with the existing legal frameworks and guidelines. However, after the joint programs are approved and put into operation, responsibility for quality assurance falls on individual institutions. As Huang (2006a, 31) observed: "in most cases, faculty members at departmental or program level are expected to be responsible for the quality of teaching and learning, though there are occasional checks by inspectors sent by the Ministry of Education or other administrative authorities." Such observations are confirmed by our study in Zhejiang province. As discussed above, our respondents are concerned about the quality assurance for these transnational education programs; this is especially so because individual institutions are gradually taking upon themselves the quality assurance responsibility. The Chinese university students are not familiar with this arrangement; they are familiar only with the state-guided quality assurance system, because the Ministry of Education has long been the only organization responsible for quality assurance in higher education.

It is against such a context that our respondents do not prefer intermediary organizations to take up the quality assurance responsibility. Nonetheless, they are equally worried when such responsibility goes to individual institutions, since there are bound to be variations in terms of quality assurance systems/mechanisms among different institutions. The issue of quality assurance is not unique for transnational higher education in China. With the rise of transnational education programs in other Asian societies, quality assurance has become one major issue for all those program-offering institutions. For instance, Australian universities have started to reexamine their quality assurance systems in order to maintain the same academic standards between the home and overseas academic programs (Meek 2006). Our filed interviews with university administrators in Zhejiang province have suggested that a preferred model in quality assurance is to set up an independent nongovernmental organization to take up the quality assurance tasks and responsibilities. Obviously, quality assurance has become increasingly important as transnational higher education programs are booming in the mainland; therefore the government must develop regulatory frameworks in governing such newly evolved programs and institutions.

Legal Status of Transnational Higher Education

Our national survey and the case study of Zhejiang province have suggested that the joint degree programs face the issue of "legal statuses" in China's higher education system. Analyzing these transnational education programs in the light of the typologies set out by GATE, we can easily find that these joint degree programs comprise only a supplementary part of China's higher education system, and not a major one. According to Huang (2006a, 8), "incoming foreign higher education activity in China is not regarded as constituting an independent part of the higher education system such as the national, public or private institutions." Unlike Malaysia, Singapore, and Hong Kong, where the governments have allowed overseas institutions to set up their branch campuses to recruit students and offer teaching programs, the Chinese government has not permitted foreign universities to establish their branch campuses on the mainland (Huang 2005a; Mok 2006c; Morshidi 2006; Yang 2006).

Even though Nottingham University from the UK has been very keen to set up its branch campus in China, a few years of efforts could only allow this foreign academic partner to found a university in collaboration with Zhejiang Wanli University. Despite the fact that the majority of programs being taught in this university have been imported from the UK, the newly established Ningbo Nottingham University has never been a branch campus, as is the case with its counterparts in Malaysia, Singapore, and Hong Kong. As Huang (2006b, 30) suggested, "it is though strongly emphasized that the University of Nottingham, Ningbo

China, which is considered as one of China's most admired new model universities with the status of corporation, is not a branch campus of the University of Nottingham, but a completely independent university owned by Zhejiang Wanli University." Since transnational higher education is still relatively new to China, our current case study has suggested that the students enrolling in these joint degree programs are worried about the social status and public recognition of these overseas institutions and programs. Such worries are well related to the Chinese government's polices toward such kind of "international cooperation."

Although these transnational education programs are considered as an integral part of China's higher education and various government policies have repeatedly stressed the importance of these programs, the existing legal documents are not clear enough to endorse their legal status. Since all these joint programs are run by overseas universities in collaboration with prestigious Chinese national universities, it seems that they are publicly owned, but actually their operation is in many respects totally different from normal programs (Huang 2006b). Similar to "second-tier colleges" being set up by major public/national universities (and also encouraged by the Ministry of Education) but run as privately run institutions, the public–private distinction is becoming even blurred and confused in Chinese higher education (Lin 2004; Lin et al. 2005; Mok 2006b). Huang (2006b) has rightly summed up the major challenge that these transnational education institutions and programs are confronted with: "it remains a big issue how they should be positioned as a new legal form of higher education activity" (30).

Discussion and Conclusion: Need for New Higher Education Regulatory Regime

This study of transnational higher education in China, in general, and the case study in Zhejiang province, in particular, has clearly shown that the higher education sector has undergone a significant transformation, especially when there is a proliferation of education providers and diversification of financial sources. If we analyze the rise of the transnational higher education in the wider context of the growing privateness of higher education in post-Mao era, especially when different kinds of *minban* or *quasi-minban* (such as second-tier colleges or independent colleges in affiliation with national universities) higher education have increased in number, we would appreciate that the diversification and marketization of higher education have inevitably challenged the conventional governance model of higher education (Lin et al. 2005; Mok and Ngok 2008). We can easily identify a few major unresolved issues such as the problem of ownership, the share of profits between the second-tier colleges and their parent institutions, the status of degrees awarded, the use of the brand names of the parent institutions, and other related issues regarding accreditation and quality assurance. All these unresolved issues challenge the existing regulatory regime, particularly as the existing legal and regulatory frameworks are inappropriate and ineffective in governing these newly formed institutions (Wu 2003). Unlike in other countries where the liberation of the market forces results in the formation of a new regulatory state by adopting corporate regulatory framework, civil society-led regulatory systems, or international benchmarking that evolves systems for governing the highly diversified sectors/markets, the Chinese government still attempts to maintain a state-oriented regulatory regime in governing the increasingly complex and diverse higher education sector.

The increasing scope of pro-competitive regulation by independent regulators and the deployment of new regulatory instruments are becoming popular trends, especially when there is increasing corporatization or privatization of state-owned public services and opening up of new markets to multiple providers (Painter and Wong 2005; Jordana and Levi-Faur 2005). On analyzing the rise of transnational higher education in relation to the increasingly diverse and complicated higher education environment in China, we see that there is an urgent need for the Chinese government to devise a new regulatory framework appropriate for governing the growing diversity in the higher education sector (Mok 2006a). More specifically, it is desirable to distinguish between the scope of state activities and the strength of state power. The former includes the different functions and goals taken on by the government, while the latter refers to the ability to plan and execute policies and to enforce laws (Fukuyama 2005). This is particularly applicable in the field of higher education provision, which has been significantly diversified and has become an increasingly complicated mix of the private and public. The Chinese government needs to redefine the relationship between the state and different educational providers, especially specifying the roles, the responsibilities and functions, and the legal statuses that are applicable to different actors and which they should perform in a more market-driven and diversified higher education scene in China's transitional economy. In conclusion, the Chinese government should develop a new regulatory regime that can respond sensitively and match appropriately the local administrative cultures and political circumstances.

Notes

1. The authors want to thank the World Bank for supporting the research project conducted in Zhejiang, China, in 2006. Special thanks are extended to all participants and participating institutions in the survey and fieldwork.
2. The number within brackets stands for the number of overseas programmes jointly run by local Chinese universities and overseas partners.

References

Chan, David, and Mok, Ka Ho. 2001. "Educational Reforms and Coping Strategies under the Tidal Wave of Marketization: A Comparative Study of Hong Kong and the Mainland China." *Comparative Education* 37 (1): 21–41.

Chen, Zhi Li. 2002. "Historical Accomplishments in Education Reform and Development." [In Chinese.] *China Education Daily*, October 17, 1–3.

Cheng, Kai Ming. 1995. "Education: Decentralization and the Market." In *Social Change and Social Policy in Contemporary China*, ed. L. Wong and S. MacPherson. Aldershot, UK: Avebury.

China Ministry of Education (CMOE). 2006. *List of Joint Programmes Leading to Degrees of Foreign Universities and Universities of Hong Kong*. [In Chinese.] Beijing: CMOE. Available online at: http://www.jsj.edu.cn.

Chinese Communist Party Central Committee (CCPCC). 1993. *Outline for Reform and Development of Education in China*. [In Chinese.] Beijing: People's Press.

Fukuyama, Francis. 2005. *State Capacity: Governance and World Order in the Twenty-First Century*. Surrey: Profile Books.

Global Alliance for Transnational Education (GATE). 1999. *Trade in Transnational Education Services*. Washington, DC: GATE.

Huang, Futao. 2005a. "Qualitative Enhancement and Quantitative Growth: Changes and Trends of China's Higher Education." *Higher Education Policy* 18 (2): 117–130.

———. 2005b. "The Growth and Development of Transnational Higher Education in China." In *Globalization and Higher Education in East Asia*, ed. K. H. Mok and R. James. New York and Singapore: Marshall Cavendish Academic.

———. 2006a. Internationalization of Higher Education in China. Paper presented at the Internationalization of Universities Conference, Osaka University, Japan.

———. 2006b. "Transnational Higher Education in Mainland China: A Focus on Foreign Degree-Conferring Programs." In *Transnational Higher Education in Asia and the Pacific Region*, ed. F. Huang, 21–34. *RIHE International Publication Series*, No. 10. Hiroshima: Research Institute for Higher Education (RIHE), Hiroshima University.

Jordana, Jacint, and David Levi-Faur. 2005. "Preface: The Making of a New Regulatory Order." *The Annals of the American Academy of Political and Social Science* 598 (1): 1–6.

Lin, Jing. 2004. "China: Private Trends." *International Higher Education* 36 (Summer): 17–18.

Lin, Jing, Yu Zhang, Lan Gao, and Yan Liu. 2005. "Trust, Ownership, and Autonomy: Challenges Facing Private Higher Education in China." *The China Review* 5 (1): 61–82.

Meek, V. Lynn. 2006. "The Role of Evaluation in Australian Universities." Paper presented at the First Session of the International Academic Advisory Committee for University Evaluation, Hangzhou Xihu State Guesthouse, China, May 9, 2006.

Merisotis, Jamie, and Jan Sadlak. 2005. "Higher Education Ranking: Evolution, Acceptance, and Dialogue." *Higher Education in Europe* 30 (2): 97–101.

Min, Weifang. 2004. "Chinese Higher Education: The Legacy of the Past and the Context of the Future." In *Asian Universities: Historical Perspectives and Contemporary Challenges*, ed. P. G. Altbach and T. Umakoshi. Baltimore and London: The Johns Hopkins University Press.

Mok, Ka Ho. 2006a. "Embracing the Market: Changing Social Policy Paradigms in Post-Mao China." Paper under review by *Social Policy and Society*.

————. 2006b. "One Country, Diverse Systems: Politics of Educational Decentralization in Post-Mao China." Paper presented at the Contemporary China Seminar Series, Institute of Oriental Studies, University of Oxford, February 2006.

————. 2006c. "The Quest for a Regional Hub of Higher Education: Transnational Higher Education and Changing Governance in Singapore." In *Transnational Higher Education in Asia and the Pacific Region*, ed. F. Huang, 127–150. *RIHE International Publication Series*, No. 10. Hiroshima: RIHE, Hiroshima University.

Mok, Ka Ho, and King Lun Ngok. 2008. "One Country, Diverse Systems: Politics of Educational Decentralization and Challenges for Regulatory State in Post-Mao China." *China Review* 8 (2).

Morshidi, Sirat. 2006. "Transnational Higher Education in Malaysia: Balancing Benefits and Concerns through Regulations." In *Transnational Higher Education in Asia and the Pacific Region*, ed. F. Huang, 109–126. *RIHE International Publication Series*, No. 10. Hiroshima: RIHE, Hiroshima University.

Ngok, King Lun. 2006. "Marketizing Higher Education in China: Critical Reflections." Paper presented at the Ideas and Universities Seminar Series, Institute of Advanced Studies, University of Bristol, March 2006.

Ngok, King Lun, and Julia Kwong. 2003. "Globalization and Educational Restructuring in China." In *Globalization and Educational Restructuring in the Asia and Pacific Region*, ed. K. H. Mok and A. Welch. London: Palgrave Macmillan.

Painter, Martin, and Shiu-fai Wong. 2005. "Varieties of the Regulatory State? Government-Business Relations and Telecommunications Reforms in Malaysia and Thailand." *Policy and Society* 24 (3): 27–52.

46   KA-HO MOK AND XIAOZHOU XU

State Council, People's Republic of China. 2003. *Regulations of the People's Republic of China on Chinese-Foreign Cooperation in Running Schools*. [In Chinese.] Beijing: State Council, PRC. Available online at: http://www.jsj.edu.cn.

State Education Commission (SEC). 1995. *Interim Provisions for Chinese-Foreign Cooperation in Running Schools*. [In Chinese.] Beijing: SEC. Available online at: http://www.jsj.edu.cn.

Wen, Bin. 2005. *Blue Book of Zhejiang 2005*. Hangzhou: Hangzhou Publishing House.

Wu, Yi Ying. 2003. "Reforming Higher education Finance." [In Chinese.] *Education and Economy*, No 3, 2003.

Yang, De Guang. 2002. "China's Entry into WTO: Some Implications for Chinese Educational Reform and Development." First Assembly of the Global University Network for Innovation–Asia and the Pacific (GUNI–AP), Zhejiang University, Hangzhou, China, September 20–22.

Yang, Rui. 2002. *The Third Delight: Internationalization of Higher Education in China*. London: Routledge.

———. 2006. "Transnational Higher Education in Hong Kong: An Analysis." In *Transnational Higher Education in Asia and the Pacific Region*, ed. F. Huang, 35–58. *RIHE International Publication Series*, No. 10. Hiroshima: RIHE, Hiroshima University.

Chapter 4

Education Within the Knowledge Industry

Deane Neubauer

Introduction

In this chapter I examine five aspects of contemporary processes of social change and develop some of the implications of these phenomena for how education (at all levels, but with a particular focus on higher education) may be "done" in the coming decade. My position is that education in its root sense is a knowledge "enterprise" and that the logics that are impelling other institutions within the overall knowledge/information environment forces will affect it as well.[1] This presents a grounding for some of the more contentious policy debates in the field of comparative and international education.

These five phenomena being examined here are familiar to many, and are indeed, to some degree, commonplace. In many ways, we have readily adapted to many of the social changes triggered by these dynamics. The position here is that, despite their commonplace character, these are transformative in ways that perhaps we have not completely examined, especially in terms of their implications for how we conceive of and attempt to produce educational outcomes. In the order of their discussion, these phenomena are:

- The increasing "boundarylessness" of our globalized world;
- The continued emergence of networks in society and of a network society;

- Re- and de-statusing as they take place within organizations migrating from industrial to information technology (IT) network models and practices;
- The revaluing of information within the new economics of digitalization as represented by the Long Tail; and
- *Search* and its implications for how we do information and how it does us.

Five Forces Changing Our World

On Boundaries

As Mary Douglas (1973) has said, boundaries define social life. They are the social frames on which the essential elements of endogeny and exogeny delineate social structure, roles and the symbolic structures that link us, create and preserve identity, and permit ordered and predictable social exchange. Thomas L. Friedman (1999), an early apostle of the increasing global interdependence that is reshaping our world, has offered an arresting and lasting metaphor for the boundary-challenging aspects of contemporary globalization by proclaiming that *the world is flat*.

The popularity of Friedman's book and the aptness of the metaphor owe much to widespread agreement on two aspects of his growing global interdependence. One, captured in the title of his first chapter, "While I Slept," points us to the extraordinary number of ways wherein by becoming "globalized" the conventional boundaries of our everyday lives have changed. The world appears to have changed in remarkable ways "while we slept," seemingly overnight, hardly within our notice. For Friedman, our world of boundaries has slipped away. The second is our everyday appreciation that, indeed, the world *is* different. Much of how we experience and "know" the world has changed a great deal in the past two decades. However, because many of these changes are incremental, we fail to "add them all up" in ways that allow us to appreciate fully the implications of these changes across many dimensions of our lives. Our customary and comfortable languages are, in the respect of aspects, obsolete—they refer to a world that in many important respects no longer exists.

In Friedman's language, this remaking of boundaries results in large part from "flatteners"—social processes that extend out from a given source, engage boundaries, and, through the various quanta of social energy engaged, force them to give way. In making his argument, he emphasizes three periods of globalization. From 1492 to about 1800, a period dominated by European voyages of discovery and conquest he calls Globalization 1.0. The second great era, Globalization 2.0, lasted roughly from 1800 to 2000, interrupted by, and in part reconstituted by, the Great Depression and World Wars I and II. It is this period that witnessed the fundamental remaking of much of the global economy by multinational companies, now commonly referred to as transnational corporations (TNCs). We are currently embarked on Globalization 3.0, the world that has been launched while Friedman, and presumably many of us, were sleeping. He invites us to contemplate in the current era ten massively transformative flatteners, "which made the world different"—in almost every conceivable way (Friedman 2005, 6–10, 48–172):

1. The fall of the Berlin Wall in November of 1989, liberating exchange between the European West and East;
2. Netscape goes public in August of 1995, signifying the launch of successful Search and significantly eroding existing boundaries in "how to find things;"
3. Work flow software, initiated in many industries whose intellectual product is produced and exchanged digitally throughout the world—a workplace without countries;
4. Open-sourcing, the development of self-organizing collaborative communities, exemplified by Apache, Lexus, Mozilla;
5. Outsourcing, exemplified by the emergence of India as a major global software producer in response to the Y2K crisis;
6. Offshoring, the massive shift of manufacturing (and services) to the cheaper labor markets of the developing world to produce complex, high-quality goods through the application of advanced technology, exemplified in particular by the rise of China as the new manufacturing colossus of the world;
7. Supply-chaining, the organization of massive supply chains of goods and materials from throughout the world to create global product and service distribution, exemplified significantly by Wal-Mart's emergence as the largest retailer in the world;
8. In-sourcing, creating third party capability to link production and consumption nodes in the world economy, rapidly, efficiently, and within reasonable cost parameters, exemplified by UPS and FedEx;
9. In-forming, the radical transformation of search and retrieval as exemplified by Google, Yahoo!, and MSN Web Search;
10. The Steroids—Friedman's phrase for the huge range and rapidly transforming universe of portable devices for accessing the digital world.

Friedman's thesis is often challenged by those who choose to emphasize the differences and particularities of the world. Illustrations of the ways in which boundaries seem to be increasing in height and impermeability include the painful and often bloody contestations of religious "worlds" and the boundaries they establish between peoples (see, for example, Gray 2005). Increasingly, these two positions, *the world is flat* versus *no, the world is round*, emphasize the two ends of the contemporary continuum. From the point of view of this essay, caveats to the contrary notwithstanding, Friedman's recent statement seems apt: "we are moving into a hyper-integrated world in which all aspects of production—raw materials, design, manufacturing, distribution, fulfillment, financing and branding—have become commodities that can be accessed from anywhere by anyone" (Friedman 2009, WK10).

Between these two positions is the inescapable fact that increasing global interdependence is resulting in accelerated processes of change, which are continuous, rapid, active, and transforming. Much of what we knew a week ago, or six weeks ago, or six months ago is in many important ways no longer "true" and will in other ways determine what we will need to know tomorrow, or six weeks, or six months from now to effectively deal with the world that is becoming.

Mary Douglas (1973) emphasizes the "work" that boundary maintenance culture "does." What it means to "learn" a culture (either to be brought up in it or to appropriate it) is to inscribe and internalize the congeries of boundaries that define our social spaces, directing us toward values and outcomes that constitute and influence identity—that literally "place" us in our world(s). We learn to recognize these boundaries across a range of "instruction" from that which is explicit and formal, such as in the socializations of family, religion, and education, to those which are informal, accidental, or seemingly unintended, such as those of the media, of casual interaction with others (especially "strangers"—carriers of exogeny). Douglas' point is that "traditionally" much of this "work" of acquiring and being directed in life by these acquired boundaries is done outside the metalanguages that might be used to interrogate the nature of boundaries. These acquisitions tend to happen within the unexamined languages of daily interaction, as part of the accepted routines of daily life.

It is precisely these boundaries—the formal, the informal, the intended, and the unintended—that are being redefined, reframed, rediscovered, and abandoned in this particular moment of global transformation. Who we are and where we are placed in relation to others is being transformed in one way or another by all of Friedman's ten "flatteners," and by more. David Harvey has called this uniqueness the "telescoping of time and space," meaning that both the scope and the pace of social change have been radically altered within this moment of contemporary globalization (Harvey 1990). A central feature of this change is the emergence from a world defined primarily in terms of structures into one defined primarily in terms of networks.

On Networks

The familiar hierarchal structures of "traditional" societies and their industrial successors were usually represented as pyramidal. Power, status, and authority were concentrated at the top among a relative few, often through generational ascriptive structures, and distributed downward through the hierarchies according to information and knowledge codes deemed appropriate to the task at hand. Within hierarchies, information and knowledge, which can be viewed as forms of currencies, move vertically, with primary values being extracted by those occupying the upper hierarchal layers.

Networks, by contrast, tend to be flatter, distributing various currencies among their constitutive nodes in response to demand. A useful definition of a network is an association, often loosely formed, of multiple nodes interacting in response to mutually beneficial purpose wherein the value added to each member through participation is larger than that which could be supplied by any node acting by itself. Manuel Castells (1996) posits that we are increasingly becoming network societies, meaning that social interactions in general take place increasingly through varieties of networks rather than hierarchies. Knowledge societies are network societies. To assert the existence of a network society is not to claim that hierarchies have somehow (magically) disappeared, but rather to assert that association through networks has become increasingly common to the point that the relative role of hierarchy in society is being displaced. Both continue to exist.

Networks formed through the utilization of electronic media have been the most obvious and transformative, a clear manifestation of Harvey's dictum that contemporary globalization results in the annihilation of time and space. Whereas the social world was much transformed by the more formal industrial age networks of the broadcast networks of radio and television, it has increasingly been the Internet that has provided the most explosive growth and depth of transformation. It is difficult on this terrain to be usefully factual, merely because it changes so rapidly. Currently, roughly one-sixth of the world's population is Internet users, with the figure rising to nearly 70 percent of the population in North America. Usage growth over the past six years has been on the order of 200 percent. Equally remarkable has been the speed with which new pathways of network association have formed within these communicative technologies (MySpace, YouTube, SecondLife, Facebook, etc., and the continuously expanding realm of social networks). The markets created by these interactive/network-facilitating devices are all the more remarkable for their global ubiquity.

Cell phones and text messages disproportionately impact who is able to connect with whom in developing societies, while in developed nations their volume continues to expand. Usage patterns of cell phones and other handheld devices are on the whole generationally biased and distinguished by exceptionally high uses within identifiable population subgroups (see, for example, Castells et al. 2006; Nyiri 2006; Telephia 2006). Whereas in developed countries connectivity is often focused directly on the Internet (as in South Korea, for example), in poorer, developing countries, which lack reliable Internet access, cell phones have radically transformed interactivity patterns, although (again) change is the constant, as broadband availability continues to grow. The Philippines is a dramatic case in point: users on average send 150 text messages a day, and report that they check their phone regularly if they have not received a message within an hour (Meinardus 2004).

If we hold that associative networks are importantly related to identity formation, it can be argued that networks become significant markers of "what one knows in the world," and are important enablers for gaining such information/knowledge. This raises two parallel issues of some importance. One, as networks increase in social and personal importance, they come to rival more traditional sources of knowledge and information acquisition. Two, the very newness of many networks means they are not much researched. Their value as providers of identity in terms of the social currency that can be associated *to them* is largely unknown. We know relatively little about how interaction with newer networks displaces or effects interactions with more traditional forms of knowledge and information acquisition.

De- and Re-statusing Organizations

One feature of the competitive environment being created by economic globalization is *managerialism*. At its core, managerialism has been a movement designed to transform corporations from the dominant organizational structures of the industrial period into forms more appropriate for the knowledge/network society. With the shift in manufacturing from mature industrial societies to the developing world, emergent transnational firms discovered that they required new organizational forms.

Increasingly they developed organization forms linking the center to its peripheral units globally through communication technology, creating flatter, more autonomous units. The annihilation of time and space permitted new forms of control, allowing the more direct command and response modalities of the industrial corporation to yield to notions of goal setting and audit. Industrial production itself shifted from the *fordist* model (so named because of its realization in the early forms of the Ford Motor Company) and the fordist mode of production that typified it (Jessop 1995).

Flexible production (or just-in-time production), which was developed during the early years of postwar Japan manufacturing recovery, has progressively displaced traditional industrial manufacturing. In flexible production the final product results from the creation and coordination of a vast network of producers of subunit components, which arrive at the assembly point just prior to their use in assembly. Flexible production revolutionized many industries by vastly reducing the amount of capital required by the end-product firm, leading to higher profit margins through cost-cutting production practices (for a definitive treatment of the Toyota model of flexible production, see Monden 1994).

In this model the transformation of managerial systems solicits the critical views of shop floor workers to be integrated into the system, resulting in a significant enhancement of quality for the end product.

Rigorous control over production runs and unit costs had the larger effect of challenging the "one-size-fits-all" modality of fordism in favor of customized production, in which units are often "made to order" for prepaid consumers. The flexible production paradigm has come to be expressed through notions of reduced inventories, rapid production turns, new shop floor production models, ideas of team production, shop floor feedback, and the emergence of management theories that promote a more decentralized, network-type structure (see, for example, Peters and Waterman 2004).

These core ideas when applied in nonspecific production settings have proved complex and complicated to put in practice. Many successes coexist with extensive dislocations of employment. When applied to the public sector, the successes of managerialism have often gone unnoticed or have been discounted for partisan political reasons. Within higher education, both public and private, managerialism has resulted in demands that universities be run "more like businesses," with consequent efforts to establish cost and profit centers and to have service units "run on their own bottom," supporting themselves out of dedicated user fees. American higher education as a whole redefined its labor force when less than 50 percent of new faculty hires were for tenure-track positions. Universities have found that the economics of shedding "bundled" personnel costs is as much a part of "their" business, just as any other organization (Kezar 2005).

The flexible production model is integral to the *network model of production* initially prevalent in information companies, but which has generalized and dispersed as an increasing number of organizations have integrated high-tech information systems and embraced their underlying logics and meta-logics—thus coming to see themselves primarily as information entities. This transformation has many traditional industries, such as banking, insurance, stock brokerage, relabeled as "financial industries" and operate in ways indistinguishable from other knowledge or information enterprises. Even medicine, long viewed as a "thing onto itself," has increasingly developed a self-understanding as an information science and practice.

For the contemporary knowledge-driven organization, it is the *idea* that matters. The lessons of organizational survival and success hold that a premium must be paid for the generation of those ideas, their early recognition, and the ability to capitalize on them in product development and market extension. In the rapidly changing world of information and knowledge, organizations re-statused their practices and structures on the basis of where and how ideas are generated. IT organizations tend to be structured around more open models of communication, Google and Amazon (the largest network retailer) having become cases in point. Any number of articles and blog posts, especially in its early organizational moments pointed to the "crazy" ways in which Google conducts its business (Lashinsky 2006).

Although statuses and roles continue to exist, derived from more conventional organizational models, in the IT network model the substance of their interactions is radically different. The organization as a whole tends to function as an active learning community with all actors posited as learners. The presumption is that at some level of idea generation and development a fundamental kind of de-statused nonhierarchy exists. Developing an organization on this model also re-statuses some of the internal roles of the organization, most particularly those directed at talent identification and recruitment. John Battelle reports on the tension evident in the early Google organization where two "institutional-bads" had to be combated simultaneously. One was founder's syndrome, in which the company's creators found it difficult to allow the organization to develop routines and customs over which they did not exercise direct control. Founder's syndrome, when not attended to, can result in stultifying issues on span of control. It was directly related to the "hiring spiral," in which the founders would hire a person they might consider an "A"—"perfect for the job, intelligent, productive, and a good cultural fit" (Battelle 2005, 130). Person A then is allowed to hire more people, who then hire more people, and so on.

Table 4.1   Elements of the Industrial and Postindustrial Organizations

Elements of the Industrial Paradigm—Fordism	Elements of the Postindustrial Paradigm—Flexible Production
Standardization and universalization—one size fits all, and a "unit" for every person	"Boutique adaptation"—design products for those who need and want them—tailor to individual needs
Linear, predictive models of cause and effect	Nonlinear, probabilistic models of association and consequence
Education based on the acquisition of relatively constant elements of agreed-upon knowledge	Education addressed for rapidly increasing knowledge quotients (knowledge explosion)
Relatively rigid professional hierarchies	Flexible associations of capabilities brought together in networks
Ideology of formal education—progress and development	World viewed as more complex—formal education is one element among many; world is a more contingent place
Concentrate productive capacity in vertically integrated hierarchies	Production distributed throughout the world to maximize economies in factors of production
Primacy of manufacturing capital	Primacy of finance capital

The problem, as Battelle relates, is that A persons rarely hire people who contest or challenge them, thereby producing a downward talent spiral, of Bs, Cs, Ds,...and so on. The company comes to be numerically dominated by C- and D-level people, "loses its unique culture and falls victim to divisive internal politics and the malaise of hierarchically driven management games" (Battelle 2005, 131.) To forestall this outcome, Google founders Brin and Page devoted an extraordinary amount of time in the extensive interviews that led to early hires.

Such a system is clearly not sustainable, and Google recognized this early. The result, as has been the case throughout the industry, however, has been a restructuring within organizations to enhance the relative role of the human relations function and processes through which people are hired. The dictum is that choice leads directly to quality. The extent to which this has become an industry-wide issue can be illustrated by an October 7, 2006, special 15-page study of *The Economist*, on the critical issue of identifying, hiring and retaining "talent," signaled by the headline "The Battle for Brainpower," which notes that "Talent has become the world's most sought-after commodity...[and] the shortage is causing serious problems" (Wooldridge 2006, 3–24). Again, Thomas Friedman, writing several years later in assessing the coming global struggle of the United States with China, conjoins the points of global hyper-relatedness with the "idea culture" by arguing that, on the face of it, China has distinct advantages over the United States—save two that cannot really be commoditized.

Fortunately, America still has one of them: imagination.

> What your citizens imagine now matters more than ever because they can act on their own imaginations farther, faster, deeper and cheaper than ever before—as individuals. In such a world, societies that can nurture people with the ability to imagine and spin off new ideas will thrive. The Apple iPod may be made in China, but it was dreamed up in America, and that's where most of the profits go. America—with its open, free, unrestricted, immigrant-friendly society—is still the world's greatest dream machine.
>
> Who would cede a century in which imagination will have such a high value to an authoritarian society that controls its Internet and jails political prisoners? Remember what Grandma used to say: Never cede a century to a country that censors Google. (Friedman 2009, WK10)

One can offer a set of suggestive propositions about the nature of the "IT organization":

- When information is of primary value, the *source* of the information is de-statused in favor of the idea itself;
- In such organizations "the leader" is a member of the learning community; a critical element of equality, reciprocity, and exchange typifies the organization;
- In overall terms, organizational focus comes to be centered on outcomes rather than on the rights, privileges, and rewards of status;
- Organizational incentives tend to be organized to reward outcomes, which, because of the fluid nature of the "idea culture," can be discontinuous and episodic rather than a result of linear tenure served in stable roles (Battelle 2005, Chapters 3 and 5);
- Incentives within the organization are calibrated to foster social climates that produce creativity, idea, "productivity," and an atmosphere of continued and positive change. (Note the blowback when such structures come to transform "banks" and "financial" companies into what are in reality information/knowledge companies! Lucchetti 2009).

IT network organizations—especially the celebrated ones such as Google and Amazon—are sufficiently new that one cannot usefully predict how these flexible organizational models will survive further success, middle age, and the continued demands of public ownership performance. Their interest to us, however, lies in the demonstration of their early success in which conjoining flatter, flexible organizational styles with processes of idea creation and production are producing revolutionary changes in how we seek and "do" information.

The Long Tail

We have so far alluded to a new "law" of labor organization, stating that if something can be digitalized, it can be outsourced. In its initial stages, this period of labor reorganization focused primarily on conventional information technology, such as clerical work. In a later stage, large financial organizations moved their "back room" activities to offshore operations. In yet another stage, shifts began to occur in the redefinition of so-called "in place services," those that were presumed necessary to be provided in place, where the service provider and service recipient were in direct contact. Medicine generally was considered an in-place service, a distinction that began to shift with the development of telemedicine. It quickly became clear that whatever could be scanned electronically could be digitized and not only transported to be reviewed at another time and place (store and forward technology) but "interpreted" by those outside the social and cultural frames of the host country as well.

In contemporary examples of digital displacement, hospitals often provide neurological surgeons with units that allow them to do a quick review of a trauma patient's condition to determine whether the surgeon needs to respond physically to the hospital or call; radiologists in India review X-ray films for hospitals in New York; and universities are developing the means by which pathologic analyses can be done on a sample anywhere in the world with sufficient broadband capacity (Zheng et al. 2003; Outsource2India 2009). Such observations may now seem commonplace to any regular reader of the technology press: technological change is producing ever more digital devices that encompass ever more applications and affect ever more aspects of everyday behavior.

The property by which "a thing" can be digitized and its storage and transmission as data become virtually costless gives rise to new notions of how market demand can be organized. The desired product-distribution curve traditionally has described a *head*, in which most of the product(s) is(are) distributed at an "effective" price (that is, one at which the producer is willing to create more products for the market), and a *tail*, in which price and volume fall as market demand decreases. Historically, this has been a highly interactive relationship, in which many producers bring a product to market seeking a "hit," during which large numbers of the product may be sold at an effective price. Ironically, as one producer creates a hit in the market, that success draws competitors seeking similar hits. In this way, the market "uses up" hits, which steadily decrease in marginal value for the production of further iterations and/or their distribution in the tail. Consequently, the availability of items in the tail become more expensive for the consumer as their small marginal value to producers leads to limiting or ending production, and for distribution to move to smaller and fewer outlets.[2]

Chris Anderson's (2006) review of the Long Tail points out that while knowledge of the phenomenon has long been noted, we appear to be entering a new era where this insight is coming to constitute both a new business and knowledge model. Rendering digital data virtually costless radically changes the economics of distribution in the Long Tail. Combined with the equally facilitative economics of search engines (hereafter referred to as Search), the result has been an increasing number of ventures from Amazon to eBay to Craigslist and beyond to other ever novel "aggregators" that make practicable markets that operate to serve highly particularistic interests of small numbers of people—matching very small amounts of demand with very highly differentiated supply. In aggregate, like Craigslist, they come to constitute a new market in and of themselves. Anderson sees the Long Tail as having transformative impacts on society.

> The theory of the Long Tail can be boiled down to this: Our culture and economy are increasingly shifting away from a focus on a relatively small number of hits (mainstream products and markets) at the head of the demand curve, and moving toward a huge number of niches in the tail. In an era without the constraints of physical shelf space and other bottlenecks of distribution, narrowly targeted goods and services can be as economically attractive as mainstream fare.... Bottom line: A Long Tail is just culture unfiltered by economic scarcity. (52–53)[3]

Anderson identifies three forces being wrought by the Long Tail. Democratizing the *tools of production* occurs through steady advances in the sophistication and capability of relatively inexpensive digital devices, leading to the phenomena we now see as MySpace, YouTube, Facebook, and other free aggregating sites.[4] The media continuum is increasingly defined at one end by the largest media producers in the history of the world that control broadcast content monopolies virtually throughout the world. These are TNCs of global media—the Big Six (Williams 2001). The other end of the continuum is increasingly dominated by the relatively chaotic "democratic" forces of production. The Big Six control the Head (although they are facing falling rates of consumption across most of their product lines); these other forces make up the Long Tail. As Anderson (2006, 54) puts it,

> Millions of people now have the capacity to make a short film or album, or publish their thoughts to the world—and a surprisingly large number of them do so. Talent is not universal, but it's widely spread: Give enough people the capacity to create, and inevitably gems will emerge.... The result is that the available universe of content is now growing faster than ever.

The other two forces are reducing the costs of distribution, largely through the mechanisms of digital aggregation and new modes for connecting supply and demand. With regard to the distribution, as Anderson points out, the PC was capable of making everyone a producer, but it was the Internet that made everyone a distributor. The third force of connectivity is obviously in its early stages. Part of it arises from the "wisdom of crowds" logic that underlies the Google algorithms of Search, part of it arises from recent organizational forms of Internet communication such as the blogosphere and the search engines that make it viable by reducing the Search costs to consumers (Surowiecki 2004; Anderson 2006, 57–59). The blogosphere itself is termed by some as a "media ecosystem" (see Hiller 2006).

The Long Tail has alerted us to a new marketplace and new ways of doing business in that marketplace. In this model the democratized tools of production lead to a vast increase in the numbers of producers—a movement that directly confronts the increasing growth and aggregation in size of the major global producers and "their" economy in which approximately two-thirds of global trade is accounted for by the top 500 TNCs. A key to this development has been what Anderson, interrogating the logic of Google, calls the "distributed intelligence of millions of consumers to match people with the stuff that suits them best," allowing them to become the new tastemakers.

Search

Moore's familiar law, first articulated in 1965 by Gordon Moore, cofounder of Intel, predicts that the number of transistors on a computer chip will double every two years. In practice, the capacity of chips has doubled roughly every 18 months, with a corresponding fall in relative prices. This exponential growth in capability has brought us to the present state in which chips, such as that announced by IBM in February 2009, will be capable of operations at 15 times the capacity of the current fastest machine (see Moore 2006). It is this exponential growth in capacity more than any other single factor that has fueled the parallel growth in capability, innovation, application, and affordability of all forms of digital devices.

In what is increasingly referred to as versions of the "law of accelerating change" (or accelerating returns), we are experiencing some of the implications of the continuous exponential growth of information; and by doing so we are acknowledging that technological change can no longer be regarded as a linear phenomenon. The world abounds with predictions, such as the one claiming that, driven by current rates of change, we will experience a century's worth of technological change in 25 years, or that, at today's rate of change, in 100 years we would get something like 20,000 years of previously measured technological "progress" (Kruzweil 2001).

Search is a result of this dynamic. Google's extraordinary success is due in large part to the genius of its founders, Brin and Page, in finding the pattern of Search technique (from keyword to complex algorithm) that allowed an entirely new version of Search to emerge from its predecessors (including Excite, Yahoo, and Alta Vista), which they then placed at the core of an advertising business model (which Google did not invent) and generated billions. Part of Google's success has been its ability to function as a Search engine within specific content modalities (for other web sites and pages) as well as new aggregational or filter "places" such as MySpace, MyPlace, or YouTube, and a seemingly endless chain of new followers (Battelle 2005). The diffusion speed of such cyber spaces and their ubiquity will continue, as can be concluded from the lessons of Moore's law, as capacity continues to expand exponentially and price continues to fall.

Search has worked so famously because it is convenient, virtually costless to the user, and has become progressively more efficient. Google's breakthrough of finding ways to target sites based on the impersonal findings of its ever more sophisticated mathematical algorithms has moved continually forward in bringing seemingly unlimited amounts of information to accessible digital retrieval, and it included the once completely outrageous project of digitizing all the books in the world. Google has become the "hare in the distance" for virtually every other Search-associated business. Virtually all of them are built on the logic of the Long Tail, allowing advertising costs to be apportioned only when triggered by users, thereby reaching the "holy grail" of advertising—spending advertising dollars only for exposure that has some probability (however small) of generating actual sales. These remarkable accomplishments were the first generation of Search.

The beginnings of many subsequent generations of Search have, without a doubt, emerged in the as yet highly imperfect world of customer/viewer/user profiling, in which all the past behavior of a given computer source is aggregated to generate a "unique" and targeted profile—a technique that has been quickly adopted by other Internet marketers and virtually the whole of the security industry, national or private. An example includes the journal *Surveillance and Society*, and especially Wood (2003). These techniques have recently been conjoined to brain research discoveries that assist in "locking products" into our "aspirational futures" (Murphy, Iles, and Reiner 2008). Certainly, the directions in which Search is taking us will do much to further erode our personal sense of privacy, just as the subscriber lists that are shopped around industries, or as the Internet that has allowed terrorist networks to employ the same technologies to their destructive ends (Holtzman 2006). All of these and much more that are even more dimly glimpsed (or not at all) are the implications of a global communications world in which every click-stream is monitored, for good or bad, in some computer somewhere. The engagement being created by these technologies and the worlds they create invite the questions: what are we doing to information and what is it doing to us?

Education in a Knowledge Society

What factors would be involved if we were to treat education, from K-20, more directly as a knowledge enterprise itself? What kinds of outcomes can be expected from such education institutions? In what ways will they be restructured or operate differently if we sought to align them more directly with the rapidly productive and transforming elements of the knowledge industry as discussed above? Here are a few directions that might be useful to pursue.

Historically, we tend to conflate education and knowledge: education as instructional practice presumes, at each level, to claim certain bodies of knowledge as appropriate and seeks to impart this to students. Functionally, it is common to see education as having performed certain traditional functions, such as knowledge transmission (the teaching function), knowledge creation (the research function), and knowledge conservation (the library function.) With contemporary computers and handhelds, a discursive shift has emerged around the insistence of separating information from knowledge as education. In this distinction, the former is viewed increasingly as a currency with its own set of tools, and the latter as a set of practices embodying categories and bodies of content formed purposively by culture and human society with the primary purpose of delineating value from mere iterative regularity (Dordick and Neubauer 1985). Within education, knowledge tends to remain distinct in many respects from information, but it is least so in those emergent disciplines organized around information theory and computing. The power of the traditional canon (differing as it will be from society to society) has been such that it has dominated the education "core," relegating innovations largely to the periphery. Within the conceit of education, knowledge was what *it* did—the appropriation of that label by the information industry was viewed largely as an unwarranted pretense.

This pretense has persisted, however, spurred in part by public policies that have driven education to serve this powerful emergent industry. Universities in particular have been viewed increasingly as sites for technology transfer, as vehicles for private sector technology partnerships, and judged in terms of their direct contributions to economic development. In what has come to be known throughout the world as the higher education "alignment issue," public and private institutions alike have increasingly come to develop partnerships and alliances within business communities, linking themselves directly to innovation centers of the economy.

However, when the public policy pressure to do this is viewed from within educational institutions, it is experienced as a less benign force. From here the endeavor seems less like becoming a major component of society's innovation centers as it does an endless struggle to "keep up" or "catch up"—a constant struggle to "make education relevant." Indeed, especially in the context of much public K-12 education, the "information discourse" often takes the form of viewing the "school" as a social institution that must be protected from the disruptive aspects of "students' private lives," which are, of course, to many degrees dominated by contemporary communication devices, games, social networking, and so on. In significant ways, schools ask students to check their lives at the door in order to concentrate fully on the work of school—the dominant paradigm proves intractable (Hawkins 2007).[5]

In seeking to track the interactive effects of information and knowledge within the received structures of education, it seems sensible to continually ask what we are doing to information and what it is doing to us. With regard to the first, we are clearly generating vastly more of it, gathering it together in novel arrays and making it available, with relatively small costs, across categories of usage that are continually expanding—the Kurzweil thesis writ large. And this dynamic is hardly likely to reverse itself.

What information is doing to us is more complicated. It is, perhaps most importantly, reidentifying us (Witaker 2000). The complex ways that we exist in data bases of all kinds that are then made available through the multitude of Search methods and devices give us identities for the world's use and misuse, in ways that we are sometimes aware but are often not. And as we are re-identified to the world outside, we interact in complex ways with the identities that we fashion within ourselves. This seems one of the primary lessons from a full generation of social networking and at least two generations of electronic gaming.

As we catalogue the many many ways that identity is formed and evolves, like the familiar categorical influences of culture, nation, and locality, language, family, and other primary identity groups (those, for example, framed around religious observance and practice, school, sport, etc.), it is increasingly difficult to construct notions of identity that do not have consumption and its status imputations at their center. And although contentions on this point are great, these tensions seem rooted in various ways in the great social thermals welling up and through Islamic societies and cultures, as well as those more typically "Western" in their emergent consumption patterns, including, in not the least case, China. Up and down the ladder of class, income, and status, what one does and does not consume as material goods and services are the primary framers of identity for both self and other. The ubiquitous world of Search and its emergent world of preferential identifiers are hardly unique in these terms. They exist as a process, a service, and interactive reality for the primary purpose of linking producers with any information quanta that define, identify, and deliver the user/consumer. Beyond that, Search seeks to identify for us "needs" and "desires," before we know that we have them, by assembling thousands—hundreds of thousands—of attributes, large and small, about ourselves and providing them as potential identity elements and potential acts of consumption even before we have made those calculations for ourselves. These traits—termed inference and intentionality by the industry—have become ubiquitous elements of Search.

As we think about the outcomes that we should expect from education (at all levels), or what might be the common elements of "international" or "global" education, it is important to argue that a primary task is to instill in students and graduates the grammars of interaction that allow them to "speak, understand and act" in a world that is being so rapidly shaped by these technologies.

Conclusion

In bringing this all too brief discussion to a close, I am going to take the easy way out by making the suggestion that higher education—as an enterprise—needs to take steps to become more like the knowledge industry that is growing around it and transforming society. This is the easy way because a powerful argument can be made that doing so constitutes nothing less than a base submission (surrender?) to the lowest of common denominators in the essential contest between information and its unre-strained growth (and as Kurzweil reminds us: information is infinite in scope). Knowledge, after all (such an argument would remind us), is some-how and irreducibly about *situating information in contexts*, which, as a result of some complex social processes, has been deemed to be either of use, or of value, or both. Knowledge and information *are* different, and universities are meant to be organized around this and other principles.

However, it is also the case that higher education is in an arrested mode with the all-pervasive alignment issue: it either effectively prepares gradu-ates for the society and economy at hand (and in the process of becom-ing one) or—at least in its given forms—it stands the risk of becoming irrelevant. If, for example, we push the current higher education funding crisis just a few years out and assume for the time being that the Great Recession is likely to be both long and slow to gain recovery, it seems not too far-fetched to posit that (a) public funding for public education will continue to fall, and (b) students will become even more vocationally oriented than ever. In this environment, the public pressures for greater alignment (to support economic growth, compete with China and India, etc.) will themselves reinforce ever more strident student demands that their evermore expensive educations actually get them jobs at the end of their education course.

One can already look across parts of US higher education to discover plentiful examples in which institutions are taking large steps to do some of the things hinted at earlier in this chapter (e.g., to whittle away tra-ditional boundaries, and especially those that define academic units and their "ownership" of portions of the curriculum): to flatten traditional academic hierarchies through the development of learning communi-ties, problem-based learning, research across the curriculum, and team-oriented instruction; to reposition "the idea" as the dominating "fact" of the organizational/educational exchange;[6] and to embrace digitalization as a normal part of the classroom environment. But, having made this claim, these instances tend to be the exception rather than the rule, and they tend to occur (as they do at the school level) where the level of resources signals an "elite" educational situation, or when the institution is already marginal by some conventional criteria. And these transformations are not just occurring in the United States. As scholars seek to draw comparisons between educational systems and the policies that guide them, they would be well advised to at least place these debates in the context of the dramatic changes that are taking place in the knowledge industry.

Ken Auletta's (2009) recent book on Google is entitled *Googled: The End of the World as We Know It*. This is a catchy subtitle, which I myself have been guilty of using on occasion. In a sense, it "works" because it allows one to talk about BIG CHANGES, and also because, in an information-exploding world, there is a self-evidential truth to it that people tend to get right away. However, for some of the reasons suggested above, the presence of Google in the world puts conventional higher educational experiences on the line in ways that they have not been before. What began two decades ago as "search," and which had challenged virtually all the received notions of how information/knowledge should be conducted within higher education, is—like one of George Lucas' films—receding rapidly into the future. May we live in interesting times.

Notes

1. A previous and longer version of this paper, entitled "Education as a Knowledge Enterprise," was presented to the 31st Annual Conference of the Pacific Circle Consortium, Honolulu, Hawaii, June 25–29, 2007.
2. Dan Bricklin describes the Long Tail relationship: "There is a classic curve with just a few of the products selling in any significant numbers compared to the others. In a traditional store or company only a subset of the products that could be sold is actually made available for sale—those to the left of the vertical dotted line. There are many reasons for this, such as cost of inventory, lack of shelf space, old fashioned telecommunications architecture, need to focus sales and support in a narrow area, etc.

     The Long Tail comes into play when the cost of making a much wider selection available drops." (Bricklin 2005)
3. Anderson (2006, 53) summarizes his views into six themes that, as per him, typify the Long Tail age.
   1. There are more niche goods than hits.
   2. The cost of reaching niches is falling dramatically.
   3. Variety does not shift demand by itself. Consumers must be given tools, such as search engines.
   4. Once variety has been massively expanded the demand curves flatten. While there are still hits and niches, the hits are relatively less popular and the niches relatively more popular.
   5. The niches add up and while none sell large numbers collectively they can develop as a market rivaling the hits.
   6. When all this has occurred, the natural shape of demand emerges without distortion of the bottlenecks.
4. In early December 2009, Wikipedia listed the following social networking sites in terms of estimates of their current members/users. I cite just a few.

The numbers obviously are in constant change and interested readers are invited to pay a visit to the site at: http://en.wikipedia.org.

1.	Facebook	300,000,000
2.	Qzone	200,000,000
3.	Windows Live Spaces	120,000,000
4.	Habbo	117,000,000
5.	Friendster	90,000,000
6.	Hi5	80,000,000
7.	Tagged.com	70,000,000
8.	Orkut	67,000,000
9.	Flixster	63,000,000
10.	Netlog	58,000,000

5. Innovation, of course, continues to challenge this bald assertion. Even such a distinguished figure of science (and at times controversy) as E. O. Wilson says that it may soon be the case that games and their underlying methodologies and meta-languages will become an essential pedagogy for engaging generations schooled by society in such ways of thought (see NPR 2009).

6. I had the great good fortune some years ago to attend a dinner honoring Amar Bose at which he told a story of teaching math at the Massachusetts Institute of Technology (MIT). First, he had lobbied for senior faculty to teach freshmen in a move that has become increasingly common wherein the telling argument is that young students should have the benefit of the best faculty in their early university learning years (and by implication should not be shunted off to graduate assistants no matter how precocious these might be). Second, he became concerned that in the "accepted" freshman math course, a first year MIT student, given the rigor of the competition to enter the university, should face the prospect of failing freshman math. After some reasoning, he decided that one size did not fit all and a new course model might be needed.

   In mid-semester (faced with several students who were likely to "fail" under the conventional organization of the course), he proposed that all students treat their existing materials as resources and that from that point to the end of the semester every class session have but one focus: each student was to prepare for class by thinking of one question to which he, as the instructor, might not know the answer. Stump the professor. In one fell swoop he managed to de-status the classroom, energize the students, and most importantly restore confidence in the "failing students." I regard it as an impressive story and emblematic of kinds of teaching styles that are working to re-status the classroom learning environment.

References

Anderson, Chris. 2006. *The Long Tail: Why the Future of Business is Selling Less of More*. New York: Hyperion.

Auletta, Ken. 2009. *Googled: The End of the World As We Know It*. New York: Penguin Press.

Battelle, John. 2005. *The Search: How Google and its Rivals Rewrote the Rules of Business and Transformed Our Culture*. New York: Portfolio.

Bricken, Dan. 2005. "When the Long Tail Wags the Dog." Available online at: http://www.dricklin.com.

Castells, Manuel. 1996. *The Information Age: Economy, Society and Culture. Volume I: The Rise of the Network Society*. Oxford: Blackwell Publishers.

Castells, Manuel, Mireia Fernandez-ardevol, Jack Linchuan Qui, and Araba Sey. 2006. *Mobile Communication and Society: A Global Perspective*. Cambridge, MA: MIT Press.

Dordick, Herbert S., and Deane Neubauer. 1985. "Information as Currency: Organization Restructuring Under the Impact of the Information Revolution." *Bulletin of the Institute for Communications Research*, Keio University, No 25, 12–13.

Douglas, Mary. 1973. *Rules and Meanings: The Anthropology of Everyday Knowledge*. Harmondsworth, UK: Penguin Education.

Friedman, Thomas L. 1999. *The Lexus and the Olive Tree*. New York: Farrar, Straus, Giroux.

———. 2005. *The World is Flat: A Brief History of the Twenty-first Century*. New York: Farrar, Straus, Giroux.

———. 2009. "Advice from Grandma." *New York Times*, November 22, WK10.

Google. 2006. "Google To Acquire YouTube for $1.65 Billion in Stock: Combination Will Create New Opportunities for Users and Content Owners Everywhere." Mountain View, CA: Google. Available online at: http://www.google.com.

Gray, John. 2005. "The World is Round." *New York Review of Books*, Volume 52, # 13, August 11.

Harvey, David. 1990. *The Condition of Post Modernity: An Inquiry into the Origins of Cultural Change*. Oxford: Blackwell Publishers.

———. 2006. *Spaces of Global Capitalism: Towards a Theory of Uneven Geographic Development*. London: Verso.

Hawkins, John N. 2006. "Higher Education Reform in Japan: The Tension Between Public Good and Commodification." Paper presented to the IFE Senior Seminar, East-West Center, Honolulu, September 6–11, 2006.

———. 2007. "The Intractable Dominant Educational Paradigm." In *Changing Education: Leadership, Innovation and Development in a Globalizing Asia Pacific*, ed. Peter D. Hershock, Mark Mason, and John N. Hawkins. Hong Kong: and Dordrecht, The Netherlands: Comparative Education Research Centre and Springer.

Hiler, John. 2002. "Blogosphere: The Emerging Media Ecosystem: How Weblogs and Journalists work together to Report, Filter and Break the News." *MicrocontentNews*, May 28.

Holtzman, David H. 2006. *Privacy Lost: How Technology is Endangering Your Privacy*. San Francisco: Jossey-Bass.

Internet World Stats. 2009. "Internet Usage Statistics—The Big Picture." Bogota: Internet World Stats. Available online at: http://www.internetworldstats.com.

Jessop, Bob. 1995. *Post-Fordism and the State.* Oxford: Blackwell.

Kezar, Adrianna. 2005. "Challenges for Higher Education in Serving the Public Good." In *Higher Education for the Public Good: Emerging Voices from a National Movement,* ed. Adrianna Kezar, Tony C., and John C. Burkhart. San Francisco: Jossey-Bass.

Kruzweil, Raymond. 2001. "The Law of Accelerating Returns." KurzweilAI.net, March 7. Available online at: http://www.kurzweilai.net.

Lashinsky, Adam 2006, "Chaos by Design: The Inside Story of Disorder, Disarray and Uncertainty at Google. And Why It is All Part of the Plan (They Hope.)." *Fortune* 154 (7): 86–98.

Luchetti, Aaron. 2009. "Big Bonuses Are Back for Many on the Street." *Wall Street Journal,* November 6. Available at: http://online.wsj.com/article/SB125737807967629459.html

Meinardus, Ronald. 2004. "Asian Tale of Two Countries." *Japan Times,* March 1.

Monden, Yasuhiro. 1994. *Toyota Production System.* 2nd ed. London: Chapman and Hall.

Moore, Gordon. 2006. *Moore's Law: Made Real by Intel Innovation.* Santa Clara, CA: Intel. Available online at: http://www.intel.com.

Murphy, Emily R., Judy Illes, and Peter B. Reiner. 2008. "Neuroethics of Neuromarketing." *Journal of Consumer Behavior* 7 (4–5): 293–302.

National Public Radio (NPR). 2009. "E. O. Wilson and Will Wright: Ant Lovers Unite! An Open Mic Discussion of Life and Games." Washington, DC: NPR. Available online at: http://www.npr.org.

Nyiri, Kristóf, ed. 2006. *Mobile Understanding: The Epistemology of Ubiquitous Communication.* Vienna: Passagen Verlag.

Outsource2India. 2009. "Outsourcing Radiology." Princeton, NJ: Flatworld Solutions Pvt. Ltd. Available online at: http://www.outsource2india.com.

Peters, Thomas J., and Thomas H. Waterman. 2004. *In Search of Excellence: Lessons from America's Best Run Companies.* New York: Harper Business Essentials.

Shiller, Dan, and Robert W. McChesney. 2003. *The Political Economy of International Communications: Foundations for the Emerging Global Debate About Media Ownership and Regulation.* Technology, Business, and Society Programme Paper Number 11. Geneva: United Nations Research Institute for Social Development.

Surowiecki, James. 2004. *The Wisdom of Crowds: Why the Many Are Smarter Than the Few and How Collective Wisdom Shapes Business, Economies, Societies and Nations.* New York: Random House.

Telephia. 2006. *Cell Phone Usage Highest Among African-American and Hispanic Users.* Tallahassee, FL: Video Access Alliance. Available online at: www.videoaccessalliance.org.

Wikipedia. 2006. *Craigslist.* San Francisco, CA: Wikipedia. Available online at: http://en.wikipedia.org.

Williams, Granville. 2001. *The Largest Six Media Companies in the World.* New York: Media Channel. Available online at: http://www.newint.org.

Witaker, Reg. 2000. *The End of Privacy: How Total Surveillance is Becoming a Reality.* New York. The New Press.

Wood, David. 2003. "Foucault and Pantopticism Revised." *Surveillance and Society* 1 (3).

Wooldridge, Adrian. 2006. "The Battle for Brainpower." *The Economist* 381 (8498): 3–5.

Zheng, Lei, Aurther W. Wetzel, John Gilbertson, and Michael J. Becich. 2003. "Design and Analysis of a Content-Based Pathology Image Retrieval System." *IEEE Transactions on Information Technology in Biomedicine* 7 (4): 249–255.

Chapter 5

Higher Education and Quality
Assurance: Trends and Tensions in Asia

John N. Hawkins

Introduction

In October of 2006 the Association of Universities of Asia and the Pacific held their 7th annual conference, the topic of which was: "Towards an Asia-Pacific Quality Assurance and Accreditation in Higher Education." Representing over 200 members from nineteen different countries, participants discussed issues of quality assurance, quality indicators, quality registers, pan-Asia accreditation, as well as other topics related to the desire of universities and colleges in the Asian region to achieve higher standards. This meeting (and the many others that have been held recently in the Asia/Pacific region) is symbolic of the preoccupation that higher educational leaders in the region have with "quality assurance" (QA hereafter). The fact that the top universities in Asia are not members of this association is also significant of the contradictions and tensions that exist in Asia when the issue of higher education QA arises. About the same time, a ministerial-level meeting sponsored by OECD was held in Athens on the topic "Higher Education: Quality, Equity and Efficiency" (OECD 2006), and another meeting sponsored by UNESCO was held in Paris. Asian participation in all of these venues was strong. Finally, as a concrete expression of how tense this issue can be, about 10,000 college students, many of them minorities, rioted and fought with police in Nanchang, China, on October 21, 2006 (*Honolulu Advertiser* 2006), because the government was not recognizing the academic credentials granted by two new private universities. This was only one of a series of such protests launched because of a lack of credentialing and accreditation of newly established *minban*, or nongovernmental universities (Jacobs 2009).

The policy context in which the heightened interest in QA occurs in Asia is worth noting. In the same way we watched the "happy anarchy" of higher education change in the United States in the 1970s and 1980s, universities in Asia are also experiencing a somewhat different shift in emphasis between themselves and their host societies. While decentralization of higher education is occurring, on the one hand, a contradictory "central" (i.e., a Ministry of Education [MOE] or other state body) obsession with QA is occurring, on the other; resulting in what some scholars are referring to as "centralized decentralization." This ambiguity has prompted both enthusiasm and cynicism for QA. The rise of QA in Asia is coincident with a number of forces and factors, including the philosophies of neoliberalism, managerialism, and corporatization, among others, all of which have contributed to the establishment of national QA or accreditation agencies, societies, associations, and other schemes to measure higher education quality. QA, it seems, is the current rage, it is ubiquitous. There are, of course, good reasons that higher education stakeholders are concerned with how their HEIs are performing. Massification plus diversity in higher education in Asia has resulted in an increased demand for more information regarding the myriad of universities and colleges that represent the higher education landscape in the region. For their part, colleges and universities can use QA for branding purposes, to find their niche in the tangle of institutions that represent the region. At the state level, governments find QA useful for increasing their control and leverage over higher education; and, increasingly, continued state funding (albeit, often diminished, as a result of decentralization) is often conditional and based on the results of various reviews.

What is clearly observable is that there has been a shift from a "bottom up" change process in higher education to an increase in external influences, a shift in the continuum of control from less to more. For most nations in the region, QA occurred on the front end, during the process by which the HEI was established, and apart from periodic demands by the MOE for quantitative data, and for approval of changes in the institution, there was little in the way of formal, regular evaluation. And as the locus of review moves toward national agencies, it has been argued that there is now more of an interest in accountability than in performance. One consequence of this movement is that "quality management" has replaced a more loosely coupled, and perhaps more academic, management style to assure that the ideas spawned from QA permeate the organization, that the data collected and the internal assessments comply with external demands. An evaluative culture has emerged in the region, for better or worse.

Some Contextual Considerations

In the pages that follow, some illustrative national examples of QA trends and issues will be presented, but first it is useful to provide a brief outline of the policy context in which this is occurring. Throughout the region, a number of factors influence the QA movement. Higher education has become more diverse, more available, and more international, but there is less money to go around, the private sector has expanded, and governance has undergone dramatic changes, all of which have resulted in more competition. The net consequence has been a demand for more accountability. QA has in some instances replaced external controls by the state, yet the state remains very much involved in the QA process.

When one examines QA policies in the Asian region, a variety of rationales emerge to justify the high level of interest in QA. Often the first item on the list is accountability of public funds. Although in most Asian nations neoliberalism and decentralization have resulted in the withdrawal of state support for public institutions such as national universities (and for some areas of the private university sector as well), increased accountability for the remaining allocated funds has not lessened. Related to this concern, but more focused inside HEIs, is the goal of better awareness about funding decisions for the funds allocated. This has resulted in internal competition among various higher education segments and divisions. On a more ideal level, a stated goal of QA is to improve the quality of higher education provision in general, and to better inform students, parents, and employers of the differential quality of HEIs in their region (the various "ranking" or league tables are related to this goal). Because of the precipitous rise in new private institutions, there is a pervasive interest in controlling for the quality of these new efforts as well. Other concerns have to do with assisting the mobility of students between institutions and, of course, for the general transfer of authority between the state and the institutions themselves.

Whatever the rationales, most nations in the region have been searching for a general model of QA that often includes, but is not limited to, some form of national coordinating body (often linked directly or indirectly with the MOE), some form of institutional self-evaluation, external evaluation by peers, published reports, and some form of follow-up. The impact of new QA processes may occur on one or all of four levels as follows: system level, institutional level, at the level of the basic unit, or at the level of the individual. And QA may function through one or all of three basic mechanisms: rewards, changing policies or structures, changing higher education cultures. In Asia, there appears to be more of a focus on QA at the system and institutional level and less interest in basic units such as departments, colleges, and schools (although there are important exceptions).

With respect to the reward mechanisms, a fundamental question being asked throughout the region is to what degree QA results should be linked to funding (a focus more concerned with persuading than with learning). One motivation to engage in a more formal QA assessment is the promise of increased funding in a climate of general reductions. Another kind of reward associated with QA is the region-wide concern with formal status-allocation or some form of accreditation. State-sponsored accreditation efforts are in competition with independent agencies as well as transnational accrediting associations. Finally, there is considerable interest, and consternation, in the region with league tables, or rankings. Most agree that rankings are useful, and many nations in the Asian region have a national goal to see at least one of their universities among the top 100. However, there is disagreement on methodology and who should conduct the rankings.

An obvious goal of QA is to provide the rationale for changing higher education policies and structures. As Burton Clark (1998) and others have argued, the more the state is involved in QA, the more the changes will be "fundamental," as opposed to the more familiar "incremental" changes that most HEIs are comfortable with. Fundamental policy changes can have far-reaching affects, such as the merging or termination of basic units within a university, or the merger or closure of the university itself. However, some argue that institutional policy changes hardly matter as entrenched interests often find ways to subvert or go around policy directives, giving credence to the notion that there are weak relationships between policies and what actually happen at institutions. Sometimes it is difficult to determine what causes what. Was the policy changed because of the evaluation, or was the policy environment ripe for change anyway because of internal forces?

Perhaps the most problematic issue that QA sometimes addresses is the culture of HEIs. All social organizations have a dominant internal culture, a symbolic side, that can either facilitate change or impede it, and universities are no exception. The shared beliefs that faculty and administrators hold help them define who they are, what they believe in, and why they behave as they do. Lyman Glenny's (1959) characterization of universities as "happy anarchies" is apt, and despite strong MOE controls in most of Asia, this has been true in the Asian region as well. QA is often invoked to change that. QA seeks to change the boundaries, attempting to realign the landscape between institutions and the state, between institutions and their faculties, between administrators and faculty, and between faculty and students. QA can attempt to strengthen one factor over another, research over teaching, for example, or the converse. Whatever the focus, QA often is meant to replace a more tribal culture with one focused on system-wide accountability measures, regardless of institutions or the "small worlds" within those institutions.

Formal QA, especially of the external variety, is a relatively new phenomenon in Asia. About two-thirds of the QA systems and mechanisms in the region have been established in the past decade (Antony 2006). In some systems, QA is as simple as recognition of a HEI as part of the national system; in others, it requires a procedure above and beyond standard regulatory measures and MOE approval. Sometimes the entire process is rather routine, with little at stake, at other times, continued or increased funding, or even institutional survival, is at risk. It is not at all clear that there is a unified view of what constitutes QA, although the conferences referred to above seek to move in that direction. A workable definition has not been agreed upon, but there is one that has been proffered by the International Network of QA Agencies in Higher Education (INQAAHE): "quality assurance may be related to a program, an institution or a whole higher education system. In each case, quality assurance is all of those attitudes, objects, actions and procedures which through their existence and use, and together with the quality control activities, ensure that appropriate academic standards are being maintained and enhanced in and by each program" (Antony 2006, 4). Of course, the key phrase here is "appropriate academic standards." As the settings vary, so do the understandings of what constitute "appropriate academic standards."

In the pages that follow, recent QA policies will be briefly explained to provide some of the flavor of this diversity in specific national and regional settings. Inasmuch as QA policies are being formed and changed as this is being written, what follows will be a snapshot in time, which will undoubtedly be dated by the time this is read. But an effort has been made to select policy issues that are relevant and are likely to continue to be addressed, even as QA policies in the future become more specifically formulated and mature.

Regional Case Examples

Two of the largest higher education systems in the Asian region are those of China and India. Yet, despite similarity in scale and complexity, their approaches to QA in higher education are quite distinct. The China MOE has played a central role in creating a regulatory responsibility system centered in one locale, rather than spread among a variety of ministries as in the past. This centralization has allowed for a more unified system of qualification standards to be applied in the areas of learning, accreditation, and awarding degrees. This has become particularly challenging and important because of the rise of the nongovernmental sector (*minban* colleges and universities such as Huang He University in Zhanzhou, Xi'an Fanyi University in Xi'an, and Sanda College in Shanghai), which has developed impressive educational capacities and have begun to challenge the notion of academic excellence (OECD 2003).

The financial self-responsibility movement has also had an impact on QA development, as HEIs now must generate around 50 percent of funds needed to cover recurrent costs and research. A question raised here is the degree to which this has helped or hindered QA. OECD noted that the movement toward the market has had mixed results and has not necessarily improved learning outcomes. It was reported that the MOE was aware of this and was taking action to "initiate further quality monitoring and assurance reforms, including providing more information to consumers" (OECD 2003, 23). The general QA system that has evolved since 2002 consists of a variety of levels of review. A five-year cycle was put in place in 2002 whereby every HEIs is to be evaluated every five to six years. The Academic Degrees Committee of the State Council (ADCSC) is responsible for defining the differentiated standards for degrees, including the BA, MA, and Doctorate, in both HEIs and research institutes. The Higher Education Department of the MOE has a disciplinary guidance committee for curricula and content. A Committee of Accreditation staffed by the Education Development and Planning Division of the MOE defines qualification procedures for assessing educational capacities for individual HEIs. Period assessments of HEIs can result in the institutions being approved, put on probation, receiving warnings, and put under suspension. While the ADCSC is responsible for overall degree standards, there is a division of responsibility for accreditation, whereby doctoral programs are accredited by the MOE, and BA and MA degree programs are accredited by local provincial, and in some cases, urban, settings (Yuan 2010).

While central, bureaucratic authorities have major responsibility for QA and accreditation in general, since 1994 there has been a movement toward independent assessment bodies such as the NGO National Evaluation Institute for Degree Granting Education (NEIDGE). However, this approach did not yield expected results, and the MOE has more recently become interested both in the US model of accreditation and agencies such as the European Foundation for Quality Management. By 2003, three basic types of institutional assessment emerged: qualification assessment, excellence assessment (*xuan yu ping gu*), and random assessment (Wang 2007). The first mechanism is focused on HEIs with recognized weak institutional capacities. Excellence assessment is reserved for HEIs with generally recognized strong institutional capacities. And random assessment is for those that fall in between these two categories. Most of the focus has been on evaluating teaching. Some provincial and urban settings have developed their own systems (e.g., Shannxi and Shanghai), and HEIs in general have been encouraged to establish their own self-assessment systems. In general, OECD concludes that this multilevel approach has increased transparency, competition, and generally functioned quite well. There is a heightened awareness of the educational market and an overall drive for innovation in teaching and research. The guidelines that were stated in the "Educational Vitalization Action Project 2003–2007" appear to be at the core of current QA efforts in China:

- Building an instructional quality assurance system
- Establishing agencies for assessment and assistance in college instruction
- Developing a system of periodic review of instructional quality
- Building links between program assessment and professional qualifications and certificates
- Formulating assessment standards and indicators
- Building data bank on college instruction
- Developing an analyzing and reporting system (Wang 2007, 3)

All this will require an even more differentiated QA approach. OECD recommends that an expanded QA system be implemented, one that focuses on educational objectives, teaching curricula and courses, pedagogic approaches, and educational methods. The emphasis should be on educational outcomes, not just inputs and outputs (e.g., do graduates find jobs, what kind of jobs, etc.). They recommend third-party accreditation and the use of "international standards," specifically International Organization of Standards (ISO 10015), a Geneva-based organization originally focused on engineering education. Section 10015 of their set of standards specifies measures for higher education quality.

In response to current needs and recommendations, such as those by OECD China's external QA, Ministry of Education policies currently focus on:

- Making policy to require all professors teach undergraduate courses and encouraging star professors to teach core curriculum courses and freshman courses

- Establishing special grants for learning resource renovation
- Establishing special grants for development of courses of excellence
- Establishing special grants for compiling textbooks of excellence
- Selecting "national outstanding professors of teaching"
- Establishing a national college instruction assessment center (Wang 2007)

The focus on teaching and learning is very evident. With respect to internal (provincial and institutional) assessment, teaching and learning are also strong components, although more institutional specific foci are also present:

- Establishment of institutional instructional assessment centers
- Formalization and implementation of student's evaluation of teaching
- Peer review both in terms of classroom supervision and faculty hiring and promotion procedures
- In-service training for teaching
- Institutional self-study procedures (Wang 2007)

The overall assessment procedures still consist of the three elements common to many procedures in the region: (1) self study and report, (2) on-site visits by specialists, and (3) correction and improvement of practices. There are both first-level indicators (such as those associated with educational philosophy, faculty, learning resources, teaching and learning, etc.), and second-level indicators (such as basic learning facilities, quantity and structure of the teaching force, majors, thesis and design, morals and values, etc.) that are considered in the overall assessment process. The system appears to be moving more toward qualitative measures than quantitative measures (e.g., written tests that were previously required for visits to campus sites are no longer part of the process), and assessment indicators are more focused on "soft" themes such as institutional philosophy, faculty issues, course development, and so on (Wang 2007).

Work on China's QA system is still in progress, and it currently consists of a mix of levels (central government, MOE, local provincial and institutional, and continued interest in the involvement of external, international agencies) and faces a number of challenges and questions (should QA be formative or terminal, how much emphasis on rankings, what should be the relationship between governmental QA and other "buffer" agencies; is there too much emphasis on competition; and how should the QA assessment be used). What seems clear is a strong policy interest in using QA to build a core of first-class HEIs.

India is the other large higher education system in Asia, of which the government has recently been harshly critical. Indian higher education has a long history of British regulatory mechanisms. The University Grants Commission (UGC) was established in India in 1994, and the National Assessment and Accreditation Council (NAAC) employs a familiar QA mechanism of self-evaluations, peer review (based on predetermined criteria for assessment), and the application of a voluntary graded five-point scale (Antony 2002). The primary problem India faces is the tradition of affiliation whereby one college takes the lead in undergraduate education and is loosely connected to other colleges and universities. As Antony (2002, 17) notes: "Most Indian universities are of the affiliating type where the affiliation university legislates on courses of study, holds examinations centrally on common syllabi for its affiliates, and awards degrees of successful candidates." Some affiliating universities have over 400 affiliated colleges, thus rendering QA a problematic exercise. Many of the affiliates are known to be substandard. An increase in private initiatives has also created difficulties for India. About 70 percent of all HEIs are run by private trusts (even though many receive substantial levels of state funding through "grant-in-aid college funds").

The scale of the "quality" problem of Indian higher education was recently divulged by the leak of a confidential report by the National Assessment and Accreditation Council, a division of the UGC. The report indicated that 123 universities and 2,956 affiliated colleges across India had been evaluated and that 68 percent of the universities and 90 percent of the colleges were found to be of "poor quality" (Neelakantan 2007b, 2). Additional QA issues were that enrollments were down, faculty positions were unfilled, teachers lacked credentials, and IT was lacking. Prime Minister M. Singh stated, "The country's university system is in a state of disrepair, we need better facilities, more and better teachers, a flexible approach to curriculum development to make it more relevant, more effective pedagogical and learning methods and more meaningful evaluation systems... (we have) a dysfunctional education system which can only produce dysfunctional future citizens. There are complaints of favoritism and corruption... we should free university appointments from unnecessary interventions on the part of governments and must promote autonomy and accountability" (Neelakantan 2007b, 3–4).

The challenges for QA in India, thus, are rather substantial. In an effort to address the issue of "affiliated non-degree granting institutions" that make up the bulk of the colleges in India, the Prime Minister further proposed that new degree-granting central universities be established in each of the 16 states that lack one. Each of these new institutions is meant to be a symbol of academic excellence; they all must maintain highest academic standards and be models of efficiency. The PM directed India's higher educational regulatory bodies and Planning Commission to prepare a strategy for the establishment of these new institutions (Neelakantan 2007a). Thus, a major higher education development effort seems to be the primary strategy to begin a more rigorous QA effort in India. The current QA mechanisms are also being questioned, but the focus is on redefining higher education in India through the establishment of new institutions that meet world standards.

India is in an advantageous position to make progress toward quality higher education, but the country also faces substantial disadvantages that the current QA system highlights but seems unable to influence. There are high quality HEIs such as the Indian Institutes of Technology, the All India Institute of Medical Sciences, and the Tata Institute of Fundamental Research, but these institutions enroll much below 1 percent of the total student population (Altbach 2005, 18). India's proposed course of action to create a new set of globally competitive institutions, thereby raising the QA level for all higher education in India, is both bold and risky (and also expensive). As Philip G. Altbach (2005, 20) notes, "without these universities India is destined to remain a scientific backwater."

While China and India struggle to push their massive higher education systems forward and at the same time raise quality standards, Japan, as the traditionally undisputed higher education leader in the East Asia region, struggles to maintain the quality that it has already attained and to redefine what it means by QA. Japan has a long history of formal accreditation that is modeled on the US system inherited as a result of the US post-World War II occupation. The Japan University Accreditation Association (JUAA) was formed in 1947 with 47 universities, and it now includes 322 universities (41 national, 28 public, 253 private). This represents 45 percent of all universities in Japan (Hokama 2005). Up to 2004, the JUAA was the sole organization for accreditation and evaluation in Japan (the MOE, of course, had the sole authority to approve the creation of all HEIs, but they stipulated the minimum standards). All HEIs were required by the MOE to undergo a self-review periodically and release the results to the public, but there was no explicit requirement that the institutions be reviewed by an external agency. JUAA accreditation was a voluntary and autonomous system of QA that many HEIs joined largely in order to help improve their pedagogical mission (Hokama 2005).

The QA process in Japan began to change in 2000 when the MOE launched its own system of evaluation by its own agency: the National Institute for Academic Degrees and University Evaluation (NIAD-EU). The NIAD-EU was modeled on a British QA system and was not an accreditation agency in the strict sense. Stimulated by WTO and the

European accreditation movement, the NIAD-EU approach "referred to trends in European countries regarding accreditation and explained the need for QA in the context of international competitive and cross border provision of education, rather than in terms of domestic requirements for quality improvement" (Yonezawa 2005, 2). The MOE had never made much use of the JUAA, but universities favored it as it symbolized participation in the international QA movement.

The *School Education Act* was amended in 2002 and proposed a new accreditation scheme to be enacted in 2004. The MOE then authorized several accreditation agencies to perform evaluations, but the process still remained centralized. Japan seems to be following the global trend of establishing national bodies of accreditation, a departure from the previous decentralized, voluntary model of the JUAA. As Yonezawa (2005, 2) points out:

> The strong insistence by the government on its ownership of accreditation in Japan has inarguably contributed to confusion regarding the concept. Currently, the only reliable model of accreditation for Japan is the American, nongovernmental one, while the Japanese approach itself corresponds somewhat to newly developing European (and some other Asian) initiatives. A sense of ownership of the accreditation system is hardly shared by the Japanese universities. The universities, especially private ones, argue that the legal requirement of accreditation as it applies to private higher education institutions is a governmental trial to intervene in the autonomy of private universities. On the other hand, Japanese higher education institutions have never consolidated to protect their ownership of accreditation after being introduced by the American forces in the mid-20th century.

This lack of perception of ownership is likely to hamstring any serious efforts by the MOE or any other accreditation agencies to gain credibility in the QA process. It is far more likely that international and local market pressures will have a much greater QA impact. The authority of JUAA has been diminished and must now report (as do all other QA agencies) to the MOE. Once again, decentralization policies toward HEIs have been countered by renewed centralization by the MOE bureaucrats. The numerous private institutions in Japan have therefore decided to launch their own accreditation agency. For-profit and even international agencies can be certified as accreditation agencies under the new legislation. One feature of the new system will be competition. If a university or college does not like the results of one QA evaluation, it can switch agencies for the next seven-year round (Hokama 2005). These developments raise questions about the seriousness of QA in Japanese higher education.

A similar search for QA alternatives is taking place in Taiwan. Since 1966, Taiwan's higher education system has expanded from 21 HEIs to 162 in 2005 (Chen 2006). The expansion, combined with the international competitive forces of globalization, have put QA on the front burner for educational leaders and analysts. The MOE has put pressure on Taiwan's HEIs to compete internationally and be able to enter the "rankings" along with high quality institutions in other Asian settings (Cheng 2006). Three basic mechanisms have been utilized to spur the QA movement forward: (1) offering HEIs more basic autonomy, (2) increased funding as an incentive for change, and (3) developing a new and better QA system to perform periodic evaluations of both institutions and programs. The institutional accreditation methods familiar in the United States influenced Taiwan early in its QA development, beginning in 1975 and up to the 1990s. The process was always centralized, with the MOE playing a central role. In 2005 the MOE commissioned a new organization called the Taiwan Assessment and Evaluation Association (TWAEA) and authorized it to conduct both programmatic and institutional evaluations. In addition, the Higher Education Evaluation and Accreditation Council (HEEACT) was established to conduct a nationwide university program evaluation and lay the groundwork for the ranking of research performance. TWAEA is a nonprofit organization founded by academics and individuals from the business sector. HEEACT is a MOE body. The latest national higher education evaluation involved a joint effort by the two bodies, with the MOE in the lead (Li 2005a). This is an ongoing process viewed by some scholars as focused more on international rankings and league tables than on improving teaching, research, and learning (Chen 2006).

The methods used are also a mix of the US accreditation approach and the experiences derived from the Bologna process in Europe. This involves more fully involving the HEIs themselves, involving students in the evaluation process, focusing on the quality and employability of graduates, and becoming competitive internationally (Li 2005b). Like Japan and China, the QA process remains highly centralized, with the MOE and its agencies playing lead roles and external agencies increasingly being involved in specific aspects of QA review (Chen 2006). At least one scholar of QA in Taiwan suggests a preferred future where the MOE would retreat to a position of assuring the integrity of the process while relying on external, more independent agencies to conduct the actual audits and evaluations.

Singapore and Hong Kong offer further examples of a QA process whereby general decentralization and increased autonomy of HEIs is coupled with a continued strong presence of the state with respect to QA. Ka Ho Mok (2000) refers to a "re-" regulation of higher education in the context of QA at the same time as the state loosens its controls of higher education in general. Hong Kong may have been the first higher education system in the region to systematize QA when in 1997 the Executive Council empowered the UGC to begin a QA process for all HEIs: "The UGC in its mission statement pledges to up hold the academic freedom and institutional autonomy of institutions while at the same time seeking to assure the *quality* and *cost-effectiveness* of their education provision, and *being publicly accountable* for the sums of public money devoted to higher education.... by the term quality assurance (the UGC means) the maintenance of the highest standards both in teaching and learning and in research and services commensurate with an institutions' agreed role and mission.... such terms as 'fitness for purpose,' 'doing the right thing right the first time,' 'value added,' performance indicators,' and so on, proliferate" (Mok 2000, 158). The focus at the central level in Hong Kong then is to determine that the HEIs in Hong Kong have the appropriate mechanisms for QA in place, rather than to assess quality by itself.

Quality Assurance Committees and Performance, Planning, Appraisal and Development offices were established within universities to focus on four meta areas of evaluation: the quality program framework (mission statements, vision, goals, etc.), formal quality program activities, quality program support, values and incentives (what is the reward structure for carrying out QA?). Hong Kong initiated (and Japan and Taiwan followed) a "center of excellence" scheme to encourage strong programs to develop and, conversely, identify weak programs. Mok concludes that "All these changes illustrate how the ideas and practices of managerialism have affected the university sector in Hong Kong. Without a doubt, university governance in Hong Kong has shifted from the traditional collegial approach to management-oriented and market models" (Mok 2005, 163).

Singapore in some ways offers a contrasting approach to QA. Whereas in Hong Kong the emphasis has been on cost cutting and efficiency, in Singapore the focus is on maintaining global competitiveness. About the same time QA began in earnest in Hong Kong (1997), Singapore's Prime Minister Goh stated, "We have to prepare ourselves for a bracing future—a future of intense (global) competition and shifting competitive advantages, a future where technologies and concepts are replaced at an increasing pace, and a future of changing values. Education and training are central to how nations will fare in this future" (Mok 2000, 163). To prepare for this competition, Singapore's two universities (National University of Singapore, NUS; and Nanyang Technical University, NTU) put in place internal QA mechanisms with the goal to transform both institutions into "world class" universities. The MOE adopted a novel approach by forming an international QA team of eleven prominent academics from highly ranked American, European, and Asian universities to conduct an external QA analysis of the two universities. The goal was to provide recommendations that would transform them into the Harvard (National University of Singapore) and MIT (Nanyang Technological University) of Asia. The reviews were conducted at the institutional level and the MOE buttressed these efforts by introducing policies that tightened up tenure rules, provided financial incentives for good teaching and research, promoted a more favorable faculty–student ratio, and so on. In the case of both the Hong Kong and Singapore, the presence of QA is very much certain, and though QA implementation has been occurring during a period of the hollowing out of the state, the state, through the MOEs, is very much involved in the process; these two cases are examples of the centralization of decentralization.

Changes in QA policy are not limited to East Asia, as it has been occurring throughout the region. QA efforts in Indonesia, Pakistan, Cambodia, Vietnam, and Thailand, to name just a few nations in the region, are keeping apace with the rest of the region, and, as was suggested in the introduction to this chapter, this is occurring amid both enthusiasm and cynicism. M. K. Tadjudin (2001), chair of the National Accreditation Board for Higher Education in Indonesia, notes that although accreditation policies date back to 1994, many stakeholders believe that more programmatic or institutional approaches to QA are not helpful. Because the higher education market is not well developed in Indonesia, students are more interested in simply obtaining the academic degree than identifying the best academic programs. Many view QA through accreditation as a somewhat foreign concept, and therefore the challenge in the immediate future is to establish a "paradigm of accreditation management (that) will also change to professionalism, transparency, accountability, and cooperation with other national and international accreditation agencies and professional organizations for better quality assurance and accuracy" (Tadjudin 2001, 17).

In Pakistan it was not until recently that the MOE established the Higher Education Commission (HEC), which in turn established a QA arm to get inside Pakistani HEIs with the express purpose of encouraging QA and bringing up Pakistani institutions to world standards. Quality Enhancement Cells (QECs) were established inside the universities to assist in creating a general awareness of modern theories and practices of QA, develop procedures to inspire quality among academics, and introduce quality measurements for continued improvement. The QECs in turn have an advisory body of university vice chancellors, policymakers, and scholars to consult with the HEIs under review. The HEC does both institutional and programmatic accreditation. In the Pakistani case, a novel feature is the significant international involvement from the

Asia Pacific Quality Network based out of Australia, the International Network of Quality Assurance Agencies based out of Berlin, and the National Accreditation and Assessment Council of India. The goal and challenge for Pakistani educational policymakers is to find a way to legitimate QA and find accreditation mechanisms that fit Pakistani national and cultural circumstances while aligning HEIs with international standards.

Finally, there are a number of settings where a centralized approach is the only approach to QA. In Cambodia, despite a large World Bank loan with preconditions that an independent accreditation system be established, the proposed Accreditation Committee of Cambodia (ACC) was launched, but it has not been an active participant in QA; however, a new agency lodged within the Ministry of Education, Youth, and Sports has instead been charged with maintaining QA (Ford 2003). A similar situation prevails in Vietnam and Thailand where a centralized structure for QA prevails. As Ford (2003, 13) notes: "the notion of an independent (accreditation committee) challenged some well-established traditions of hierarchy and power." The decentralization policies urged by the World Bank (and other globalization forces) have been experimented with, but the urge to recentralize seems powerful, especially when it comes to QA for higher education. In the case of Cambodia, Ford (2003, 13–14) suggests that:

> It remains to be seen how the new ACC will function. Due to chronic shortages of human resources, people with the necessary expertise are not available locally, and without external funding, it seems unlikely that they will be easily recruited. Most of the original draft law remains unchanged. The requirements for accreditation are still in place—including definitions of institutions, minimum standards, and the necessity for a foundation year, credit transfer, and transparent financial procedures. If they are applied fairly, then the new law may still achieve its intended purpose of providing a regulatory framework for the sector. But if the ACC simply becomes a paper tiger—or worse, a toll gate—then official accreditation may have little effect on improving the quality of the higher education sector.

Discussion

The foregoing discussions and comments are meant to provide a flavor of the complexity, diversity of policy issues, and motives of QA in the Asia region. A few observations seem warranted here and may provide some topics for further discussion. QA in Asia seems to arise from a variety of impulses and motives. There are examples of countries where the goal of becoming globally or regionally competitive in higher education seems to be the priority (Singapore, China, Japan, Taiwan), and there are those cases where more local/national interests prevail (Indonesia, Cambodia, Vietnam, Thailand). There are some examples where developing "world class" model institutions seems to be the primary goal of QA (India), and there are other examples where "efficiency" prevails (Hong Kong). While the motives are mixed, QA is naturally assumed to be part of the new higher education landscape.

On another axis, the mechanisms of QA are as diverse as the motives. There are those examples of highly centralized approaches (Cambodia, Vietnam, Thailand, perhaps Indonesia), a basically centralized approach with some decentralization gestures (Japan, China, Taiwan), a mixture of decentralization and centralization (India, Singapore, Hong Kong, Pakistan), and some cases where the novelty of involving international QA agencies is beginning to take hold.

Finally, little has been said thus far about the issue of cross-border QA. The globalization of higher education is still in its initial stages, but it will not be long before many nations in the region will have to weigh the interests of national higher education against entrepreneurial global interests. The Asian Pacific Quality Network survey has found that while many nations have developed an internal QA capacity, only a few nations in the region have the capacity to ensure the QA of imported educational services (Antony 2006). The future of QA, both conceptually and practically, will likely be characterized by a lively discussion as educational policymakers, academics, students, and other stakeholders attempt to determine what is meant by higher education and how to conceptualize the university, and also how to determine what is meant by that illusive concept, "quality."

References

Altbach, Philip G. 2005. "India: World Class Universities?" *International Higher Education* 40 (Summer): 18–20.

Antony, Stella. 2002. "Institutional Accreditation in India." *International Higher Education* 27 (Spring): 17–18.

———. 2006. "Globalization in Higher Education: Ensuring Quality Across Borders." *UNESCO Bangkok Newsletter* 4, August 2005: 4–5.

Batool, Zia. 2006. "Quality Assurance in Higher Education: A Shifting Paradigm." Paper published in Higher Education Council, Islamabad.

Burke, Joseph C., ed. 2004. *Achieving Accountability in Higher Education: Balancing Public, Academic and Market Demands*. San Francisco: Jossey-Bass.

Chen, I. R. 2006. "Pursuing Excellence: Quality Assurance in Taiwanese Higher Education." Paper presented at Clifton House, Bristol, UK, July 12, 2006.

Clark, Burton. 1998. *Creating Entrepreneurial Universities: Organizational Pathways of Transformation*. Oxford: Pergamon.

Ford, David. 2003. "Cambodian Accreditation: An Uncertain Beginning." *International Higher Education* 33 (Fall): 12–14.

Glenny, Lymen. 1958. *The Autonomy of Public Colleges: The Challenge of Coordination*. New York: McGraw Hill.

Hokama, Hiroshi. 2005. "Transformation of Quality Assurance System of Higher Education in Japan." Paper delivered at the International Conference on QA, Athens, Greece.

Jacobs, Andrew. 2009. "Beijing Students Pressed to Stop Protesting Lecturer's Detention." *New York Times*, September 21, A13.

Li, Shiaau-Rurng. 2005a. "Learning from the European Higher Education Area." Paper presented at the Third Conference on Knowledge and Politics, The Bologna Process and the Shaping of the Future Knowledge Societies, Bergen, May 18–20, 2005.

———. 2005b. "The Latest Higher Education Evaluation in Taiwan." Paper presented at the Higher Education and Research and Development Society of Australasia, Sydney, July 3–6, 2005.

Messick, Samuel J. ed. 1999. *Assessment in Higher Education: Issues of Access, Quality, Student Development and Public Policy*. Mahwah, NJ; Lawrence Erlbaum Associates.

Mok, Ka Ho. 2000. "Impact of Globalization: A Study of Quality Assurance Systems of Higher Education in Hong Kong and Singapore." *Comparative Education Review* 44 (2): 148–174.

Neelakantan, Shailaja. 2007a. "India's Prime Minister Assails Universities as Below Average and 'Dysfunctional.'" *Chronicle of Higher Education*, June 25.

———. 2007b. "Indian Prime Minister Promises to Establish Many More Universities and Colleges." *Chronicle of Higher Education*, June 4.

OECD. 2003. *OECD Review of Financing and Quality Assurance Reforms in Higher Education in the People's Republic of China*. Geneva: OECD and Centre for Co-operation with Non-Members Directorate for Education.

———. 2006. *Meeting of OECD Education Ministers—Higher Education: Quality, Equity, and Efficiency*. Paris: OECD, Programme on Institutional Management in Higher Education (IMHE).

Shavelson, Richard, and Liu Huang. 2003. Responding Responsibly to the Frenzy to Assess Learning in Higher Education. *Change* 35 (1): 10–19

Tadjudin, M. K. 2001. "Establishing a Quality Assurance System in Indonesia." *International Higher Education* 25 (Fall): 16–18.

Wang, Yingjie. 2007. "Building Quality Assurance System in Chinese Higher Education: Recent Progress." Paper presented at Quality Assurance of Higher Education in China and Switzerland Conference, April 17–18, 2007.

Yonezawa, Akiyoshi. 2005. "The Reintroduction of Accreditation in Japan: A Government Initiative." *International Higher Education* 40 (Summer): 20–22.

Yuan, Li. 2010. "Quality Assurance in Chinese Higher Education." *Research in Comparative and International Education* 5 (1): 58–76.

Chapter 6

A Policy Framework for Higher Education in Lebanon: The Role of Strategic Planning

Hana Addam El-Ghali, John L. Yeager, and Zeinab F. Zein

Introduction

Lebanon, located at the crossroads of the Middle East, possesses a rich, diverse history reflecting the ebb and flow of the many nationalities that have all left their unique imprints on the country's social, political, and cultural development. These historical events frame the critical influences of the country's current development and operations. Of particular importance in this development process is the overall educational sector: basic, secondary, and higher education. This subsector is central and pivotal to Lebanon, which prospers primarily on the wealth of its human capital. It is recognized that education is an essential foundational base on which the nation must depend for its economic and future well-being, particularly when situated in the context of a volatile international marketplace and an unstable global economy.

While the basic and secondary education subsectors in Lebanon are well established, the higher education subsector has experienced a relatively uncoordinated pattern of growth and development, which has resulted in sporadic, piecemeal development based on changing national and institutional agendas, most which can be attributed to the country's changing political and economic climates. This development has brought a rich diversity to the sector, as well as a sense of fragmentation. To a large extent the government has historically played only a modest role in coordinating and directing the development and operations of the higher education sector. This has led to an emphasis on an individual institutional entrepreneurial development approach that has resulted in a mix of institutional types and a perceived submaximization of potential outcomes. The question then is about the capacity and desirability of the government to facilitate the development of this sector through more active and direct involvement.

One of the widely used mechanisms that has been employed by several countries is the development of national policies to support the coordination of higher education activities through the implementation of various forms of national strategic plan, as in the examples of China, Mongolia, Canada, and several African countries. If a country wishes to maximize the scarce resources it is applying to the higher educational sector, it must have a strategic planning, which is one of the most appropriate mechanisms for the development and implementation of strategies and achieving desired goals.

In the case of Lebanon, the government and higher education institutions must develop an effective partnership in order to develop and implement a higher education plan. Potential partnership models involve the creation of a higher education consortium, encouraging collaborative institutional planning efforts, and the Ministry of Education and Higher Education (MEHE) assuming more direct control of higher education plans and policy. Given the existence of a large and diverse private higher education sector and only a single large public university, the authors believe that the Directorate General of Higher Education should foster the development of a voluntary, cooperative planning consortium that is comprised of all the higher education institutions in the country, duly supported by government policy, to serve as a vehicle for initiating and coordinating cooperative institutional projects, academic activities, and policy initiatives.

Many may argue that Lebanese higher education institutions should continue to essentially operate independently and autonomously from the MEHE. However, in these times of unstable global economy, turbulent regional political scenario, and critical local developments, there is a pressing need for coordination to maximize the availability of scarce resources to the higher education subsector. Under these conditions, the major question that persists is, "how best can the MEHE and the Lebanon's universities cooperate to meet the country's needs?"

This chapter will address these issues through the presentation of a brief history of the subsector, a description of the current higher education system, and a proposed consortia strategic planning model to develop and align MEHE and institutional planning activities.

History of Lebanese Higher Education

Since its inception in 1866, the Lebanese higher education sector has been growing, evolving, and changing, reflecting the country's development and its educational needs. El-Amine (1977) categorized the growth and development of the Lebanese higher education system into three stages: Foundation, Nationalization, and War. However, Hana El-Ghali (2008) has proposed a fourth stage, the Revitalization Stage, spanning from the 1990s to the present.

During the first stage, the Foundation Stage, 1866 to 1950 (El-Amine 1997), foreign missionaries established two universities in Lebanon, the Syrian Protestant College, which in 1920 became the American University of Beirut (AUB), and the University of St. Joseph (USJ). The role and influence of AUB, founded in 1866, as an institution of higher learning extended beyond Lebanon, serving youth from across the Middle East region. AUB was, and still is, strongly affiliated to supporters from the United States, from where it receives a majority of its funding. In 1875, USJ was founded by a group of monks, and it has maintained strong ties with the University of Lyons in France (El-Amine 1997). During the latter part of the Foundation Stage, three other higher education institutions were founded. The American Junior College for Women, today known as the Lebanese American University (LAU), was founded in 1924; this was followed by the Lebanese Academy for Fine Arts (ALBA) in 1937. ALBA was the only higher education institution that had no foreign affiliation when it was founded. The third institution to come up was the Near East School of Theology. This is one of the few higher education institutions in the region to prepare students in the study of theology.

The Nationalization Stage was initiated with the founding of the Lebanese University (LU) in 1951 (El-Amine 1997). The Lebanese University, the only national university in the country, is a government-run public institution with five campuses: East and West Beirut campuses, Tripoli campus, Sidon campus, and Zahle campus. LU is made up of 17 faculties with 47 branches in various locations across the country. While originally founded with the primary purpose to train teachers for secondary schools, it has greatly expanded its program offerings to include training for a number of other professions. In 1959 it was granted a license by the Lebanese government to teach all of its study programs and award LU graduates bachelor's, master's, or PhD degrees. Instruction is relatively free, students pay only minimal fees for registration, and those enrolled in teacher training programs receive stipends. The University follows the French model of higher education in most of its colleges and institutes, and in a few cases it employs the United States course credit system. As a public institution, the government provides approximately 98 percent of LU's revenues; the balance comes from student fees and publications (El-Amine 1997; UNICEF 2005). Salaries consume the major share of LU's budget, while expenditure for research and libraries represents a very small proportion. Expenses for students at private universities are two to five times the expenses at LU. For example, tuition fees at AUB for the 2007–2008 academic year ranged between US$10,080 and US$10,680 per year, whereas tuition fees *and* total expenditures at LU for the academic year 2007–2008 reached a maximum of US$1,000 per year (International Colleges and Universities 2008). The Beirut Arab University (BAU), a private institution of higher education, was also established during the Nationalization Stage in 1960. It is financially supported by the Alexandria University of Egypt and operates under the auspices of the Moslem Philanthropic and Benevolent Society of Beirut. Accordingly, BAU's entire decision making is controlled by its Council based in Egypt.

It was during the Nationalization Stage in 1961 that the government passed the first Lebanese law regulating higher education, later modified in 1967 by the Supreme Advisory Council of the MEHE, specifying new licensing procedures and regulations. From 1975 until the present time, 21 private universities were founded and recognized by the Lebanese government. These procedures were again modified in 2007 to legitimize new institutions founded in the past decade.

The Nationalization Stage was followed by the War Stage. Throughout the history of higher education in Lebanon, the country passed through long periods of civil war that seriously damaged its civil infrastructure, businesses, and human resource base. The war inflicted large losses in terms of human lives and the social and physical displacement of people, causing poverty and social inequality in Lebanon. During these difficult times, higher education pursuits shifted from a local-country bias to an external focus, with foundations and families encouraging and funding students to study abroad.

The Revitalization Stage shifted higher education pursuits back to responding to internal local demands. During this stage, the higher education subsector witnessed significant growth in terms of the total number of institutions, programs offered, students enrolled, and those who graduated. Overall student enrollment in higher education increased 34.2 percent since 2001, with 167,165 students having enrolled in the Lebanese higher education subsector during the academic year 2007–2008 (Center for Research and Development 2009). While the public sector, represented by the Lebanese University, remained relatively stable, the growth in student demand to attend higher education resulted in a major expansion of the private sector. Student enrollment across universities in Lebanon was marked by an unequal growth between 2001 and 2007. As student enrollment continued to steadily grow in the Lebanese University, enrollment in private universities grew at a faster rate (Center for Research and Development 2008). Despite this growth, in the absence of national policy, signs of instability arose in the sector. Both public and private institutions shared organizational and governance difficulties, and the subsector at large struggled with issues of accountability and quality assurance.

In 2002, MEHE, which played a significant role in specifying and enforcing regulations in the higher education subsector, crafted a strategic plan for the subsector. The plan contained several strategic initiatives, among which was the identification of new challenges in higher education and the need for new national policies to overcome them. MEHE outlined a number of policy initiatives in its strategic plan to address these challenges. These policy initiatives were as follows: build the capacity of the Directorate General of Higher Education, review and modernize current higher education policies, promote and strengthen the role of the Lebanese University, establish quality assurance standards for higher education, establish a new country agenda for the subsector, regulate the licensing of new institutions and the equivalency of their degrees, and promote and develop scientific research in higher education institutions. These initiatives served as the foundation for the development of the subsector's strategic plan.

Current Status of Lebanon's Higher Education Subsector

Types of Institutional Organizational Structure

The diversity of Lebanon's higher education system provides a variety of institutional and program options to the students seeking higher education. After completing the Lebanese baccalaureate, students have the option of pursuing either a university degree or a technical degree in higher

education. Those who select to pursue a university degree have several
options, such as a obtaining a bachelor degree in science, arts, or in engineering. Those pursuing a university degree can eventually obtain a doctorate in an academic discipline or a medical doctorate. Those following
the technical track can choose from a variety of technical majors offered to
obtain technical licensure. The variety of degrees and the diversity of the
institutions that are available to students present multiple opportunities
and mechanisms for students to pursue advanced study.

Ministry of Education and Higher Education

The first Ministry of Education in Lebanon was established in 1955.
This ministry was founded for the purpose of establishing and regulating
the following: the Ministry's central office, the Lebanese University, the
directorate of elementary and intermediate education, the directorate of
vocational education, the directorate of secondary education, the teacher
preparation program, the physical education program, the cultural program, the national institute for music education, and the national publishing house. These responsibilities defined the new role the Ministry played
in regulating the sector.

However, it was not until six years later, in 1961, that the first law governing higher education in Lebanon, the *Higher Education Act* by the Ministry
of National Education and Fine Arts (MNEaFA), was passed within the
context of strongly competing political influences (Matar 2003). Several
regulations and multiple decrees followed to further organize the higher
education subsector in the country; however, this initial law remains intact
and is the foundation for later regulations. In addition, several regulatory reforms followed MNEaFA's founding, which resulted in changes in
its name and the areas of focus. The most recent regulatory reform was
passed in 2000. This reform not only changed the name and agenda of
the MNEaFA but also divided it into several ministries and added a new
directorate that specifically addressed higher education. The new ministries included the Ministry of Education and Higher Education (MEHE),
which now includes the Directorate of Higher Education; Ministry of
Culture; Ministry of Technical and Vocational Education (MaTVE); and
Ministry of Youth and Sports (MoYS).

MEHE has several governing bodies that regulate the subsector, such as
the Higher Council of Universities, Lebanese University, National Center
for Scientific Research, National Center for Research and Development,
and Directorate General of Higher Education. The Directorate General of
Higher Education, in turn, has several councils and committees reporting

to it, from which it seeks advice and inputs. While private institutions do not directly report to or are controlled by MEHE, there exists a long-standing, informal relationship between MEHE and these institutions, which permits them to enjoy total autonomy of governance and at the same time maintain a liaison role that facilitates communication and cooperation. MEHE does not have direct control over the private universities.

Current Challenges

As a growing subsector, higher education in Lebanon has experienced both successes and challenges in the past decade of the country's reconstruction and restoration efforts. Both public and private efforts have been made toward keeping the subsector moving steadily forward amid roiling local, regional, and global instability. New plans, policies, and regulations have been put forth in the hopes of creating a better national higher education system. Despite these efforts, many difficulties remain and new ones have emerged.

Ambiguity of National Policies

One major obstacle facing higher education in Lebanon is the ambiguity of national policies governing the subsector at large and the private institutions in particular. This vagueness in policies has created opportunities for many institutions to enter into what can be called the "higher education market" of Lebanon. It has been over 40 years since the first state policy governing the private higher education subsector was passed. During this period, numerous institutions were founded and new regulations generated to govern the procedures of initiating and founding new institutions. Despite these efforts, certain weaknesses emerged that pertain to educational administration at new institutions, the licensing procedures, accountability, and quality inspection. For example, since 2002, new efforts have been ongoing in an attempt to modify the current policies to address the emergence of international academic standards.

Lack of Quality Assurance

This challenge has resulted in the urgency for Lebanon to establish a quality assurance system, particularly after the rapid growth the higher education subsector experienced in terms of the number of institutions and programs. This need was further heightened with the growing number of university graduates who were increasingly unable to find employment. In an effort to realize this QA policy, partnerships have been initiated since

2002 between the Lebanese government and the European Commission (EC).

Issues pertaining to quality assurance in higher education emerged from several factors influencing the subsector. The poorly regulated process of determining the equivalency of higher education degrees conferred by the various private higher education institutions is a complicated and contentious process. With the emergence of a large number of private higher education institutions in the past few years, this process has gained increased attention. Many of these institutions have manipulated current regulations to benefit their own organizations and have been granting student degrees that the MEHE does not provide equivalency or accept. In addition to verifying the degrees earned at these local resident institutions, The MEHE also had to determine the equivalency of degrees earned through distance learning. Both these factors required MEHE to issue new equivalency regulations that addressed these quality issues.

Lack of Program and Institutional Diversification

In spite of the expansion of the subsector, there still existed a lack of diversification of institutions and program offerings. This has been manifested at two levels. First, current policies regulating the subsector for the variations between levels of higher education and the corresponding degrees offered are not clear, making it difficult for students to transfer between institutions. Another manifestation of this challenge appears in the emergence of highly specialized institutions that attracted students to programs because of their narrow focus but which did not meet the demands of local, regional, and global markets. For example, most of the higher education institutions licensed between 1996 and 2000 were offering only variations of business and IT majors.

Problems within the Lebanese University

The establishment of new programs by LU presented another difficulty for private higher education institutions, because it offered the largest number of programs of studies in Lebanon. The University had experienced steady growth in faculties and students since 1951. However, this growth was accompanied by a state of instability due to either legal, organizational, financial, academic, or political hindrances. This insecure and troubled situation of the LU presents a more pressing issue than at other institutions because 48.1 percent of students are enrolled at the this University. Furthermore, due to its size, LU is one of the major vehicles for creating access to higher education and, consequently, for social mobility in the country.

High Performance Expectation

The Lebanese society has grown to expect that the higher education sub-sector will play a pivotal role in the advancement of the country. In recent years, with the growing regional and global economic crises, these expectations have heightened. The higher education institutions are expected to be among the most influential drivers of an economy that depends heavily on its primary source of wealth: human capital. They are no longer only expected to create an educated citizenry but to also address the country's social and economic needs and to develop its production and service sectors. These new roles are now emphasized owing to the limited capacity of existing institutions to provide opportunities for nontraditional learning/teaching and avant-garde programs. It is anticipated that new universities will be able, through partnering with international institutions, to provide a wider and more innovative array of programs.

Minimal Support of Scientific Research and Development Activities

A further perceived role of Lebanon's higher education institutions is that of advancing knowledge through scientific research and development. This component of activities had been neglected due to the long periods of war the country experienced, which resulted in a brain drain, the absence of a research infrastructure, and lack of basic financial support to effectively establish research and development programs. This has led to a drastic decrease in the number of professional and scientific journals and articles published in Lebanon. However, in the past few years, there has been a noticeable change in the engagement of higher education institutions in scientific research, as a number of them have initiated partnerships with international institutions. Further, it is recognized that the mission statement of universities needed to be expanded to include a commitment to research. This commitment can be reinforced by introducing new standards based on performance and auditing; the introduction of more graduate programs, particularly, doctoral programs; and by funding postdoctoral students and centers that engage in research and development efforts. The expressed need for an increase in these efforts supports the new direction of higher education in Lebanon in developing a knowledge-based economy to facilitate the country's competitive position in a global economy. The challenge of creating a knowledge-based economy pertains to all constituencies of the society, but it can only be achieved through the existence of a quality higher education system to provide well prepared, competent citizens to carry forward these efforts.

Limited Capacity to Lead and Support Change

To overcome these obstacles, it is critical for Lebanon's higher education institutions to partner and cooperate with MEHE and with each other. MEHE can play a critical leadership role through the creation and initiation of incentive programs to stimulate collaboration. To this end the role of MEHE's currently established councils need to be more clearly defined and they must receive additional support to meet their management roles and responsibilities through such activities as management training, provision of adequate numbers of support staff, and sufficient program funding. For example, among the critical councils supported by the Directorate General of Higher Education are the Technical and Equivalence Committees that make decisions as to which institutions are to be licensed and which degrees are to be approved. These Councils currently rely heavily on members of the private sector to serve on their boards and provide appropriate human resource support. Furthermore, new councils need to be developed to address new and emerging needs of the subsector, such as a quality assurance council and a modified licensing committee. These needs entail a major overarching challenge involving limited financial resources, which has been a serious subsector limitation ever since the founding of the first higher education institution in Lebanon. Limited governmental resource availability presents private institutions with limited access to them, thereby forcing them to create their own sustainable funding. It should be noted that these resource limitations not only affect the private institutions but also the LU and MEHE, restricting their capacity to address the many challenges they confront in a fast paced, changing globalized society.

Role of MEHE in Addressing Higher Education Subsector Challenges

MEHE plays a key role in addressing the emerging issues that face higher education. The Directorate of Higher Education, while relatively small in terms of staffing and funding, has however managed to accomplish its mission through the several committees and councils it appoints. Discussed below are examples of some of these issues and the strategies MEHE has designed to address them.

MEHE has acknowledged the ambiguity of many national policies governing the subsector at large and the private institutions in particular. In response to this, MEHE has initiated the development of a strategic plan as one of its highest priorities along with the need to establish new policies to govern the higher education subsector. In addition, MEHE has started working in partnership with the EC to establish a quality assurance framework. Among the activities they are conducting are issues involving program accreditation and institutional licensure, which have begun to directly affect private universities. These quality assurance challenges have placed a heavy burden on the government to issue new equivalency regulations.

The Director of the Directorate General of Higher Education has stated that there is a growing concern for the increasingly limited choices students have in selecting higher education degree programs (Jammal 2008). This trend could in the near future result in a crisis as students realize that the expertise they are gaining through their higher education does not meet the current and evolving demands of the market. It was thus crucial for MEHE to create a clear policy that licenses institutions offering appropriate programs. Private higher education institutions are expected to play a pivotal role in the advancement of the country, and MEHE has urged higher education institutions to take on the role of advancing knowledge through scientific research and development. In support of this role, MEHE has begun funding programs to support research initiatives, although these programs have not developed a sufficient potential to have any major impact as yet. This expressed need for increased research and development matched the policy initiative set forth by MEHE for directing higher education in Lebanon toward a knowledge-based economy to compete more effectively in the global economy. To overcome obstacles in its implementation, it is critical for higher education institutions to partner and cooperate among each other and with MEHE. Among the efforts that MEHE could foster in this direction is the creation of incentive programs that could be developed to stimulate collaboration. Finally, MEHE acknowledges that there are limited financial resources available for the subsector, which limits the private institutions' expectations of securing governmental resources and having to face the challenge of relying on their own creative means for generating funds essential for sustaining research activities. In response to this situation several private universities, such as the American University of Beirut and the Lebanese American University, have taken on the lead in securing funding from private parties and small businesses in order to become self reliant.

The major challenge of limited financial resources is pervasive and takes precedence over other concerns, for it not only affects private higher education institutions but also to a greater extent the public sector represented by LU and MEHE. Thus, lack of funding is well documented and addressed through the strategic plan that MEHE developed in 2002. The

plan was initiated because of the need for planning that arose after MEHE
licensed over 23 new private higher education institutions in the 1990s.
The Directorate of Higher Education explained that these institutions
were licensed according to requirements based on a decree passed in 1961,[1]
which lacked critical quality assurance standards. Another challenge that
emerged, transnational higher education, also encouraged MEHE to proceed with putting together a plan for the subsector.

The duration of the strategic plan was "variable" because of the nature
of the goals set forth and often owing to the county's political atmosphere.
For example, while there was a recognized need for new regulations during
2005, the process was held back because the authorizing body, the House
of Parliament, did not convene for almost two years due to the heightened
political situation that existed at the time. MEHE's strategic plan also faced
several implementation impediments, which resulted in the specified time
durations set out for the implementation of certain regulations becoming unviable. The plan was initially funded by UNDP and UNESCO
for the first stages of data collection and self-assessment. Later the EC
supported the plan, heavily funding initiatives such as quality assurance.
The Directorate of Higher Education incorporated the participation of the
private sector through continuous workshops and seminars held for the
purpose of engaging universities and disseminating the plan. Although
no official evaluation process has been developed and implemented, primarily due to the lack of sufficient funding, the Directorate General of
Higher Education oversees the progress of the implementation of MEHE's
strategic plan. The Directorate of Higher Education deems necessary the
strengthening of the partnership between the private and the public sectors, particularly in planning, in order to better address the development
of the higher education subsector (Jammal 2008).

Assessment of Current Status of
Higher Education Planning

One key to the development of a fully integrated higher education subsector
is the cooperative development of a national strategic plan for higher education supported by individual institutional strategic plans. The alignment
of planning activities assists in the maximization of resource utilization,
the application of resources to priority activities, and a reduction in the
overlap and duplication of activities. A major advantage in the cooperative
development of a coordinated set of plans is that it permits all participants

to obtain an understanding of the major external factors impacting the higher education subsector as well as potential individual institutional responses. This cooperative approach also permits a detailed assessment of the major strengths and challenges of the MEHE and the individual institutions. The analysis of this information provides the framework for the consensus development of MEHE and institutional plans and the coordination of strategies and activities.

As demonstrated, the challenges are formidable, particularly in light of the severe economic and political issues confronting the nation. These conditions reinforce the need for all elements of Lebanese society to cooperate in an effort to maximize utilization of scarce resources. To be successful, it will be particularly important that Lebanon's higher education subsector assumes a leadership position in providing the necessary educated manpower that is one of the primary drivers for the economic, political, and social growth of the country. This will become even more important in the coming decades if Lebanon is to assume a national and regional leadership position and effectively compete in an increasingly international economy.

The first step necessary to establish a national cooperative agenda for the higher education subsector requires the development and articulation of a multiyear strategic plan that provides for a unified approach for higher education institutions to actively engage with MEHE. The plan resulting from this cooperative agenda should be developed in an open, participative process that promotes and enhances new educational opportunities, provides new academic and technical programming, and fosters the country's economic development. As has previously been noted, MEHE had in 2002 developed a planning agenda that outlined an initial approach to serve as a basis for the propagation of nationwide strategic planning activities encompassing all institutions of higher education.

To understand the current status of institutional strategic planning and the degree to which MEHE's strategic plan is influencing institutional planning, the authors conducted a preliminary review of the status of planning activities at MEHE and at public and private higher education institutions through the study of public information presented on institutional and MEHE web sites and publications. The review examined all universities in Lebanon, which included one public university and 27 private universities.

It is important to gain an understanding of the context in which planning takes place in order to better understand the opportunities and challenges confronting higher education institutions. The authors identified a wide number of issues and trends that present a number of challenges and opportunities. These trends were assembled in several categories as presented in table 6.1.

Table 6.1 Examples of Major Trends Occurring in Lebanon's Higher Education Subsector

Financial	Student	Academic Quality	Curriculum/ Programs	Political
1. The challenge of Lebanon's continuing economic development	1. Growing student enrollments	1. Increased concern in the quality of educational programs offered	1. Increased emphasis on market-driven outcomes; alignment of curriculum with requirements of the market	1. Political instability resulting in security concerns
2. Increase in cost to students attending private institutions of higher education	2. Increased competition for quality students	2. Proliferation of institutions claiming higher quality programs and opportunities for students than can be delivered	2. Needs of the market dictate course selection by students	2. Liaise faire mode of governance at state level leading to a rapid and chaotic expansion of private institutions
3. Lack of sufficient funds to provide financial aid to students	3. Development of a more student centered programming	3. Recent attention to the development of quality assurance processes	3. Excessive emphasis on marketable degrees	
4. Lack of sufficient institutional operating funds	4. Lack of employment opportunities on graduation	4. Increased demand for accountability	4. Development of international partnership	
5. Private institutions have relatively few income streams and are almost totally dependant on student tuition fees			5. Slow growth and poor development of institutional research programs	
6. Large growth in the number of private for-profit institutions of varying standards			6. Increased emphasis on American style of education	

The trends depicted in table 6.1 are a sample of the issues that are confronting higher education in Lebanon. To address these issues, some private institutions have begun to engage in institutional strategic planning activities. A review of the institutional web sites and documents indicated that at least eight universities have developed multiyear strategic plans within the last five years, and many have established planning offices to coordinate these activities. Although it is difficult to ascertain the causes of development of these strategic plans, the recent interest in institutional accreditation and quality assurance activities may provide a partial explanation, particularly within a broader context of developing competitive programs at the national and regional levels.

The majority of those institutional plans contained elements typically found in most strategic plans worldwide: external and internal assessment, vision/mission statement, goals/objectives, and strategies. Although written copies of plans were not always available, most institutional plans examined a large range of issues and considered a comprehensive array of planning elements.

Major goals of these institutional planning activities focused on a number important areas, such as alignment of curriculum with market needs, desire to become a world class institution, enhancement of the quality of all institutional programs, selective program development, and the creation of centers of excellence, with a few institutions indicating or referring to a goal of enhancing international programming and relationships. In addition, the plans of several institutions indicated strategies that would be employed in pursuing these goals.

It is evident from an examination of the individual institutional plans and accompanying documents that these institutions clearly understood the needs of both the society in which they operate and whom they serve as well as their own specific institutional needs, and they are actively in the process of attempting to develop appropriate responses. In one sense, while the composite of these plans represents, to a limited extent, a response by the private higher education subsector to societal needs, they nevertheless lack the cohesiveness of a unified planning framework, which could possibly only be provided by some form of leadership from the MEHE.

An examination of the institutional strategic plans and the MEHE strategic plan indicated that the following goals were mutually supported: reevaluate the roles of several of the National Higher Education Councils for equivalency of degrees in a way that meets the local and global needs of higher education; promote quality in higher education; enhance educational cooperation, exchange of faculty, and scientific research; establish new educational rules and regulations for regulating the subsector; support scientific research and development; and address citizenship development, human capital development, and issues of employability in higher education institutions. Although the university plans that were examined had several goals in common, they were not all aligned with those of the MEHE.

Although MEHE and several higher education institutions have developed strategic plans, the next challenge that confronts them is the successful implementation of these plans. As noted in the literature, a large number of institutions have developed strategic plans but have failed to successfully implement them (Peterson et al. 1997; Presley and Leslie 1999). Successful implementation requires the identification of funds, the ability to change old habits and practices, and to provision of incentives to encourage such actions. In particular, the institutions are challenged by such factors as national instability, political polarization, low employee motivation, old-fashioned middle management, inadequate staff, lack of commitment among senior staff, and resistance of some faculty and staff to change.

It is imperative that if MEHE and universities are to successfully execute their plans, they lay out a formal guideline for plan implementation by specifying activities to be carried out, time frames for completion, assignment of responsibilities, and an assessment process.

The inability of higher education institutions to successfully implement new strategic plans in response to changing internal and external conditions weakens the country's overall ability to develop and improve its higher education subsector. This negatively impacts the country's economic, social, and political development.

In spite of the fact that many higher education institutions have not developed formalized plans, it does not negate the fact that all institutions engage in some form of planning process, as exemplified by the development of new curriculum, programs, and services. However, it is important that if MEHE and higher education institutions are to maximize their potential, formalized written plans will be important instruments for sharing information and developing cooperative programs.

Suggested Coordination of Lebanon Higher Education Subsector

As has been discussed, while MEHE has developed a national higher education subsector planning agenda, few of Lebanon's higher education institutions participated in its development; most did not use the agenda to guide their own institutional planning and a number of them denied having received information about what the plan included. It is this fragmentation of planning information that greatly limits the higher education subsector from progressing and achieving a high level of operation and maximization of its resources and strengths.

The major limitations to achieving a coordinated approach to the development of an effective national higher education strategic plan can be traced to a number of factors, the primary being the lack of national laws or regulations creating a strong MEHE. There are no regulations that permit MEHE to be responsible for licensing institutions, provide program approvals, and provide funding to incentivize the existing universities to meet national needs. A second factor is that only one among the 28 institutions is in the public sector, the rest have long histories of being private institutions, and this is further complicated by many of the institutions having religious or international affiliations. These factors have resulted in each institution developing a high level of independence. Without government sponsorship, the state had little control over the private institutions and in most instances could only make recommendations in terms of programs, enrollments, and quality.

In recognition of the potential benefits that can be obtained from selective forms of cooperation, it is recommended that effective communication channels be established between MEHE and private higher education institutions for the purposes of information sharing and joint planning. It is not imperative that a high level of centralization be developed, but rather a possible cooperative consortium model be adopted whereby institutions could share in the areas of in-service training development seminars for faculty and staff, cooperative quality assurance and evaluation projects, and research activities. We believe that it is only through such cooperation that Lebanon's higher education can maximize the individual potential of its higher education institutions to fully realize their mission and serve the nation's needs. This recommendation is based on the assumption that a broad planning agenda could be framed that is supported by the majority of institutions and in which they participate in implementing. Such a cooperative endeavor would permit MEHE to provide leadership, maximize resource utilization, and permit all higher education institutions to retain their well-entrenched governing structures.

Note

1. The 1961 *Higher Education Law* is the main law that regulates the private higher education subsector in Lebanon. As a result of this law, the Council for Higher Education was established with the main responsibility of licensing new higher education institutions. The law regulates the establishment of an

institution of higher education, its organizational structure, faculty size and qualifications, and facilities. A number of decrees were subsequently issued to regulate the subsector. The most significant one was issued in 1996, which modernized the 1961 law and set new conditions and criteria for a higher education institution to be legalized, to be given the permission to operate, and to be audited through special technical committees (Traboulsi 2010).

References

Alfred, Richard L. 2006. *Managing the Big Picture in Colleges and Universities: From Tactics to Strategy.* Westport: Praeger Publisher.

Bryson, John M. 1995. *Strategic Planning for Public and Nonprofit Organizations: A Guide to Strengthening and Sustaining Organizational Achievement.* San Francisco: Jossey-Bass.

Daher, Fouad. 2005. "Higher Education in Lebanon: Current Situation and Perspectives." Paper presented at the Order of Engineers and Architects Conference in Tripoli, Beirut, Lebanon.

Educational Center for Research and Development. 2008. *The Distribution of Students in the Higher Education Institutions in Lebanon.* Beirut: Educational Center for Research and Development. Available online at: http://www.crdp.org.

El-Amine, Adnan, ed. 1997. *Higher Education in Lebanon.* Beirut: Lebanese Association for Educational Studies.

El-Amine, Adnan, and Muhammad Faour. 1998. *University Students in Lebanon.* Beirut: Lebanese Association for Educational Studies.

El-Aouit, Henri. 1997. "Legislation of Private Institutions." In *Higher Education in Lebanon,* ed. A. El-Amine. Beirut: Lebanese Association for Educational Sciences.

El-Ghali, Hana A. 2008. "Equity in Socioeconomic Status of Students and Higher Education Enrollment in Lebanon." *Comparative and International Education Society Newsletter* 148.

El-Ghali, Hana A., and John L. Yeager. 2009. "The Influence of Context to a National Strategic Planning Effort: The Case of Lebanon." Paper presented at the annual conference for the Comparative and International Education Society, Charleston, SC, March 23, 2009.

Haidar, Nabil F. 2003. "Higher Education in Lebanon: Reality and Hope." Paper presented at the ARAB-ACRO 24th Annual Conference, Beirut, Lebanon, March 31, 2009.

Jammal, Ahmad. 2008a. "Higher Education in Lebanon." Paper presented at the Quality Assurance Framework of Higher Education in the Arab States Workshop, Cairo, Egypt, November 2–3, 2008.

———. 2008b. Interview by Hana A. El-Ghali, Beirut, Lebanon, December 12, 2008. Jammal is the Director of the Directorate General of Higher Education.

Matar, Suhail. "Higher Education in Lebanon: History, Responsibility, and Freedom." Paper presented at the ARAB-ACRO 24th Annual Conference, Beirut, Lebanon, March 31, 2009.

Ministry of Education and Higher Education (MEHE). 2009. *Directorate General of Higher Education.* Beirut: MEHE. Available online at: http://www.higher-edu.gov.lb.

Nauffal, Diane I. 2004. "Higher Education in Lebanon: Management Cultures and Their Impact on Performance Outcomes." PhD diss. University of Birmingham, Birmingham, UK.

Peterson, Marvin W., David D. Dill, Lisa A. Mets, and Associates. 1997. *Planning and Management for a Changing Environment: A Handbook on Redesigning Postsecondary Institutions.* San Francisco: Jossey-Bass.

Presley, Jennifer B., and David W. Leslie. 1999. "Understanding Strategy: An Assessment of Theory and Practice." In *Higher Education Handbook of Theory and Practice,* ed. J. C. Smart. New York: Agathon Press.

Rowley, Daniel James, and Herbert Sherman. 2001. *From Strategic to Change: Implementing the Plan in Higher Education.* San Francisco: Jossey-Bass.

TempusLebanon. 2005. *Overview of the Higher Education System in Lebanon.* Beirut: TempusLebanon. Available online at: http://www.tempus-lebanon. org.

Traboulsi, Berge J. 2010. "Ethical Challenges in Today's Higher Education Institutions in Lebanon: A Stakeholder Analysis." Paper presented at the 2nd Global Conference on Ethics in Public Life: Understandings, Applications, Controversies, Salzburg, Australia, March 15–17, 2010.

UNESCO. 1998. *Beirut Declaration on Higher Education in the Arab States for the 21st Century.* Beirut: UNESCO.

———. 2005. *Education in Lebanon.* Beirut: UNESCO Institute for Statistics.

———. 2005. *Notes on Lebanon's Higher Education System from the World Higher Education Database.* Beirut: International Association of Universities.

Chapter 7

ICT-Driven Curriculum Reform in Higher Education: Experiences, Prospects, Trends, and Challenges in Africa

Christopher B. Mugimu and Connie Ssebbunga-Masembe

Introduction

The growth of information and communication technologies (ICT) in recent years has transformed all aspects of life in the world. Although ICT is still in its infancy in Africa, it has the potential to contribute to the continents' political, social, and economic development. ICT should offer new possibilities to transform education in terms of making it more accessible, equitable, and efficient. Education is a human right (UNESCO 1990), and therefore governments have the obligation to make it available to all, but many have fallen short in this responsibility, particularly in Africa. As such, Africa's greatest challenge is to ensure that all its citizens have access to quality education and are able to participate fully. This goal is often undermined by the weak economies of most African countries; hence financing quality education in Africa remains a mirage, particularly at secondary and tertiary levels, given the ever rising institutional operation costs. This is further compounded by the declining government funding to public services, especially in health and education. Higher education is the most adversely affected, given that extremely few individuals in Africa are able to access it at their own expense.

Traditionally, most African governments have supported their citizens through higher education; this has, however, changed in recent years. Higher education is currently considered to be more of a private good rather than a public common good. Given that families are the primary beneficiaries when their relatives graduate from college, individual families have the obligation to support their own children through higher education. However, this approach may not favor most families, especially those without the capacity to pay for the higher education of their children. Consequently, the existing social inequalities between the "haves and have-nots" are instead exacerbated, which is contrary to the core values of education for all (EFA) and the millennium development goals (MDGs) (Ahmed 2007). Higher education continues to be extremely costly, and it is therefore prohibitive to the majority of individuals who would otherwise wish to access it. It is hoped that ICTs will extend new possibilities to reduce the cost of higher education and thus make it more affordable and accessible to the growing numbers of individuals than ever before. Therefore, setting up national ICT policies in education, improving ICT infrastructure, and integrating ICT in the higher education curriculum and courses should become a policy agenda with top priority in many African countries. Subsequently, many HEIs would be encouraged to align ICTs with their curriculum reforms, with the hope that such efforts will bring knowledge to more people (Richards 2005).

Theoretical Framework

Our research was informed by the constructivism theory, which states that knowledge is constructed-reality rather than discovered (Smith and Ragan 1999). Learners construct their own knowledge and experiences through free interaction with the ICTs. ICTs should promote student-centered learning and assist them to take responsibility of their own learning through their engagement with the curriculum content delivered with the help of ICTs.

The principles of constructivism have a lot to inform ICT educational policies as they strive to establish and nurture active, problem-based, collaborative, situated, experiential, meaningful, cost-effective, and authentic learning, drawing on the support of emergent ICT tools (Karagiorgi and

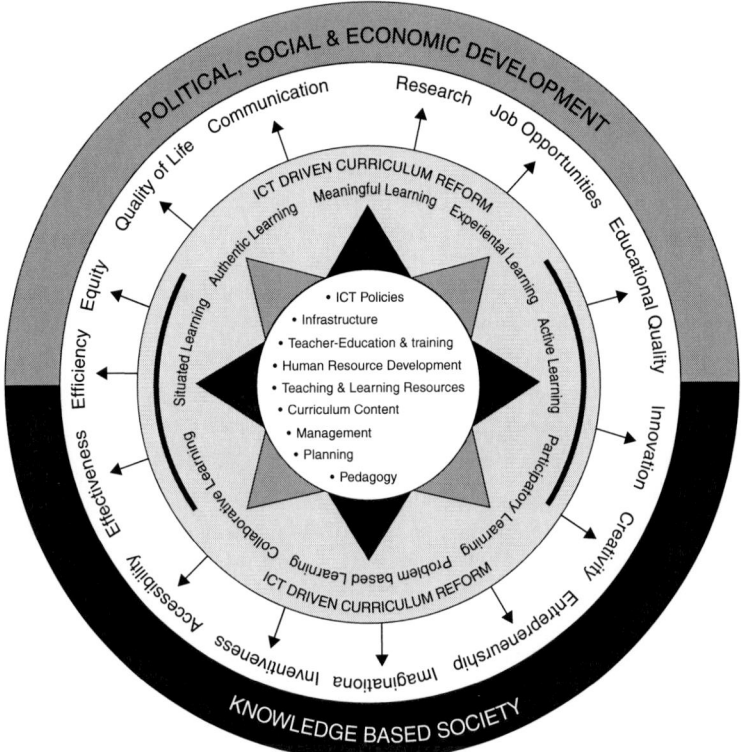

Figure 7.1   ICT-Based Constructivist Theoretical Framework

Symeou 2005; Barnett and Coate 2006; Day and Sachs 2009). ICTs as tools can render the acquisition of knowledge more dynamic and interesting for the learners. Therefore, ICTs enable them to become active recipients of information. The ICT-based constructivist theoretical framework is depicted in figure 7.1.

The Relevance of ICTs in Education

ICTs offer extensive potential contributions to the education sector in general and higher education in particular. This section highlights some of the critical contributions of ICTs.

Management of Information

ICTs can enhance HEIs to serve large student numbers, since they are capable of improving the capacity of HEIs in Africa to store and retrieve large volumes of information. This has always been a major constraint in Africa and has often resulted in uncalled for inefficiencies and low productivity. Mostert and Nthetha (2008, 25) indicated that "ICTs are important resources that can be used to reorganize schooling and as well serve as tools that can assist whole-school development. ICTs are, therefore, tools for management, administrative tools used to increase productivity; resources for curriculum integration; communication tools, and collaborative tools for teachers and learners."

Planning and Delivery of Information

ICTs can also enhance the management of institutions in terms of tracking students' information such as admission, attendance, assessment, payments, and so on. This can improve the planning and the delivery of educational services offered, which can result in improved productivity and performance (Evoh 2007). On this basis, African countries should set up ICT policies to help them transform into knowledge-based societies. Establishing the necessary ICT infrastructure should be a priority in Africa. At the same time, ICT policies are needed to support ICT infrastructure and human-capacity building (Ahmed 2007).

Curriculum Integration

ICTs can be important resources in curriculum integration in higher education. In fact, many of the developed countries across the world have formulated or are in the process of formulating specific ICT policies to initiate and support ICT programs (Burnett et al. 2008). These programs should improve educational quality as well as promote their national development agendas. HEIs should, therefore, lobby governments to include components of education and curriculum innovation in their national ICT policies. ICT policies should support curriculum reforms that can enable HEIs to increase opportunities for participation to a growing number of students. Recent years have seen increased student enrollments in HEIs globally; that is, 138 million students in 2005 compared to 93 million students in 1999 (Burnett et al. 2008). Although this trend may also be true in many African countries, the majority of individuals are denied entry into higher education because of the prohibitive tuition. Interestingly, modern technologies are increasingly becoming cheaper and therefore more affordable.

Reducing the Cost of Higher Education

ICTs can reduce the expenditure for HEIs —by minimizing transportation costs, recruiting fewer employees, and reducing telephone bills, which could assist HEIs realize substantial savings. For instance, with the help of ICTs, fewer employees will be required for maintaining students and financial records in HEIs. Given that the biggest portion of institutional budgets goes to staff salaries and allowances, these can be reduced substantially if they are complemented with ICT use in management, curriculum delivery, students' records, and so on. The ICT policies should encourage HEIs to utilize advanced ICTs, particularly mobile technologies, to serve the growing number of students. The use of mobile technology could be a practical solution to reduce the cost, improve equity, and gain access to higher education in Africa. Given that most people stay in rural areas, usually without reliable electricity and telephone lines, the ICT policies should address the possibilities of utilizing alternative power sources such as solar energy, nuclear energy, and wind energy, which are needed to support the mobile technologies.

Making Education More Flexible and Accessible

ICTs, especially mobile technologies, are capable of making education flexible and accessible in many amazing and unlimited ways. This will get even better in the near future. ICTs can overcome distance and remove geographical barriers, two factors that often prevent students from acquiring the necessary education they need.

Creating New Job Opportunities

ICTs can enable people everywhere and at any time to access important information for acquiring new skills or seeking better job opportunities in Africa. It is also becoming a widely accepted belief that "specializing in ICT enhances the possibilities of getting and retaining a good job" (Ministry of Works, Housing and Communications [MWHC] 2004, 100). It is not uncommon to find people in countries such as India and China outsourcing work from companies based in the US and UK and working from home in their own countries. This may not be the case in Africa, given the poor ICT infrastructure and lack of human capital. Without these facilities it is very unlikely, therefore, that the people of Africa will compete favorably in the globalized knowledge-based economy. Without Africans actually gaining the competences needed to utilize ICTs, their economic and social development potential will be compromised and she will continue to lag behind the rest of the world. However, ICTs can transform Africa into a knowledge-based society through research and improved human capacity building, and doing so will contribute to the eradication of poverty and improvement of the quality of life for the people.

Making Outsourcing of knowledge in Higher Education Possible

Africa's improvement of human capital in ICTs should make the outsourcing of knowledge in higher education sector possible. Currently, outsourcing of knowledge in higher education is not only rapidly growing but is also proving to be a good source of revenue. Many HEIs of the world have already provided ICT services–enabled education (World Bank 2008, 52). For instance, it is reported that the United States has earned US$10.7 billion in 2003 from foreign students through these innovative means. ICTs should offer opportunities for "outsourcing services such as e-tutoring or outsourced exam grading" in the education sector. The Open University (UK) is also serving more than 250,000 off campus students worldwide. ICT policies should also encourage HEIs in Africa to attract international students from all over the world. The African Virtual University (AVU) based in Nairobi, Kenya, and the Open University in Tanzania both provide programs to students from many countries in Africa and other parts of the world. This should not only enhance global cooperation but also boost the incomes of these institutions. Therefore, ICTs should offer new possibilities for African HEIs to create new markets irrespective of their geographical boundaries. This implies that HEIs will have to improve their ICT infrastructures and human resources in order to serve the diverse student populations from anywhere on the globe. However, ICT policies should take precautionary measures for the likely security issues regarding the safety and privacy of the digitized information on students and administrative information, such as results, certificates, and so on. It is also important to consider issues involving copyright laws on e-content, risks on hacking, pornography, and so on.

Supporting the In-service Training of Faculty

The need to integrate ICTs in the higher education curriculum is extremely vital, but there are currently few African academics with the expertise to be able to do so (Unwin 2005). There is a need for training African academics in ICT integration competences to enhance higher education curriculum reforms. Governments will have a big role to play; in particular, their political will and commitment are critical to support these efforts (Hepp et al. 2004). Policies that encourage outsourcing specialized knowledge from other countries, particularly in ICTs integration in the higher education curriculum, may be necessary. This could give African academics the opportunity to access specialized expertise in these areas via the Internet at relatively affordable prices rather than having to go overseas to study.

Supporting Teacher Education

ICTs can also support teacher education in Africa. For instance, with the help of ICTs, many teachers can be trained through self-directed learning, especially in how to use open learning resources (OLRs) to reach out to the marginalized populations (Gaible and Burns 2005). The national ICT policies should make ICT integration mandatory in all teacher education programs. This could particularly provide both preservice and in-service teachers with the basic skills on how to integrate ICTs within the mainstream curriculum. Training and retraining educators will be necessary for them to gain confidence and positive attitudes toward the use and integration of ICTs in what they do.

Teachers are the major players in the curriculum reforms and cannot be replaced by ICTs, so it is rather critical to bring them on board. It is also necessary to recognize their individual differences, such as their interests, concerns, and competences for ICTs. Competent and effective teachers could lead to effective and good schools that are capable of offering quality education. This has important implications to teacher preparation and capacity development in terms of providing teacher trainees with basic skills in ICTs.

The focus of ICT policies "should reside on people and how to improve and develop their skills and practices with the help of ICTs; ICT policies should be closely related to curriculum, for teachers to use them for learning practices in classrooms" (Hepp et al. 2004, 2). The curriculum reforms should, therefore, be in support of the teachers' and learners' daily routines. This may also imply the need to look into the possibilities of improving the conditions at homes and schools in terms of raising opportunities for access to ICTs.

Using ICTs in Assessment of Teaching and Learning

ICTs can be important tools for assessing teaching and learning. Marsh (2009, 73–75) pointed out that ICTs are capable of "giving students and teachers more opportunities for feedback and reflection. Technology-assisted assessment is a relatively new phenomenon and it is developing rapidly." Many students can be simultaneously assessed through their activities and projects submitted with the help of ICTs (Miller, Imrie, and Cox 1998; Oosterhof, Conrad, and Ely 2008). The challenge is how to verify whether the projects are true representations of the students' ability. Making basic skills in ICTs examinable at all levels of education, particularly at the HEIs, will be a good assessment strategy.

Levels of ICT Education Policies in Africa

Most countries in Africa are in their initial stages of developing their own national ICT education policies. Farrell and Isaacs (2007, 6) indicated that out of the 53 African countries surveyed, 39 had established ICT in education policies. ICT policy formulation and integration in higher education is, therefore, a recent phenomenon in most African countries. For instance, Botswana and South Africa established their national ICT policies as recently as 1995; Senegal and Burkina Faso did so by 2000; Angola and Central African Republic, in 2002; Uganda, by 2003; and Benin, in 2005. According to Farrell and Isaacs, national ICT policies are important in that they act as catalysts for ICT in education policy development (2007, 6). Nevertheless, it is critical that as governments develop ICT policies, they should be aware of the fact that ICTs could exacerbate the existing social inequalities in local communities. Governments in Africa are therefore challenged not only to bring ICTs to those that cannot afford it, but also to provide them with the basic skills needed to use ICTs in meaningful and productive ways. ICTs are therefore just tools; it takes apprenticeship to use them profitably, irrespective of which ICTs may or may not be of any benefit.

The Rationale for Funding ICTs in Education

To bail Africa out of its present political, social, and economic crisis, there is a need for improving the quality of its citizens through education and enabling them to become a knowledge-based society through advancing their competences in ICTs. ICTs can improve educational quality through improved information sharing and delivery. Information is power, and all people, particularly the marginalized groups, should have a right to timely information. Accessing important information enables the citizens to acquire new skills as well as good job opportunities. Without access to ICTs it is very unlikely that people in Africa will compete favorably in the globalized knowledge-based economy.

Since many more teachers can be trained through self-directed learning with the help of ICTs, teachers will become more effective in their work and improve the quality of education. ICTs should make the outsourcing of knowledge in the higher education sector possible. As earlier indicated, ICTs, especially mobile technologies, can make education provision flexible and accessible in unlimited ways.

If Africans do not actually gain the competences needed to utilize ICTs, it will hinder the economic progress of Africa and undermine the quality of life for its people. Africa's greatest challenge is to ensure that all its citizens have access to quality education and are able to participate fully in its development. Investing in ICTs in education is the sensible way to progress and is a worthwhile goal for Africa.

Current Trends in Funding ICTs in Education in Africa

Four trends currently characterize the ICT movement in Africa: donor-driven support and funding, the goal toward sustainable financing strategies, market-driven curricula, and equity and access issues at all education levels. Each trend is introduced in brief in this section.

Donor-Driven Support and Funding

Governments have played a major role to attract funding from international donor agencies and NGOs for the ICT policy formulation and ICT use in education in Africa. In fact, most of the funding to support ICT initiatives in education in Africa comes from external donor agencies and NGOs. International donor agencies have provided support for the establishment of ICT infrastructure and human capacity development in many African countries, including support through bilateral cooperation between donor agencies and governments to promote ICT. However, with the current economic depression this may not be sustainable, as many donor agencies and NGOs are cutting down their international expenditure.

Establishing Sustainable Financing Strategies

Governments are therefore challenged to establish sustainable financing strategies to support the digital reform in Africa. The ICT policies should provide environments that encourage the participation of the private sector in the mobile phone industry, which is rapidly growing in many African countries. Increasingly more people are able to access mobile phones and Internet cafes—at the pay-as-you-go arrangement with private service providers, such as Mobile Telephone Networks (MTN) and Zain, which operate in countries such as South Africa, Democratic Republic of the Congo (DRC), and Uganda.

In order to enhance national development in the context of poor economies, governments have also embraced economic liberalization policies to encourage the participation of the private sector in all fields, including in health and education. Uganda is a good example where economic liberalization policies have worked. In Uganda, the private sector is currently the major provider of education at all levels (i.e., primary, secondary, and tertiary), as well as a major investor in the ICTs sector. This may also be true in many other African countries. To increase their competitive advantage, institutions are also increasingly integrating ICTs in their courses to attract more students and realize higher revenue collections. The need is enormous for African governments to work with their development partners to establish favorable conditions to facilitate a meaningful ICT integration into the higher education curriculum. As such, suitable conditions, such as the required modern ICT infrastructures and appropriate human resource training in basic ICT skills, are needed for curriculum integration. Governments also need to encourage the private sector to establish ICT training institutions.

Market-Driven Courses and Curriculum Content

Most universities have introduced market-driven courses, such as computer-related courses. Today computer knowledge is recognized as a critical leverage for individuals in the world of work. This is based on the assumption that acquiring basic skills in ICTs and modern technology can facilitate improved production, efficiency, and collaboration. These efforts could contribute to the social and economic development in Africa.

Equity Issues Related to ICT Access at Primary, Secondary, and Higher Education

While many African countries have made no provisions to use ICTs to reduce gender inequities in education, several countries, such as South Africa and Uganda, have done so. Studies on gender equity and ICTs in education indicate that female students are likely to find it difficult to access computers compared to men. Girls and women are more likely to drop out of schools compared to boys and men; therefore there are higher rates of illiterate women and girls compared to men and boys in Africa. In the eventuality of high prevalence of HIV/AIDS in Sub-Saharan Africa (SSA), girls are more likely to stay home to nurse their relatives than boys. Consequently, in order to reduce these gender inequalities through ICTs, there is need to lobby for gender inclusion in ICT policies (Farrell and Isaacs 2007). In Uganda, in order to encourage more women to access higher education, incentives have been given to women by waiving stringent admission requirements in some courses and adding extra points for female students seeking admission. Similarly, while in Angola, Botswana, and Burkina Faso there is little affirmative action for empowering women and the girl child, Cape Verde has achieved more enrollments for girls than boys. Likewise, in South Africa an NGO called WomenNet promotes gender equality through the use of ICT by providing training and dissemination of content to women, girls, and women's organizations (see Fall 2007a).

In general, a good ICT policy should consider issues such as access, equity, affordability, benchmarking, quality control, curriculum content development, and intellectual property rights. It should, according to Gunga and Ricketts (2007, 903), "not only reduce the waste occasioned by duplication but also improve the return on investment through improved accountability and information sharing while promoting investment initiatives and liberalization of the ICTs." These are critical considerations, since individuals for whom the benefits from curriculum reforms are intended may often not be able to do so. This is because Internet provisions may be available only in affluent communities where people can afford to pay for the services. It is also true that weak communication and social infrastructure not only block information flows in most SSA countries but ultimately stifle social and economic development (Ahmed 2007, 353). Hence there is a need for policymakers and governments to intervene in situations such as war torn areas (e.g., Northern Uganda, Somalia, Sudan, Ethiopia, Eritrea) and marginalized communities (e.g., Bakonjo and Karamojongo in Uganda; Turkana and Chagga in Kenya) through education policies so that ICT services are made available to such groups via satellite centers (cf. Ahmed 2007; Mutonyi and Norton 2007).

ICTs Integration in the Higher Education Curriculum in Four African Countries

This section presents the state of ICT integration in the higher education curriculum in four African countries: DRC, Senegal, South Africa, and Uganda. We also attempt to highlight the various ICT policies enacted by these countries to integrate the ICTs with curriculum reforms in higher education.

Democratic Republic of the Congo (DRC)

ICTs remain largely undeveloped in DRC due to lack of a national ICT policy. According to Gjerstad (2006), the process of implementing ICT integration in higher education in DRC has been compromised by the lack of a national ICT policy, poor ICT infrastructure, lack of government commitment and political will to support ICT initiatives, lack of public funding, and shortage of human resources. It is not surprising that the private sector dominates the efforts to support ICT use in education. However, the Multi Sector ICT Dynamic Project was established with the aim of democratizing access to ICTs in the DRC as well as enhancing social and economic development (Fall 2007b). HEIs in DRC have also attempted to incorporate ICTs in their programs. For example, the virtual Francophone Campus coordinates with other HEIs through distance training courses, research, and technology. Together with seven other universities, the University of Kinshasa and the University of Lubumbashi participated in research to identify the needs and opportunities to strengthen ICT capacity in the DRC.

Furthermore, the University of Kinshasa enacted a project supported by the Belgium government to interconnect all Congolese universities through distance education programs. Costs for connectivity and for maintenance of these links are still too high. However, negotiations with the African Virtual University (AVU) are underway to reduce these costs (Fall 2007b).

Given that the landline telephone infrastructure in Congo is in bad shape, like that of other countries in Africa, there has been rapid expansion of the mobile phones in DRC, and by 2006 there were approximately 3.5 million subscribers (Gjerstad 2006). Today cellular phone subscribers have exceeded 5 million, and there are four major mobile phone companies (Vodacom, Zain, Tigo, and Congo Chine Telecom) serving more than 288 towns.

Senegal

The Senegalese government has put in place a national ICT policy and has showed its commitment toward ICT use in education. Fall (2007a) pointed out that the Ministry of Education has partnered with the private sector to provide computer hardware and networks as well to digitize content and training materials. Donor agencies such as USAID and UNDP have supported ICT initiatives in Senegal. In 2004, Microsoft and the Ministry of Education partnered to provide affordable computer software in many Senegalese institutions. HEIs in Senegal are also playing a significant role for ICT use in education through the support of bilateral agencies such as the African Virtual University (AVU). The AVU disseminates training courses across twenty-eight countries in Africa. SchoolNet Africa also supports ICT efforts in the University of Cheikh of Dakar. The Canadian International Development Agency (CIDA) is the leading funding agency in Senegal supporting and promoting ICT use among the youth and women through distance education. Arrange University Francophonie based in Dakar also provides a digital access center for students and offers training and Internet network of 635 HEIs worldwide. With the boom in mobile telephone usage and multitudes of operators in the telephone sector, Senegal has travelled a long way in integrating and using ICTs in schools. The access to ICTs and high-quality content in Senegal presents other major challenges (Fall 2007a, 1–11).

South Africa

The Government of South Africa has played an active role in regulating a national ICT policy, thus recognizing the role of ICT in the enhancement of economic growth, job creation, social development, and global competitiveness (Isaacs 2007, 5). South Africa had formed an educational ICT policy in 1995 and therefore enjoys higher rates of ICT penetration compared to other African countries. For instance, according to the African Economic Outlook report (2009) it was pointed out that the mobile phone penetration in South Africa is 100 percent while that of fixed line penetration is 55 percent.

A lot of emphasis has been devoted to the professional development of teachers, and they have been trained in skills needed to integrate ICT within the curriculum content (Isaacs 2007, 15). NGOs and international donor agencies have also significantly contributed to ICT use in education; SchoolNet and the Educator's Development Network (EDN) have promoted online communities of teachers to share information and learn from each other. Teachers completing six of the EDN modules receive certification from the University of KwaZulu-Natal. The Intel project offers preservice and in-service teachers with skills to integrate ICT in the teaching and learning process to help learners develop a high level of critical thinking skills while at the same time enhancing active learning.

Many universities in South Africa have embraced and contributed to ICT use in education. Tshwane University of Technology offers computer and ICT programs. The University of KwaZulu-Natal offers an advanced certificate in education and ICT integration for teachers. The University of Johannesburg has integrated an ICT course in the Bachelor of Education program. With support from Intel, the University of Pretoria provides a Post Graduate Diploma in Education (PGDE) course. The University of Fort Hare and the Central University of Technology in Free State have also used Intel's help to teach numerous staff development programs.

Like in many other African countries, in South Africa too there is no coherent coordinated policy at the higher education level. Institutions are instead forced to establish their own ICT policies and master plans. Lack of a comprehensive ICT policy in higher education and tertiary education in South Africa has to some extent undermined the effective implementation of ICT in higher education.

Uganda

Uganda developed its initial national ICT policy framework in 2003 to exploit the potential opportunities of the ICT sector. The government recognized the potential of ICT in stimulating social and economic development (GOU 2003). With the introduction of the economic liberalization policies, Uganda has seen massive expansion of the private sector in ICTs and mobile technologies (i.e., cellular phone networks, radio communications, etc.).

The National ICT policy was catered for the education sector with the aim to increase the levels of ICT functional literacy in all sectors, build human capacity, and encourage and support research and development in ICT. Greater emphasis has focused on integrating ICTs in the mainstream curricula as well as providing equitable access to learners at all levels.

In light of these ICT strategies, the Ministry of Education and Sport (MOES) has expanded its focus on the use and application of ICTs.

The MOES has developed guidelines on the use of ICTs for institutions in Uganda, introduced a mandatory ICT budget for all secondary schools, and signed agreements with private providers (i.e., Microsoft, Uganda Telecom [UTL], MTN, ZION, etc.) to subsidize software licenses and services for educational institutions. The MOES has also embarked on the training of teachers in ICT skills and designed an ordinary level curriculum on ICT and made it an examinable subject by the Uganda National Examinations Board (UNEB). The draft of the ICT education sector policy on ICTs was considered and passed by Cabinet in 2008. The draft policy applied to all education subsectors, including nonformal education, and was focused on the development of ICT competencies as well as using it to teach across the curriculum. The draft policy also emphasized the development of teachers' ICT competencies and skills needed for the development of digital learning content.

Many HEIs in Uganda have recently established their own ICT policies and master plans through their own initiatives. For instance, Makerere University established an ICT Policy and Master Plan in 2001, which was intended to leverage and enhance the ICT capacity for faculties by using ICT in pedagogy, research, and development (Musisi and Muwanga 2003). Mbarara University of Science and Technology (MUST) and Uganda Martyrs University (UMU) have used ICT to improve their organizational and management capacities. Our recent interviews with system administrators in four HEIs in Uganda revealed that there is an attempt by institutions to ensure that all students and academic staff are trained on a continuous basis to equip them with the basic ICT literacy skills to fully exploit the digital learning environment (DLE) in the different disciplines (Amos 2009; Kalema 2008; MUK 2003, 2). Distance education programs are run at MUK, Kyambogo University (KYU), and UMU.

The E-learning and Teacher Education (ELATE) project sponsored by the British Council also creates and disseminates open learning resources (OLRs) for teacher trainees and practicing teachers. More than 1000 CD-ROMs have been distributed to secondary schools in Uganda and more than 40,000 people have visited the ELATE web site. Similarly, UMU and MUST are supported by the Nuffic IT Project in collaboration with the Dutch Government. UMU is also supported by the Ava Project aimed at developing capacity in e-learning. These initiatives have been partly funded with support from the allies of UMU, in particular the University of Delf in Netherlands, the University of Western Cape (South Africa), and the University of Notre Dame (Kalema 2008). Other additional revenues are generated through cost sharing for the ICTs and Internet services rendered to the private sector by the university.

What comes out clearly from the study of cases in the above four countries is that Francophone HEIs seem to coordinate their efforts in establishing ICT policies and the use of ICTs in education better than the Anglophone HEIs. However, in the four countries, international donor agencies and NGOs have played key roles in supporting ICT use in education. The implementation and sustainability of these policies in practical terms in schools and HEIs of Africa will continue to remain a challenge, at least in the foreseeable future.

Challenges to ICT Integration in the Higher Education Curriculum in Africa

The majority of African HEIs are constrained with poor connectivity and outdated infrastructures. Poor infrastructure is a serious limitation confronting Africa as the continent attempts to embrace ICTs. However, "wireless networks are emerging as a cost effective way of establishing connectivity among and within the HEIs" (Farrell and Isaacs 2007, 10). Farrell and Isaacs also pointed out that the majority of African HEIs lag behind the rest of the world in terms of knowledge, technology, and economic aspects.

Access to technology and ICT in many of Africa's institutions remain a challenge; it is particularly difficult to access computers and find teachers specialized in teaching ICT-related courses. It is obvious that in a few years teachers in Africa will need to use ICT skills extensively in schools. Integrating ICT in the curriculum in higher education is thus a high priority area. Sustainability of ICT use in education will depend upon the extent to which HEIs in Africa embrace this technology and train enough human capital.

In short, there are a number of hindrances to obtaining full benefits of ICTs in the African classrooms. There is lack of access to technology, lack of computer literacy among teachers, lack of properly developed curriculum for integrating ICTs into subject teaching, need for student-centered learning approaches, and shortage of electricity. Broadband penetration rates are still very low, downloading speeds are also equally low, and the cost of equipment and Internet services are quite high, which are bottlenecks that undermine the efforts to improve education through the integration of ICT in the curriculum (Farrell 2007; Isaacs 2007; Mostert and Nthetha 2008).

Furthermore, our in-depth interview with the system administrator at MUST also revealed that there was shortage of financing to purchase equipment and human capital especially in the ICT support unit, and there were serious shortcomings in the provisions for training the technical support unit (Personal Communication in March 2009). Nevertheless, given that we will continue to see an increased use of computers and ICTs in schools, academic staff in tertiary institutions and school teachers in Africa will be required to have reasonable pedagogical competencies in using ICTs in teaching and learning (UNESCO 2006).

Future Prospects of ICT in Higher Education in Africa

In general, ICT policies for higher education stipulate that ICT should be integrated into the curriculum. The policies should also provide incentives to academic staff in higher education to encourage them to embrace ICTs, such as offering them the certification required for promotion and salary raise. Launched in 2001, the University of Botswana eLearning (UBel) Programme has provided training to all faculties on how to integrate ICTs in the curriculum. The bottom line that needs to be appreciated is that professional development of teachers is critical to the future prospects of ICT in higher education in Africa, which should be informed by the principles of the constructivism theory.

Conclusion

This chapter has highlighted the policy discourse in ICT integration in education in general and in higher education in particular across Africa. It is quite clear that ICT can enhance the access, equity, and quality of higher education in Africa in a number of ways. The future of quality education in Africa is in the hands of teachers. ICT can play a significant role to enhance the quality of teachers and education standards. Therefore, getting teachers to use ICTs in their innovative instructional delivery and teaching (pedagogy) is vital. More serious attention is needed regarding improving human capacity in curriculum development and implementation of good classroom practices and pedagogies. Preservice and in-service training of teachers will need to be conducted in order to cultivate positive attitudes and motivate them to gain skills to integrate ICTs into the teaching and implementation of curriculum content. The processes of implementing ICTs into the higher education curriculum should be guided by the epistemological underpinnings of the constructivism theory, especially when it comes to introducing modern participatory pedagogical approaches to the delivery of the curriculum content.

ICT education policy must become a top priority agenda in higher education in Africa and should rotate around the following: adequate preparation of teaching and technical staff; curriculum reform; establishing ICT infrastructure and other facilities needed for teaching and learning; HRD policies; sustainable financing for the use of ICTs in education; soliciting donor support and bilateral cooperation; and monitoring standards and evaluating performance. Through research and curriculum reforms, ICT can transform Africa into a knowledge society. Given that ICTs are here to stay and will continue to cut across all sectors in our daily lives, African governments should exploit the benefits that accrue with the integration of ICTs in higher education in terms of improving the quality of citizens and ensuring their full participation in the knowledge society.

References

Ahmed, Allam. 2007. "Open Access Towards Bridging the Digital Devide—Policies and Strategies for Developing Countries." *Information Technology for Development* 13 (4): 337–361.

Albion, Peter. 2000. "Setting Course for the New Millennium: Planning for ICT in a New Bachelor Degree Program." In *Proceedings of Scoiety for Information Technology and Teacher Education International Conference 2000*, ed. D. Willis. Chesapeake, VA: Association for the Advancement of Computing in Education (AACE).

Barnett, Ronald, and Kelly Coate. 2006. *Engaging the Curriculum in Higher Education* (2nd ed.). Berkshire, England: The Open University Press.

Burnett, Nicholus, Nicole Bella, Aaron Benavot, Marieta Buonomo, Fadila Cailaud, Vittoria Cavicchioni, Alison Clayson, Catherine Ginisty, Cynthia Guttman, Anna Haas, Keith Hinchliffe, Anais Loizillon, Patrick Montjourides, Claudine Mukizwa, Delphine Nsengimana, Ulrika Peppler Barry, Paula Razquin, Isabela Reullon, Yusuf Sayed, and Suhad Varin. 2008. *EFA Global Monitoring Report*. Oxford: Oxford University Press.

Chisholm, Linda, Rubby Dhunpath, and Andrew Paterson. 2004. *The Use of ICTs in the Curriculum in Botswana, Namibia, and Seychelles*. South Africa: SACHES commissioned by The Southern African Development Community Education Policy Support Initiative (SADC APSI).

Czerniewicz, L., and C. Brown. 2005. "Information and Communication Technology (ICT) Use in Teaching and Learning Practices in Western Cape Higher Education Institutions." *Perspectives in Education* 23 (4): 1–18.

Davidson, Judith. 2003. "A New Role in Facilitating School Rreform: The Case of the Educational Technologist." *Teachers College Record* 105 (5): 729–752.

Day, Christopher and Judith Sachs, eds. 2009. *International Handbook on the Continuing Professional Development of Teachers* (3rd ed.). Berkshire, England: The Open University Press.

Evoh, Chijioke J. 2007. "Collaborative Partnership and the Transformation of Secondary Education through ICTs in South Africa." *Educational Media Intenational* 44 (2): 81–98.

Fall, Babacar. 2007a. *ICT in Education in Senegal: A Survey of ICT and Education in Africa Country Report.* Washington, DC: infoDev, World Bank. Available online at www.infoDev.org.

———. 2007b. *ICT in Education in the Democratic Republic of Congo (DRC): A Survey of ICT and Education in Africa Country Report.* Washington, DC: infoDev, World Bank.

Farrell, Glen. 2007. *ICT in Education in Uganda: A Survey of ICT and Education in Africa Country Report.* Washington, DC: infoDev, World Bank.

Farrell, Glen, and Shafika Isaacs. 2007. *Survey of ICT and Education in Africa: A Summary Report, Based on 53 Country Surveys.* Washington, DC: infoDev, World Bank.

Gaible, Edmond, and Mary Burns. 2005. *Using Technology to Train Teachers: Appropriate Uses of ICT for Teacher Professional Development in Developing Countries.* Washington, DC: World Bank.

Gjerstad, Lina. 2006. "Democratic Republic of the Congo (DRC)." *Global Information Society Watch*: 140–143.

Government of Uganda (GOU). 2003. *National Information and Communication Technology (ICT) Policy.* Kampala: GOU.

Gunga, Samson O., and Ian W. Ricketts. 2007. "Facing the Challenges of e-learning Initiatives in African Universities." *British Journal of Educational Technology* 38 (5): 896–906.

Hepp, Pedro K., Enrique S. Hinostroza, Ernesto M. Laval, and Lucio F. Rehbein. 2004. *Technology in Schools: Education, ICT and the Knowledge Society.* Washington, DC: World Bank.

Isaacs, Shafika. 2007. *ICT in Education in South Africa: A Survey of ICT and Education in Africa Country Report.* Washington, DC: infoDev, World Bank.

Kalema, Peter. 2008. Personal Communication on the Implementation of ICT Policy at UMU Nkozi Campus, Nkozi, Uganda, September 26, 2008.

Karagiorgi, Yiasemina, and Loizos Symeou. 2005. "Translating Constructivism into Instructional Design: Potential and Limitations." *Educational Technology & Society* 8 (1): 17–27.

Loughland, Tony, and Bob Meyamn. 2003. "Information Technology across the Teacher Education Curriculum: More Claims than Evidence." *Change: Transformations in Education* 6 (2): 102–108.

Madon, Shirin, Nicolau Reinhard, Dewald Roode, and Geoff Walsham. 2009. "Digital Inclusion Projects in Developing Countries: Processes of Institutionalzation." *Information Technology for Development* 15 (2): 95–107.

Makerere University Kampala (MUK). 2001. *Makerere ICT Policy and Master Plan*. Kampala: Makerere University.

Marsh, Colin J. 2009. *Key Concepts for Understanding Curriculum* (4th ed.). New York: Routledge.

Miller, Allen H., Bradford W. Imrie, and Kevin Cox. 1998. *Student Assessment in Higher Education: A Handbook for Assessing Performance*. London: Kogan Page Limited.

Ministry of Works, Housing and Communications (MWHC). 2004. *E-Readiness Assessment Abridged Report*. Kampala: Techno Brain (U) Ltd.

Mostert, Janneke, and Mduduzi Nthetha. 2008. "Information and Communication Technologies (ICTs) in Secondary Educational Institutions in the uMhlathuze Municipality, South Africa: An Insight into Their Utilisation, Impact, and the Challenges Faced." *South African Journal of Library and Information Science* 74 (1): 23–40.

Musisi, Nakanyike K, and Nansozi K Muwanga. 2003. *Makerere University in Transition 1993–2000: Opportunities and Challenges*. Kampala: Fountain Publishers in Partnership in Higher Education in Africa.

Mutonyi, Harriet, and Bonny Norton. 2007. "ICT on the Margins: Lessons for Ugandan Education." *Langauge and Education* 21 (3): 264–270.

Oosterhof, Albert, Rita-Marie Conrad, and Donald P. Ely. 2008. *Assessing Learners Online*. Upper Saddle River, NJ: Pearson Education.

Preston, Christina, and John Cuthell. 2007. *Education Professionals' Perspectives on ICT CPD: Past, Present and Future of the Experienntial Learning of Advisers Responsible for School Teachers' ICT CPD Programmes*. London: Institute of Education (IOE), University of London.

Richards, Cameron. 2005. "The Effective Design of Effective ICT-Supported Learning Activities: Examplery Models, Changing Requirements and New Possibilities." *Language Learning & Technology* 9 (1): 60–79.

Smith, Patricia L., and Tillman J. Ragan. 1999. *Instructional Design* (2nd ed.). New York: John Wiley & Sons.

Trucano, Michael. 2005. *Knowledge Maps: ICT in Education*. Washington, DC: World Bank.

UNESCO. 1990. *World Declaration Education for All*. New York: World Conference of Education for All, UNICEF House.

———. 2006. *Work on UNESCO's ICT Competency Standards for Teachers Enters Final Phase*. Paris: UNESCO. Available online at www.unesco.org.

Unwin, Tim. 2005. "Towards a Framework for the Use of ICT in Teacher Training in Africa." *Open Learning* 20 (2): 113–129.

World Bank. 2008. *Improving Competitiveness and Improving Growth in Uganda*. Washington, DC: infoDev, World Bank.

Part 3

Education Policy Debates with Lasting Consequences

Chapter 8

Making Gender Matter: Paradigms for Equality, Equity, and Excellence

Maureen K. Porter

Introduction

International policy analysis and practice has been reshaped by scholars and advocates who offer new paradigms for thinking about the essential role that gender plays in program design, implementation, and assessment. Early feminist work that fundamentally affirmed the contributions of girls' schooling to economic well-being has grown to become a multifaceted, multinational, networked discourse about the very meanings of gender and education. Spurred on by international summits, declarations of human rights, and interagency collaborations, women and men who work in international education policy now can draw on a set of complementary paradigms that offer guidelines and tools that can help us to achieve success.

This chapter will highlight three major paradigms that have been, and continue to be, influential in revealing the essentially gendered nature of education and reform. Women in Development (WID) frameworks, Gender and Development (GAD) frameworks, and Gender Mainstreaming (GM) have different principles and priorities. They diverge in significant and complementary ways, but they also share several attributes in common. Each challenges us to question the gender status quo. Each way of conceptualizing the underlying problems continues to motivate advocates to work for equality, equity, and excellence. Together, these paradigms reveal high-potential realms for direct intervention and draw attention to ways that we could make formal schools more welcoming, inclusive, and responsive places where both boys and girls can persist and thrive.

Criteria for Effective Paradigms

The international nongovernmental organization (NGO) Femmes Africa Solidarité (FAS) defines gender as

> the different roles and responsibilities attributed to men and women in society. It does not only mean the biological definition of sex as male and female, but also how these biological definitions are constructed in a social context, subject to historical and cultural change. During conflict, women and men may have different roles, concerns and priorities.

This definition provides an entry point for understanding gender as linked to sex and sexuality, but also as a social, political, and cultural construction. The gender of students, teachers, policymakers, and fieldworkers is an integral part of their embodied human existence.

Consequently, gender matters in education practice, policymaking, and theory-building. The United Nations' *Millennium Development Goals Report* highlights unresolved disparities in participation and performance in many geographic subregions of the world (2008). The following factors show the gendered nature of the problem. Gender comes into play in families when the adults are trying to decide how many children to have, or even whether or not the mother or the father has the right to input into this decision. Gender matters in children's wellness, access to nutritious food, and preventative care. When children reach school age there are school fees and related costs to consider, and gender matters when deciding which child is the most promising and is most likely to provide a good return on the investment for the family. Young boys and girls also have different kinds of expectations and obligations for participating in housework in the family home, laboring in the streets or in the fields, and rearing of other siblings. Gender matters when we consider the kind of access that youth and older adolescents have to well-paid work. Gender also is one attribute considered by those who would forcibly conscript young civilians into warfare. Gender expectations and sexual identity become factors as young men and women grow older, seek out sexual health services, and practice self-determination and seek dignity in intimate relationships. Gender also matters in young people's abilities to leave the confines of a household, whether alone or under supervision, and how much they are expected to, or able to, participate in the public domain. As adults, gender matters when we think about mobility, and the ability, to travel for employment. Gender matters when we look globally at peoples' ability to exercise civil rights and to fully participate in governing bodies, whether as voters or as elected representatives.

We know that gender matters in education and development policy. So why are we still primarily talking about girls and women as the ones who are being placed at a disadvantage? Aikman and Unterhalter (2007) highlight significant gender gaps. More than half of the 100 million children who quit school annually are girls (55 percent). The disparity between men and women is even more striking at the adult level: 100 million of the 800 million adults worldwide do not have basic literacy skills, and 64 percent of this comprise women. We know that mothers of the most influential family members determine about their own children's participation in formal education, or whether or not girls are to be retained at home to do work in the household. And finally, even where girls complete secondary school at the same or greater rate than boys, they are less likely to have the chance to turn this into fair paying, diverse (beyond agriculture, sales, and teaching) forms of employment that are financially and personally rewarding.

When are the educational worlds of boys and men gendered such that they are placed at risk? Boys are affected by school practices and social pressures that constrain their participation in schooling and that reinforce stereotypes of the gendered worlds of war, work, and sexuality (Lingard and Douglas 1999; Ruxton 2004). They are impacted by bullying and harassment at school and may be subjected to greater corporal punishment by teachers. Boys face pressures to enter the workforce early and to leave school; this effect is compounded in the United States by race and ethnicity. Boys, like girls, have to counter stereotypical constraints on the fields of study that are deemed appropriate for their gender. Boys are also at greater risk of being conscripted for warfare, including the irony of being rounded up when they attend school. Boys also need to be explicitly taught about the ways they are encouraged and even rewarded for perpetuating gender-based violence and harassment on the basis of sexuality and sexual identity performance. Young men need to be part of the solution of the HIV/AIDS epidemic; they need frank discussions about how expectations of masculinity and male promiscuity can contribute to their own health risks and risks to others.

Given the significance of gender, what would it mean to successfully integrate a gendered analysis into educational policy and practice at all levels? In order to answer this question we will need to select a meaningful set of criteria that can help serve as focusing lenses for our energies. We can

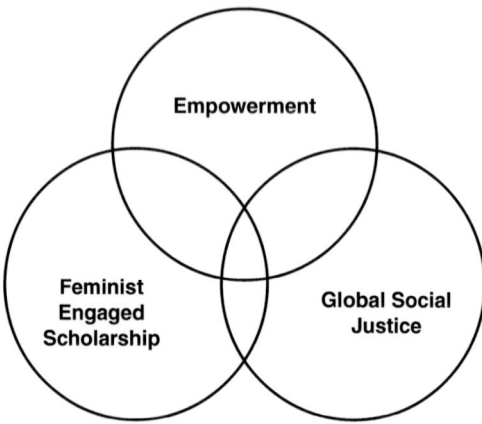

Figure 8.1   Convergent Lenses for Discerning Effective Paradigms

imagine this point of convergence as the overlap between three spheres: working toward global social justice for men and women, continually striving to empower individuals and communities, and using the discipline and analytical tools of feminist engaged scholarship to help refine praxis. By aligning this system of lenses, we can aim a targeted beam of light that will reveal important features of our selected paradigms.

Metaphors of light are common in policy rhetoric that aims to spotlight a worthy goal and to illuminate a preferred path to achieve those ends. However, centralized or generic exhortations to kindle "a thousand points of light" through education may miss the mark and fail to inspire particular audiences. Elsewhere I discuss the potentially problematic geopolitical nuances of using such diffuse imagery, noting that parents and teachers in marginalized and stigmatized regions, such as the Appalachian mountain range in the south central United States, saw such metaphors as connoting that they lived in an unenlightened hinterland, or that they could barely hold a candle to the reforms and outcomes of more urbane areas of their home state (Porter 2001). Local activists refused to accept passive roles as recipients of externally generated wisdom, measures of success, or governance. They were not simply "candles to be lit" by suspect flatlander experts. The lesson for this chapter is not that such metaphorical language is inappropriate, but rather that the underlying values of "light" and "dark" correspond to larger notions of good and bad, up and down, developed and underdeveloped, donor and recipient, model and imitator (Lakoff and Johnson 1980). It is exactly because the metaphor of light has such intensity that it is deeply meaningful and useful for guiding this critique.

As educators concerned with the implications of gender for policy and theory, our ultimate aim is to design conceptual paradigms that will help us to achieve the greatest degree of targeted success. Aligning the three complementary lenses is a strategy to examine the paradigms more closely and to gain a new level of fine-grained clarity about their distinguishing features. The goal of this chapter is not to criticize any one particular reform initiative or local program, but rather to identify the distinguishing contours of each paradigm. By comparing and contrasting the paradigms in terms of a common set of lenses, we are able to pinpoint flaws that are only apparent when one shifts perspective and applies a set of shared standards. Each lens reveals part of the picture, and each offers guidelines that can serve as crosshairs for refining our aim. By concentrating our efforts on meeting these orientation criteria, we gain a three-dimensional sense of perspective and, therefore, greater depth of vision.

The first lens provides the tool with which to examine the constituent parts of an effective paradigm. The goal of empowerment provides the impetus for dual, coordinated action. Just as light is both an energized particle and a coherent wave, genuine empowerment is at once a dynamic state of being as well as a holistic, far-reaching pattern. Empowerment happens at micro and at macro levels; each of these profoundly affects the conditions of the other. Paradigms that wish to pass this gatekeeper's test have to meet these dual criteria. By using this lens as a portal, policymakers have to rise to the challenge of acting on both the individual and collective levels to transform the very conditions of oppression that have led to unequal, inequitable experiences by gender.

The Task Force on Education and Gender Equality of The UN Millennium Project sees empowerment as "related to gender equality but distinct from it." They note the requisite elements:

> to be empowered women must not only have equal capabilities (such as education and health) and equal access to resources and opportunities (such as land and employment), they must also have the agency to use those rights, capabilities, resources and opportunities to make strategic choices and decisions (such as are provided through leadership opportunities and participation in political institutions). And to exercise agency, women must live without the fear of coercion and violence. (Grown, Rao Gupta and Kes 2005, 3)

This definition is important because it points to the multiple levels of power that a person can be subjected to and/or can exercise. It asks us to think about the role of violence or persecution in keeping young students, as well as innovation-minded administrators or faith-based NGO workers, in line. Further, this rich definition firmly locates our criteria of empowerment relative to the debate about the meanings of equality, equity, and excellence in educational provisions.

Just like the light that passes through this lens, we can observe the effects, if not the essence, of this concept through its reflection in agents of change, whether these be teachers, the staff of micro-loan offices, or leaders of international organizations. We speak of leaders who empower others and of those people whose gifts of reflection and discernment are able to harness the energies of other people into unified movements for social change. We honor local elected leaders and nonprofit community organizers who show the long-term dedication to stay the course. Sheila Aikman and Elaine Unterhalter (2007) note that countries and organizations that are able to sustain programs demonstrate political will, the "sustained commitment of politicians and administrators to invest the necessary resources to achieve specific objectives. It is the *willingness* of these actors to undertake reform and implement policy, despite opposition" (61). They outline the constituent elements of political will: commitment, leadership, and responsiveness. These provide the environment for grassroots empowerment to grow (Grown, Rao Gupta, and Kes 2005).

If a paradigm is to refract, that is, to alter the course of a social convention or assumption and, instead, to empower previously marginalized gender groups, it has to provide a different medium for continued effort. As experience in the United States with Title IX continues to demonstrate (Sadker, Sadker, and Zittleman 2009), it is not sufficient to rely on legal declarations of equal access and funding alone; these must be coupled with local school administrators' proactive and constructive intercession. Just as water refracts light streaming into it from the surrounding atmosphere, new development paradigms need to inspire local actors to establish conditions that change the milieu of rewards, sanctions, and opportunities.

One of the critical steps in redirecting our efforts away from a downward spiral of powerlessness and fear toward a generative cycle of hope is to rethink the meaning of power. Francis Moore Lappé (2007) offers a way to think of "relational power" as shared, collectively generated momentum that keeps us on track for achieving global social justice. A shared sense (and the active practice) of empowerment, rather than entitlement or estrangement, can help to foster what she calls a "living democracy." Lappé's summary of the features of empowerment has set high and relevant standards for paradigms and the advocates who depend on them to transform schools, communities, and policy milieus.

Feminist engaged scholarship provides a second lens with which to discern the appropriateness and effectiveness of a paradigm. Engaged scholarship with a feminist underpinning offers guidelines for identifying the critical components of "scholarship" and sets the standards for viable, respectful modes of collaboration and research. The lens of feminist engaged scholarship challenges us to look at the complementary roles of academic scholars and applied scholars, and clarifies the interdependence of all actors as they work in tandem for sustainable, culturally responsive policies. By concentrating analysis on how well a particular theoretical paradigm serves to further critical praxis, we can set our long-term sights on the social relevance of theories, policies, and models.

Praxis is at the center of transformative action. It is the effective combination of theory and practice, two complementary endeavors, which combine in "a spiral in which critical reflection and action continuously inform each other in the service of individual and personal transformation, central to liberatory education" (Villaverde 2008, 14).

Feminist research emphasizes, among other key definitive principles, hands-on applications of knowledge, reciprocal partnerships across lines of power and position, honoring gendered ways of knowing and expressing them in new art /media forms, and building networks for grounded social change. Shulamit Reinharz (1992) notes that in order to accomplish such goals of engagement and social justice, feminist scholars should be willing to tackle "multiple methods research" using the diverse tools of oral history, ethnography, content analysis, action research, and more.

Academic calls for recognizing diverse modes of being a scholar have accompanied ongoing efforts to achieve this ambitious set of research intentions. When looking holistically at the academy as one partner in creating knowledge, the somber old triad of research, service, and teaching seem poorly suited to the broader goal of contributing to effective, culturally-inclusive reforms in the field. In the Carnegie Foundation special report, Ernest Boyer (1990) reclaims "scholarship" to include four key elements. Meaningful paradigms that can inspire gender-sensitive policies and that can help refine practice share many of these same attributes. By setting these as the sub-criteria for a multifaceted feminist engaged scholarship, we affirm the contributions that scholars of many talents can make to the field.

- The "scholarship of discovery" is at the heart of knowledge-building. This includes creating models, identifying what constitutes a meaningful problem, and naming new categories of responses. In terms of gender and education, this has meant using paradigms to question the gender status quo, publishing new models of assessing familial and public returns to early marriage, critiquing assumptions about the "nature" of boy-on-boy violence at school, and questioning long-standing organizational structures that disadvantage those who would combine family and work.

- The "scholarship of integration" is the process of positing relationships and discovering larger patterns. In practice, this has meant being explicitly critical about the workings of patriarchal social systems and family dynamics that seemingly legitimize underinvestment in girls' education or pulling boys out of school prematurely in order to earn money or serve in a militia. This attribute is important in maintaining a sense of purpose and seeking out global, intercultural perspectives with which to imagine wider possibilities for action.

- The "scholarship of application" values relevance and diligence in taking discoveries and program models into the field, be that in the primary schools of another country, in the executive boardroom of a philanthropic foundation, or at a town hall meeting. Education professionals who advocate for more sophisticated gendered analysis of policies value collegial feedback about the viability of their work, and see such exchanges as essential elements of their scholarly life.

- The "scholarship of transmission" builds on the traditional understanding of teaching as essential to learning, and esteems the kinds of exchanges that can grow through collegial discourse. This can include formal teaching and learning in courses as well as systematic yet informal encounters that foster face-to-face dialogue. By sharing promising gender-explicit reforms at international convocations, sponsoring professional development workshops, publishing field-tested gender training manuals, and building virtual social networks, feminist scholars around the world have transmitted key lessons about the principles and priorities that give their work meaning. By critically engaging in discourse about the dominant paradigms, scholars have begun to decenter Western educational models and started to contribute as equal colleagues to a more inclusive, reflective, and culturally diverse discourse on social change (Mather Saul 2003). Using the paradigms presented in this chapter as sources of shared vocabulary and motivation, they have developed a common basis for action.

This list was further refined in the follow-up article by Boyer, who added the "scholarship of engagement" (1996). This fifth element helps to integrate and extend the others. In brief:

> The "scholarship of engagement" affirms that the work of universities and scholars is to further social justice, serve the public good, and foster creative civic life. Engagement is about nurturing relationships, "creating a special

climate in which the academic and civic cultures communicate more continuously and more creatively with each other." (20)

This aspect of scholarship can serve as a further standard for assessing a paradigm's power to motivate, connect, and reward.

In this chapter I use the phrase "engaged scholarship" to refer to the specific features of this additional component as well as to embrace the professional literature (including benchmarks for community-engaged scholarship and guidelines for promotion and tenure) that takes the term to holistically include all of these interlocking pieces of scholarship. This inclusive definition dovetails with the feminist research goals of gender advocates and scholars.

Andrew H. Van de Ven (2007) favors thinking beyond the opposition of basic research and practice, in which too often research is only valued in terms of how it can serve applied needs. Rather, he emphasizes the complementarity of the pair. Just as advocates at all levels need to extend a hand *to* one another to achieve reciprocity (Porter and Monard 2001), engaged scholarship means working *with* rather than *for* others: "Engagement means that scholars step outside of themselves to obtain and be informed by the interpretations of others in performing each step of the research process: problem formulation, theory building, research design, and problem solving" (10).

Use of the goal of contributing to feminist engaged scholarship as one of the three lenses through which to appraise the success of a paradigm leads us to focus on the collaborative roles that professionals in the field, in the academy, and in global organizations play as a team. By emphasizing the shared goals of discovery, integration, application, transmission, and engagement, we can continue to grow as members of an educational "community of practice" (Lave and Wenger 1991).

The third criterion through which we can refine our focus is global social justice. It sets benchmarks for excellence that are common to empowerment and engaged scholarship as well. These areas of overlap most notably include: an emphasis on incorporating, but not homogenizing, diverse perspectives and culturally-nuanced worldviews; recognizing people located at the furthest margins as equally important partners with those at the centers of formal power in international funding and governance institutions; validating multiple modes of research and fully utilizing emerging media as viable and effective routes for publication; and acknowledging that schooling choices are meaningless if options are not financially, culturally, geographically, or linguistically accessible.

In addition to these shared starting points, a lens of global social justice challenges us to think globally and act locally. This lens challenges us to act on an international scale and to humbly offer our ideas as part of an ongoing, reciprocal global discourse geared toward generating lasting gender justice. This form of global citizenship requires us to proactively seek out divergent voices and case studies. James A. Banks (2006) warns of thinking of citizenship in assimilationist terms, requiring development actors in non-Western locations (both politically and geographically) to conform to dominant norms. Rather, he calls on those who hold up the standard of working for social justice to incorporate pluralistic, democratic, and inclusive means of contributing to the global public interest.

Unterhalter (2007) outlines current debates about the very basis for achieving social justice. She challenges advocates of sophisticated and responsive gendered policies to balance institutionalized statements of rights and obligations (as laid out in treaties, declarations of universal human rights, international agencies' development goals, and governmental regulatory mechanisms) and local sentiments about, and support for, egalitarian gender relationships. She cautions that enhancing the status or privileges of one group can lead to a false sense of social justice being considered as retribution, in which winners and losers are engaged in a zero-sum game. Instead, she sets forth the goals of working collectively across artificial national borders and thin notions of citizenship to create alliances based on shared meanings and aspirations. "Gender equality in education as an objective of global social justice is thus an open global dialogue which entails practice" (32).

Holding up a lens of broader social justice compels us to ask larger, tactical questions about the cultural contexts in which reforms are proposed and implemented. Gender advocates working toward social justice also need to link practical needs (such as scholarships to fund girls' school fees) to strategic interests (e.g., the allocation of household work and perceptions of the value of girls' education) (Centre for Development and Population Activities 1996). In this manner, this lens reinforces the dual attributes of praxis.

Successful gender reform strategies need to meet the benchmarks set by our focal criteria: contributing to global social justice, fostering empowerment, and cumulatively adding to feminist engaged scholarship. Taken as orienting points for targeting best practices, these lenses help us to appraise the strengths and weaknesses of different policy frameworks. Further, they help us retain a long-term focus on fundamental social change and establish challenges for actors and institutions to meet. We can now take a closer look at how three influential paradigms have helped advocates redefine problems, set priorities, and propel reforms.

The Three Paradigms

Women in development (WID) frameworks, gender and development (GAD) frameworks, and gender mainstreaming (GM) each offer principles and strategies that can help us to refine a gendered analysis of education reform. These paradigms can motivate us to strive for equality, equity, and excellence.

I have selected these three policy paradigms because they have been, and continue to be, influential. The three movements came about in roughly this same order, each one growing out of dissatisfaction with development practices, funding priorities, and organizational management strategies that were dominant. Each policy model proffers a retooled approach to refine and target gender-specific reforms. Each subsequent paradigm has enabled advocates to respond to frustrations over missed opportunities, to inappropriate governance structures that did not empower women and gender advocates, and to continued resistance to developing the political will for change. The three policy orientations build sequentially, starting with the most fundamental issues of access and equal economic opportunity, continuing with equity human rights, and extending to building capacity for sustaining a diverse array of excellent programs and creating deep social change.

Paradigms are, according to Thomas Kuhn (1970, 43), the "set of recurrent and quasi-standard illustrations of various theories in their conceptual, observational, and instrumental applications." That is, reigning paradigms fundamentally shape our underlying rationalizations, seem to legitimize rules, inspire certain modes of research, and inform instruments for assessing progress. These usually implicit ways of understanding the world inform scientific traditions and underlie legislation. Explicit questioning and debate about the assumptions of certain paradigms render them vulnerable to modification, even radical change. He notes that this shift in the sanctity of a dominant paradigm, for example, from the hegemony of equality as a goal to a more socially just concept of equity, precedes (even precipitates) broader scientific revolutions. Paradigms are frameworks for elaborating and prioritizing problems. Murray Edelman (1998, 12) expands on the social construction of problems, noting:

> they signify who are virtuous and useful and who are dangerous or inadequate, which actions will be rewarded and which penalized. They constitute people as subjects with particular kinds of aspirations, self-concepts, and fears, and they create beliefs about the relative importance of events and objects. They are critical in determining who exercise authority and who accept it. They construct areas of immunity from concern because those areas are not seen as problems.

This view of paradigms, and their constituent problems, as socially constructed and embedded in power hierarchies recognizes the unequal positions held by different agents of change. Advocates at all levels have the authority to accept or reject these paradigms and to flesh out these frameworks with images, symbols, characters, and origin stories that give them locally-sanctioned meaning. Indeed, as Andrea Cornwall, Elizabeth Harrison, and Ann Whitehead chronicle in their edited book (2008), feminist gender advocates need to be able to "make strategic choices, including which linguistic and presentational forms will best get particular gender issues addressed, prioritize, and resourced" (16). Feminists need to be able to tap into and make explicit the *Weltanschauung*, folklore, icons, and implicitly sexist language that colors the policy realms where they wish to make an impact. Authors, such as Tsitsi Dangarembga (1988), also know how to convey the entwined personal and transnational sagas of colonialism, a rural sense of place, enduring kinship obligations and traditions, and the hunger for literacy and knowledge into novel forms that call out in a compelling manner to readers and policymakers alike.

All three paradigms are currently in use and none has been so fully achieved that it can be abandoned as passé. We still face fundamental conceptual and logistical challenges in trying to move beyond the gender gap (Heward and Bunwaree 1999), starting with actually counting how many girls and boys are in school, and in determining adequate and meaningful measures of school participation and attainment (Maslak 2008). In both former colonial powers and in postcolonial states, from pan-African organizations to Pacific Rim networks, educators struggle to legitimate and to implement curricula that expand opportunities rather than reinforce narrow and patriarchal gender stereotypes.

Women in Development (WID)

Unterhalter (2007, 3) argues that the ways policymakers have defined the very concept of "gender" have had a significant impact on deciding what matters most. She distinguishes three distinctive approaches: understanding "gender" as a noun, as an adjective, and as a verb. The Women in Development (WID) paradigm is firmly anchored in, and has benefitted from, the first and most fundamental of these, that is, counting singular instances of men, women, girls, and boys. When gender is a noun, schooling is first and foremost about granting equal access for both males and females.

WID-oriented reforms have defined the problem as the exclusion of girls from even the most basic levels of schooling and as disparate outcomes in retention, achievement, and returns to education. This paradigm has continued to form the foundation for the Education for All (EFA) movement, which has at its basis the principle of equality. The WID paradigm has informed feminist engaged scholars' arguments that women are not anomalous or supplemental to an unchallenged male norm. Rather, girls and women should be incorporated as equal and essential. Therefore you cannot simply add women into male-defined and male-priority systems and expect such from more than a few token or "exceptional" women. WID paradigms have helped establish a priority on facilitating access. Parents are more likely to send their daughters to school, particularly secondary school, when there are schools nearby, when there are gender segregated sections or classes, when there are secure, public means for transit to and from school, and when there are rules against sexual harassment and exploitation from other students and adult male teachers. Safety issues *en route* to school and in class are priorities in Women in Development programs. Another WID-inspired emphasis has been on increasing the number and proportion of female teachers. They can serve as role models of what one could do with a school-leaving certificate as well as how to thrive and even lead in mixed-gender settings.

WID's contributions to global social justice have come through scholars' recognition that women's work is often unpaid and in the nonformal sector, but it is nonetheless critical for household well-being (Boserup 1970). Furthermore, women's labor is also relatively undervalued and underpaid, thus artificially compressing the apparent value of their contributions. Therefore we cannot assess the returns to schooling for women over a short term or base it on narrow definitions of public labor and wages. WID-motivated studies ask us to consider investments and assessment tools that recognize all forms of women's labor.

While this shift in willingness to recognize women's actual reproductive as well as productive work has had considerable advantages, it can also lead to undue essentializing about women's roles as mothers, daughters, and wives. WID programs may invest heavily in micro-loan schemes run by cooperatives of women community leaders, or may provide incentives to keep girls in school. Directors have noted that when women participate in schooling they share their love of learning and of content knowledge to siblings and offspring, cultivating a multigenerational positive attitude toward schooling. However, these initiatives are not radically empowering if the underlying message is that women are the means to others' prosperity. Gender matters in the WID paradigm in that educated women become the conduit for the welfare of men and children.

The WID paradigm has contributed to global social justice in that theorists and administrators now place greater "value" on women's work, moving it from the private domain of invisible labor within patriarchal households to "counting" as part of transnational indices of well-being and economic vitality. Education becomes the means to prosperity. Scholarship inspired by this paradigm emphasizes the responsibilities of international agencies and monitoring bodies to actually record relevant data, starting with the not so simple task of ascertaining the numbers of girls being enrolled and boys being retained in primary schools. Educators motivated by this paradigm have established new bases for accountability and have set up ranking systems for financial interventions. WID has also made a difference by affirming the importance of having both women and men serve as teachers and administrators. This paradigm posits that positions, like curricula, should be gender-blind and open for supposedly fair competition. While few places enjoy parity in the number of women and men educators (e.g., primary schools are still considered the domain of women teachers, and upper levels of administration and ministry posts are still predominantly held by men), we have made progress in providing role models from among both genders who bring a range of talents and styles to the positions they hold (Shakeshaft 1989).

Continuing to work toward shared power and a living democracy (Lappé 2007) remains a goal that our orienting lenses of empowerment and social justice challenges us to achieve. Empowerment is both a process and a product, a cycle that can gain momentum as it is further enhanced by feminist policymakers and educators' engaged scholarship. WID advocates work at both individual and transnational levels to demand accountability and to highlight progress. Scholarly work done by degreed professionals and lay leaders alike has contributed to better understanding the implications of this paradigm. Community mapping and resource inventories have helped reveal the overall distributions of power and authority and gendered contexts of economic, familial, and political systems (Heward and Bunwaree 1999). The goals of WID programs are to provide gender-blind choices open to both men and women who compete for equal opportunities.

Among other critiques, feminist engaged scholarship on WID has revealed some of the shortcomings of a paradigm primarily focused on assuming that women are important because they are the means to others' (e.g., their patrilocal families') economic prosperity. Scholarship, broadly defined to include teaching, application, and public engagement, helps us continue to push those working primarily within this paradigm to question patriarchal assumptions about women's and men's appropriate adult roles. It helps us to articulate the structural and symbolic ways that school reify rather than rectify the social and economic inequalities that result from gender hierarchies of power.

The next paradigm commences from another starting point, and thus it puts us on a somewhat different trajectory as we set out to meet the criteria associated with global social justice, empowerment, and feminist engaged scholarship. However, both have the long-term aim of effecting sustainable, responsive change to benefit both men and women. Both recognize that when it comes to education, gender matters.

Gender and Development (GAD)

Following Unterhalter's progression of ways of understanding "gender," the shift to Gender and Development (GAD) paradigms can be associated with her insight that gender can be an adjective as well as a noun. In this framework, it is important but not sufficient to simply count participants by sex. In this expanded definition, gender encompasses not only individual choices and attendance, it is also the driver for the dynamic and highly charged relationships between young girls and boys, and between adult men and women. In this relational definition, individuals retain agency and responsibility; their actions gain meaning as the sum of their private choices unfolds.

GAD advocates believe that gendered attributes and roles are at the heart of long-standing social relationships and deeply-held values that fundamentally shape support for formal schooling. In this framework, both boys and girls have gender, rather than seeing "gender problems," primarily in terms of adding women and girls to an extant male norm. Understanding gender as an inclusive descriptor encourages us to clarify assumptions about each sex's "natural" traits. Using this stance, policymakers can use "gendered" as an adjective to describe the institutional practices that favor one sex or the other, or to pinpoint those enduring excuses that overlook problematic boys' or girls' behaviors. GAD advocates recognize that equal opportunities are insufficient to redress external sexism. This paradigm prompts us to articulate the stereotypes that seem to rationalize differential expectations and treatment of girls and boys once they come to school.

In the GAD framework, gender becomes significant as a social construction that privileges and normalizes hierarchical power relations between students or, by extension, male administrators and female teaching corps. Therefore GAD-inspired policies take a proactive approach to global social justice by identifying implicit forms of bias and holistically redesigning curricula and schooling to compensate for the sexism and segregation that is part of students' daily lives. Rather than adopting a stance of being gender-blind, advocates recognize that the curricula can, intentionally or not, primarily acknowledge and reward one group's experiences and ways of knowing. Gender advocates using this paradigm note that gender should have a bearing when designing programs, such as for boarding schools or for evening classes, that are responsive to the differential social expectations for young people's paid work and unpaid family labor. Offering gender-inclusive opportunities is necessary but not sufficient; GAD-motivated advocates note that compensatory programs that are gender-responsive may be required to offset the unequal burdens placed on youth based on their gender. They note that access to secondary school is compromised if girls have to deal with widespread acceptance of early marriage, rape, and teen childrearing. Foregrounding this relational aspect of gender in educational policy and practice helps to propel policies based on the principle of equity rather than simplistic notions of equality.

WID programs have placed an emphasis on access; GAD-inspired praxis has redefined the next pressing problem as one of retention. Schools should be places where boys and girls should not only feel safe, learn, and survive, but where children can also thrive. WID programs had established safe school and safe conduit as the prerequisites; GAD programs go beyond this to state that safety is as much about harassment and sexual abuse as it is about making it to school unaccosted. Laws and regulations outlining safe and welcoming schools are not enough. Educators need to act as intercessors, proactively empowering kids (and one another) to stand up to abuse and bullying that feeds gender-based harassment.

The GAD paradigm entreats us to define the underlying problem as one of gender hierarchies and marginalization. Rather than just appending women and girls into institutions and professions that remain designed around an implicit male norm, GAD programs value the impact that reforms can have on balancing power relationships between the sexes. They value work as a means of personal dignity and access to resources, social exchange, and public spaces. Such reformers see women and women's work not just as the means to greater familial and community prosperity, but also as ends in themselves.

The GAD framework draws strength and authority for these programmatic strands through its grounding in universal human rights. Rather than seeing education primarily as a means to (others') prosperity, in GAD, gender is a fundamental dimension of all people, all of whom deserve respect. This is a shift away from the relative value of an individual in a competitive, equal marketplace to a stance of human rights, and it confers inherent dignity as well as integrity of the body. It treats a man or woman as an ends in himself or herself and sees the complementarity of the contributions made by each gender.

GAD advocates have contributed to theory-building by enriching the international discourse on women's ways of knowing. Scholars have honored women's cultural forms of expression and use of education, whether via pottery or via multimedia web design. Program evaluators have examined women's unique leadership styles and modes of organizing for social justice through women-led micro-loan cooperatives and traveling nonformal health courses. Masculinity studies were also carried out, building gender-responsive programs that spoke in the languages, activities, and forms of creative expression that engage boys of varied class and cultural backgrounds. Both sets of experts worked in collaboration to prepare teachers who could teach in gender-inclusive, fair, and affirming ways that challenge stereotypes and bias about what the future should hold for young men and women.

In summary, the Gender and Development paradigm has helped educators achieve high standards of equity by contributing to global social justice. By first articulating and then strategically activating an international discourse on human rights and gender rights, proponents of this paradigm displayed a powerful tool with which to propel and channel reforms. By redefining the problem of empowerment as one of relational power, this paradigm can reveal complementarities between girls and boys as well as men and women. Numerical equality (or parity or even proportionality) is now not enough; the call is now for compensatory means of equity that takes uneven power in other domains into account. The focus on access to education turns to issues of retention. Gendered policies become centered on (re-)balancing power relationships and achieving interlocking modes of equity in the curriculum, pedagogy, school structures, fee incentives, and courses.

Empowerment becomes a more dynamic concept through GAD, one that is energized by dialogic exchanges and gender-responsive policies that encourage both groups to bring their unique, sometimes even essentialized, attributes to the table. Advocates working within GAD can make use of the paradigm's conceptual priorities and ask appropriate questions that can help foster community ownership and engagement. They look to men and women educators to be intercessors for youth, to serve as role models for gender-responsive pedagogies and non-stereotypical career paths.

GAD draws more than ever on worldwide networks on feminist engaged scholars who have continued to refine what equity would require in diverse cultural contexts. This paradigm takes gender seriously as a dimension of praxis, not only for school children but for the reformers as well. GAD reinforces the importance of conducting feminist engaged scholarship with an eye to the embodied, situated, power-fraught nature of inquiry and action. The perceived gender (and generation, race, religion, language skills, etc.) of scholars and fieldworkers can become resources as well as impediments to effective praxis. While scholars, politicians, and development specialists alike continue to work through the culturally-specific implications of particular Gender and Development initiatives, we turn to the next influential framework.

Gender Mainstreaming (GM)

The third definition of "gender" that Unterhalter offers is as a verb. Just as Gender Mainstreaming (GM) builds on the institutional accomplishments and international discourses that have arisen from WID and GAD paradigms, adding this elaborated understanding of gendered policy to our repertoire helps to further expand our conceptual tool set. This social construction of gender as performance highlights the process of becoming a masculine or feminine person, a lifelong task that is always achieved in relationship to the "opposite sex." Young people learn, at school and in numerous other settings, how to appropriately perform a gendered identity that is congruent with social expectations. Conversely, they also learn the consequences for divergent modes of gender expression and social expectations for forming normative and "alternate" family constellations. They learn that education has a great deal to do with preparing young adults to enter the segregated world of work, in which professions are sorted into "pink collar," "blue collar," or "white collar" (themselves wonderfully gendered metaphors for the kinds of clothing stereotypical for a particular field). These expectations are further enriched, and entangled, by being part of class, ethnic, racial, political, geographic, and religious groups. Understanding gender as a verb, in addition to being available for use as an adjective and a noun, provides an important shift away from static social hierarchies to a stance of malleability, action, and transformative praxis.

Building on the fundamental, and still inconsistently achieved, requirement of equality in provisions of and returns to schooling, and coming on the heels of international demands for equity in human relations and rights, the paradigm of Gender Mainstreaming sets high expectations for gender-explicit policymaking and partnerships. GM looks at excellence as a core principle in design, collaborations, and assessment. I do not mean to suggest that the other paradigms are not concerned with quality outcomes. By excellence I mean finesse, superiority, and dexterity, that is, "going from good to great" (Collins 2001). Using this simplified moniker to distinguish GM does not diminish the contributions of the other paradigms that are concurrently operating. Rather, it highlights the systematicity and synchronicity required for large-scale organization and social change. Excellence, like GM, is necessarily multilevel; gender must be explicitly integrated as a dimension in achieving the empowering goals of recognizing human rights, establishing shared governance, and facilitating full participation.

As advocates from women's organizations and networks from around the world continue to collaborate with the United Nations, and as world conferences in Cairo and Beijing have sustained discourse and strategic action plans, the GM paradigm for policy has gained ground. Gender Mainstreaming is an explicit organizational and institutional planning framework that highlights the gendered experiences, needs, and lived experiences that could impact "design, implementation, monitoring, and evaluation of policies and programmes." In this regard, GM represents a "comprehensive and holistic" (Pietilä 2007, 83) approach to educational policymaking. Coordinated leadership and organizational redesign depends on using GM well as a "strategy for making women's as well as men's concerns and experiences an integral dimension of the design, implementation, monitoring and evaluation of policies and programmes in all political, economic and societal spheres so that women and men benefit equally and inequality is not perpetuated" (Division for the Advancement of Women 1997, 2). The GM paradigm builds on the complementary, but not identical, goals of equality and equity in order to build a system of excellence amenable to thoroughly embedding a gendered analysis into policy and practice.

The overall rationale for implementing wide-ranging GM programs is building capacity for institutional and social change. If, put simply, WID is often about investing in individuals as the means to group prosperity, and GAD emphasizes offering complementary programs to develop human beings for their own sake, GM inspires advocates to develop educational opportunities as a systematic means for including everyone and fostering the diverse, creative talents of all people. GM meets standards of working toward global social justice in that this focus on capacity-building reinforces gender as a mode of doing, being, contributing, and inventing.

GM programs are about organized, integrated, and proactive strategies for accountability and partnership. They are about coordinated leadership, tethering large-scale change to top-down mandates and governing bodies and grounding it in bottom-up skill building. GM paradigms emphasize that educators who are able to use a sophisticated gender lens and who want to work for social justice need to be in place at all institutional levels of power. Therefore, this principled way of approaching praxis inspires us to put men and women in leadership positions who are able to recognize the likely long-term consequences of policies, including when there are likely to be divergent or congruent outcomes for each gender.

In GM, both individuals and organizations are responsible for change. However, it is easy to become enamored with establishing formal university commissions for women's (or gender) equity, underrepresented gender mentoring programs (such as outreach for male students in early childhood education or women in school leadership), and new family leave policies.

Once finally enacted, they provide gratification and can lull administrators into thinking that the "problem" has been "solved." The challenge is to couple these top-down, organizational strategies with changes in long-standing school culture and norms of individual disengagement or entitlement. By making these initiatives gender-explicit, excellence becomes a shared goal, not the sole responsibility of actors at one level or another.

A final important feature of GM arises out of this principle of coordinated leadership. GM can contribute to shared authority and networked hubs of empowered agents of social change. This can happen if the full range of scholarly work, from discovery to application to transmission, is built in and recognized as part of a diversified approach to praxis. Feminist engaged scholars recognize via GM that "gender" is not a separate branch or subfield of development. It is not a charitable form of reaching out to the disenfranchised but an essential aspect of effective development policy. "First world" feminists need to make sure that the proliferation of material available for gender advocates is not simply a surplus of the same content, but that it offers useful and novel ways of building paradigms and contributing to social justice, broad-based empowerment, and feminist engaged scholarship. The current diversification of publications and publishing houses, training manuals, web sites, conference sponsorships, service-learning encounters, formal academic degree programs are signs that GM, coupled with WID and GAD, are having a cumulative effect on education and are contributing to inclusive, global networks (Mather Saul 2003). Gender advocates are becoming savvy users of new media and communications to share their diverse stories, and the field is not the same as it was at the advent of "women in development" debates.

In summary, Gender Mainstreaming alters and extends the course of education reforms by making explicit the ways that gender continues to matter. GM advocates are not just arguing the complementarity of the parallel demands that men and women place on the education system. They wish to move beyond accommodation and compensatory programming to find sites of congruence. For example, this may mean recognizing the pitfalls of offering a generous, but ill-fated, "mommy track" for women that allows extended time out of the full-time workforce but harshly penalizes such a "choice" by segregating returnees and relegating them to the lower ranks of their profession. Whether designing a childcare contract in a small weaving studio, a university, or a global bank, the GM paradigm has led advocates instead to consider the advantages of extending "family leave" to all parenting workers as part of establishing a comprehensive family-friendly environment. GM is, at heart, about building capacity, about implementing strategies that meet the benchmark of effectively linking individual and institutional levels of accountability. It honors both the

Table 8.1 Simplified Areas of Divergence between the Three Gender Paradigms

	Women in Development	Gender and Development	Gender Mainstreaming
Focus:	Equality	Equity	Excellence
Gender is a:	Noun	Adjective	Verb
Stance on gender:	Gender-blind	Gender-responsive	Gender-explicit
Core Problems:	Access	Retention	Diversification
Establish:	Role models	Intercessors	Coordinated leadership
Women's labor:	Means for group prosperity	Ends in itself	Well-being
Rationale:	Prosperity	Human rights	Building capacity
Gender roles:	Competition	Complementarity	Congruence

grassroots and the corporate aspects of empowerment, coupling bottom-up and top-down reforms. Constructing gender as a verb, that is, as a mode of performance and identity formation, GM advocates recognize the authority of diversely-situated actors to create their own routine. As engaged scholars working with this paradigm, reformers celebrate the collective imagination and creative powers of the global community of educators who are making gender matter in policy and practice.

Summary

In conclusion, we can think of gender in educational policy and planning as primarily a matter of counting person, places, and things in order to achieve equality. We can also expand that definition to include gender as an adjective and use it as a tool to reveal the power relationships and institutional structures that differentially privilege and reward participants and impact the quest for equity. Further, we can widen our conceptual repertoire and think of gender as a verb, as the act of pursuing excellence at the individual, collective, and institutional levels.

Fundamental work in realizing the best intensions of the WID, GAD, and GM paradigms is happening at all levels. While much needs to be finished, we have made substantial progress in breaking down gendered barriers of access, authority, and advocacy. Grassroots educational activists are challenging external authorities' generic mandates. Professionals in elected office, political bodies, and policymaking institutions are generating the leverage and political will to implement and sustain thoughtful, thorough reforms that take gender seriously. Experts from academic, analytical, and applied professions have begun to recognize one another as legitimate partners in reform. Internet and print journals are identifying, publishing, and promoting empirical studies from a global array of contributors. New media and virtual social networking sites provide new forms of praxis that further facilitate the international webs of collegial relationship that are hallmarks of the third wave of feminism (Baumgardner and Richards 2005). What scholars of all forms and in fieldsites need in order to live up to the highest ideals of empowerment, feminist engaged scholarship, and global social justice are integrity, perseverance, and courage (Glassick, Taylor Huber, and Maeroff 1997).

The education reform paradigms featured in this chapter at once emerge from and in turn can be used to continually polish our critical lenses. Collectively, the three current paradigms exhort us to expand our definition of global social justice to include human rights, economic prosperity, and institutional capacity. Each fulfills part of the charge of fostering empowerment, challenging us to change not only who is regularly at the table but also which resources and evidence they are able to bring to bear on the problems at hand. Finally, using the standards of feminist engaged scholarship charges us to recognize and reward the integrated scholarly modes of discovery, integration, application, transmission, and public engagement. These, in turn, can serve as well-positioned levers for change. We need to continue to keep complex and transformative conceptualizations of gender front and center in order to mobilize the resources and political will for broad-based ownership and sustained investments in multipronged programs. Karen Hyer and colleagues (2008, 146) exhort us to remember that "the current political priorities and agendas say more about collective values and philosophical commitment to gender parity in education than they do about the capacity to provide it." Paradigms are powerful tools in this continuing mission.

As advocates continue to apply their energies to conducting increasingly sophisticated gendered analyses of education policy, perhaps a new framework will emerge that builds on the insights and unanswered questions of the WID, GAD, and GM paradigms. By testing this new paradigm against the three standards in this chapter, we can hold it up to the light and examine its viability as a sustainable means to achieve the harmonizing goals of gender equality, equity, and excellence.

References

Aikman, Sheila, and Elaine Unterhalter. 2007. *Practising Gender Equality in Education.* Oxford: Oxfam.

Banks, James A. 2006. "Democracy, Diversity and Social Justice: Educating Citizens for the Public Interest in a Global Age." In *Education Research in the Public Interest: Social Justice, Action, and Policy*, ed. G. Ladson-Billings and W. Tate, 141–157. New York: Teachers College Press.

Baumgardner, Jennifer, and Amy Richards, eds. 2005. *Grassroots: A Field Guide for Feminist Activism.* New York: Farrar, Straus and Giroux.

Boserup, Ester. 1970. *Woman's Role in Economic Development.* New York: St. Martin's Press.

Boyer, Ernest. 1990. *Scholarship Reconsidered: Priorities of the Professoriate.* The Carnegie Foundation for the Advancement of Teaching. San Francisco: Jossey-Bass.

———. 1996. "The Scholarship of Engagement." *Journal of Public Service & Outreach* 1 (1): 11–20.

Centre for Development and Population Activities. 1996. *Gender Equity: Concepts and Tools for Development.* Washington, DC: Centre for Development and Population Activities.

Collins, James Charles. 2001. *Good to Great: Why Some Companies Make the Leap...and Others Don't.* New York: HarperBusiness.

Cornwall, Andrea, Elizabeth Harrison, and Ann Whitehead, eds. 2008. *Gender Myths and Feminist Fables: The Struggle for Interpretive Power in Gender and Development.* Malden, MA: Blackwell Publishing.

Dangarembga, Tsitsi. 1988. *Nervous Conditions: A Novel.* Seattle: The Seal Press.

Division for the Advancement of Women. 1997. "Gender Mainstreaming." Report of the Economic and Social Council. New York: United Nations Department for Economic and Social Affairs.

Edelman, Murray. 1998. *Constructing the Political Spectacle.* Chicago: University of Chicago Press.

Femmes Africa Solidarité. n.d. *Glossary of Terms.* Geneva: Femmes Africa Solidarité. Available online at: http://www.fasngo.org/terms.html.

Glassick, Charles E., Mary Taylor Huber, and Gene I. Maeroff. 1997. *Scholarship Assessed: Evaluation of the Professoriate.* San Fransisco: Jossey-Bass.

Grown, Caren, Geeta Rao Gupta, and Ashlihan Kes. 2005. *Taking Action: Achieving Gender Equality and Empowering Women.* London: Earthscan.

Heward, Christine, and Sheila Bunwaree, eds. 1999. *Gender, Education, and Development: Beyond Access to Empowerment.* London: Zed Books.

Hyer, Karen, Bonnie Ballif-Spanvill, Susan Peters, Yodit Solomon, Heather Thomas, and Carol Ward. 2008. "Gender Inequalities in Educational Participation." In *Inequality in Education: Comparative and International Perspectives*, ed. D. Holsinger and W. J. Jacob, 128–148. Hong Kong; and Dordrecht, The Netherlands: Comparative Education Research Centre and Springer.

Kuhn, Thomas. 1970. *The Structure of Scientific Revolutions.* 2nd ed. Chicago: University of Chicago Press.

Lakoff, George, and Mark Johnson. 1980. *Metaphors We Live By.* Chicago: University of Chicago Press.

Lappé, Francis Moore. 2007. *Getting a Grip: Clarity, Creativity, and Courage in a World Gone Mad*. Cambridge: Small Planet Media.

Lave, Jane, and Etienne Wenger. 1991. *Situated Learning: Legitimate Peripheral Participation*. Cambridge: Cambridge University Press.

Lingard, Bob, and Peter Douglas. 1999. *Men Engaging Feminisms: Pro-Feminism, Backlashes and Schooling*. Buckingham: Open University Press.

Maslak, Mary Ann. 2008. "Using Enrollment and Attainment in Formal Education to Understand the Case of India." In *Inequality in education: Comparative and International Perspectives*, ed. D. Holsinger and W. J. Jacob, 240–260. Hong Kong; and Dordrecht, The Netherlands: Comparative Education Research Centre and Springer.

Mather Saul, Jennifer. 2003. *Feminism: Issues and Arguments*. Oxford: Oxford University Press.

Pietilä, Hilkka. 2007. *The Unfinished Story of Women and the United Nations*. New York: United Nations Non-Governmental Liasion Service.

Porter, Maureen. 2001. "We are Mountain:" Appalachian Educators' Responses to the Challenge of Systemic Reform. In *Policy as Practice: Toward a Sociocultural Analysis of Educational Policy*, ed. M. Sutton and B. A. Levinson (Sociocultural Studies in Educational Policy Formation and Appropriation, Vol. 1), 265–294. Westport, CT: Ablex Publishing.

Porter, Maureen, and Kathia Monard. 2001. "Ayni in the Global Village: Building Relationships of Reciprocity through International Service-Learning." *Michigan Journal of Community Service Learning* 8 (1): 5–17.

Reinharz, Shulamit. 1992. *Feminist Methods in Social Research*. Oxford: Oxford University Press.

Ruxton, Sandy, ed. 2004. *Gender Equality and Men: Learning from Practice*. Oxford: Oxfam.

Sadker, David, Myra Sadker, and Karen Zittleman. 2009. *Still Failing at Fairness: How Gender Bias Cheats Girls and Boys in School and What We Can Do about It*. New York: Scribner.

Shakeshaft, Charol. 1989. *Women in Educational Administration*. Updated Edition. Newbury Park, CA: Sage Publications.

United Nations. 2008. *The Millennium Development Goals Report 2008*. New York: United Nations.

Unterhalter, Elaine. 2007. *Gender, Schooling and Global Social Justice*. London: Routledge.

Van de Ven, Andrew H. 2007. *Engaged Scholarship: A Guide for Organizational and Social Research*. Oxford: Oxford University Press.

Villaverde, Lila E. 2008. *Feminist Theories and Education*. New York: Peter Lang.

Chapter 9

Leaps or One Step at a Time: Skirting or Helping Engage the Debate? The Case of Reading

Luis Crouch and Amber K. Gove

Introduction

In a paper that deserves a wider recognition, Deon Filmer, Amer Hasan, and Lant Pritchett (2006) call for a "Millennium Learning Goal" as a way to focus the international community's attention on quality in education. They call for indicators that could do for quality what access and completion indicators have done for the access. The international community is responding, gradually. Three years after this paper's appearance, the Fast Track Initiative (FTI) appears to be the first major international entity to have declared something like a set of international quality goals (The EFA-FTI Secretariat 2009, 11). In the meantime, attention to quality issues seems to have increased at UNESCO as well. In 2008, UNESCO launched an initiative called "Learning Counts" aimed at, among other things, producing a set of indicators to focus attention on the quality issue in the same way that the EFA and Millennium Development Goal (MDG) access and completion indicators focus attention on those issues.[1]

One reason many countries (explicitly or implicitly) focused on the access goals of EFA established in Jomtien and reaffirmed in Dakar is simply that enrollment rates are easily measured. The estimating of these rates was well established (if not always reliable) in nearly all countries at this point; UNESCO's Institute of Statistics maintains information on nearly all countries going back to the 1970s.[2] Quality, by comparison, is amorphous; as Goal 6 states: "Improving all aspects of the quality of education and ensuring excellence of all so that recognized and measurable learning outcomes are achieved by all, especially in literacy, numeracy and essential life skills" (UNESCO 2000). The most concrete phrase, "recognized and measurable learning outcomes," is sticky at best, contentious at worst. "Recognized" implies agreement, yet there is no universal standard as to what constitutes learning outcomes in literacy, numeracy, and life skills. "Measurable" indicates not only the political agreement implied by "recognized" but technical consensus on psychometric rigor, reliability, and validity. At this point in 2000, TIMSS and PISA (PIRLS did not begin until 2001), the leading international assessments of literacy and numeracy, were administered in just seven developing countries, so an agreed upon standard of measurement for what constituted learning outcomes in the developing world remained elusive.[3]

In all this, it seems important to establish some key facts related to the relative lag of low-income countries, relative to high-income ones, in learning-outcomes as opposed to access. A review of 2007 data on access (using the World Bank's EdStats data query system) shows that the ratios of the low-income countries' mean to the high-income country means in the primary gross enrollment rate and primary school completion rate are 97 percent and 66 percent, respectively. At the secondary level the ratio of gross enrollment rates drops to 43 percent. But the differences in learning outcomes seem much larger. Unfortunately, there are few assessments where both high-income and low-income countries participate, so one has to make a judgment as to low-income countries' performance on the basis of a few countries such as Ghana, Morocco, South Africa, or the Philippines. The latter three are not even low-income, so estimates are optimistic. Taking the average percent correct answers in the latest rounds of TIMSS and PIRLS, the ratio of average percent correct answers in low-income countries to that in high-income countries is around 30 percent (about 19 percent correct answers in the former versus 60 percent in the latter).[4] A dramatic estimate shows where, in the high-income country distribution, the *median* child in a low-income country would fall. The most pessimistic result can be derived assuming that the distribution in the high-income countries is normal throughout the distribution. Under this assumption, the median child in countries such as South Africa, Morocco, the Philippines, or Ghana is placed at *less than the first percentile* of the distribution in rich countries. The most optimistic assumption uses a distribution-free approach, using Chebyshev's inequality, which leads to the estimate that the median child in the poorer countries is somewhere around the 8th percentile of the distribution of children in high-income countries. But it is this procedure that produces the most conservative results possible. Finally, if one fits a polynomial to the scores at the 5th, 25th, 50th, 75th, and 95th percentiles in TIMSS or PIRLS, the score of the median child in the same countries (only one of which is actually low income) is lower than the extrapolated score of a child at the first (second in the case of the Philippines, in TIMSS) percentile in the rich country distribution.[5] All this, the chapter argues, is remarkable and represents both a failure and an opportunity to improve. Furthermore, this chapter will argue that taking one step at a time (that is, demonstrating what is possible in one subject, in a few grades, and focusing on the key actor, namely, the teacher), rather than aiming for massive leaps in quality in all grades in entire systems all at once, might be the most fruitful way to engage this debate on quality. Some might think that such an approach skirts the debate. We will argue that this may be in fact the most productive way of truly engaging in the debate, and that attempting a wholesale attack on the quality front results in, if not skirting, at least prolonging the debate unnecessarily, and rendering it too abstract for action.

Early Grade Reading: An Entry Point?

In the midst of increasing questions about the tradeoffs between access and quality (Could quality be achieved while rapidly expanding access for all? Would parents, lured by the elimination of school fees, reject schooling once they learned their children were not actually learning anything?), a growing number of voices called for simple, clear ways to measure quality.[6] As Daniel A. Wagner (2003) posits, assessments of quality and, in particular, literacy need to be:

- *smaller*: "just robust enough" to respond to key policy and instructional needs;
- *quicker*: completed in real time to meet country needs and political cycles; and
- *cheaper*: low cost, to facilitate participation in resource-constrained environments.

In response to this demand and building on a pilot experience in Peru (Abadzi et al. 2005), the authors, with support from USAID, developed a draft protocol for an individual oral assessment of students' foundation reading skills, including recognizing letters of the alphabet, reading simple words, and understanding sentences and paragraphs. To obtain feedback and to confirm the validity of the overall approach, a meeting of cognitive scientists, early-grade reading instruction experts, research methodologists, and assessment experts was convened; a group that would become a community of practice with the goal fostering the development and use of early reading assessments for improving learning outcomes in developing countries.

A product of that meeting was the Early Grades Reading Assessment (EGRA), a tool designed to complement traditional written assessments and respond to the needs of developing countries. At issue, however, was how best to use the tool and for what purpose.[7] International donors wanted to use EGRA to compare across languages and countries; nongovernmental organizations (NGOs) wished to evaluate programs; ministries felt its best use would be for formative assessment in the classroom; while some foundation and advocacy leaders wanted to use it as a tool to spur governments and civil society into action.

As it would happen, due to the open source nature of the tool, countries were determined to use it in whichever way best fit their needs.[8] In 2007, the World Bank supported an application of the draft instrument in Senegal (French and Wolof) and The Gambia (English), while USAID supported the application in Nicaragua (Spanish). In addition, national governments, USAID missions, and NGOs in South Africa, Kenya, Haiti, Afghanistan, Bangladesh, and other countries, developed their own versions, totaling nine applications in all. The following year brought 13 additional applications; and in 2009, there were 27 uses of EGRA or EGRA-like instruments reported (see Figure 9.1).

What emerged in this process was the adaptation of the instrument for different uses along four categories: (1) "snapshot" or a quick assessment for informing policymakers; (2) thorough national or system level diagnostics; (3) program evaluation; and (4) classroom-based continuous assessment. Each of these approaches and example countries is described in Table 9.1. Common to all of these approaches is the emphasis on use of information for making systematic improvements, not just testing for the sake of testing.

As EGRA became more widely used, with assessments for multiple purposes in more than 30 languages and countries, there was a need for guidance regarding the potential uses (and misuses) of EGRA. While we had considered the tool useful for our on purposes, we never expected to

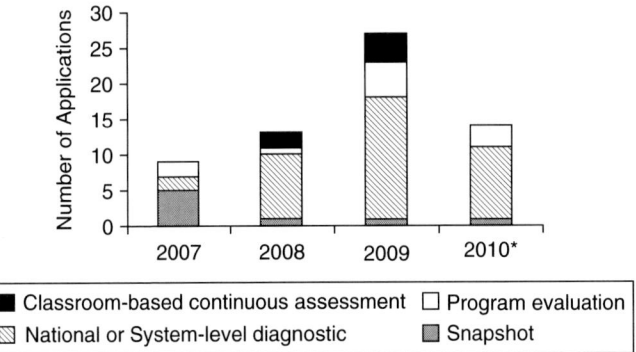

Figure 9.1   Evolution of the Use of EGRA Since 2007

Note: Applications in 2010 refer to planned uses of EGRA or EGRA-like tools. Applications are counted if the authors receive notification that a country or project will be using EGRA or developing an early reading assessment based on the EGRA tool. Some countries have multiple applications for different purposes.

Source: Authors' calculations, 2009.

see more than 50 applications of EGRA within a three-year time frame. The Early Grade Reading Assessment Toolkit, published as part of a joint USAID-World Bank collaboration, was an effort to meet this need, as well as respond to critique of the approach (Gove 2009).

First, EGRA is frequently criticized for its single-minded attention to reading in the early years. While reading is not the only skill students should acquire in the early years, it is a key component and is foundational to everything else students will do in school. Despite persistent beliefs to the contrary, the ability to read and write does not develop naturally, but requires careful planning and instruction (IRA and NAEYC 1998). Reading also acts as an indicator of school and system health; it is hard to imagine a school in which students are performing well in mathematics or science but cannot read. Furthermore, focusing change efforts in one key area—in our case reading—can be more effective than seeking to overhaul the entire system; concrete early wins can then act as a fulcrum for leveraging whole school or system-level improvements (Brinkerhoff and Crosby 2002).

Second, EGRA is criticized for deriving much of its research base from the National Reading Panel (2000) and studies conducted in the United States and other wealthy nations (Adams 1994; Snow, Griffin and Burns 1998; Fuchs et al. 2001; Sprenger-Charolles et al. 2003; Tibi 2005; Linan-Thompson and Vaughn 2007; Jiménez and O'Shanahan 2008).

Table 9.1 Potential Uses of Early Grade Reading Assessment

Approach	Purpose	Summary of key steps for implementing assessment	Example countries
Snapshot	Quickly examine reading levels to raise awareness and spur policymakers, donors, and civil society into action	1. Adapt instrument (develop if new language) 2. Train Ministry staff to apply (use several pilot schools as training exercise) 3. Draw small sample of schools (~25) 4. Conduct assessment, enter subtest data in excel 5. Conduct analysis and report and disseminate results	The Gambia Jamaica Peru India
National or System-level diagnostic with rigor	Thoroughly examine lacunae in reading competencies among students (and instructional approaches among teachers) to inform on the improvement of teacher professional development and preservice programs	1. Adapt instrument (develop if new language) drawing from word lists created from graded material 2. Train and select assessors based on quality of administration (include tests of inter-rater reliability) 3. Draw pilot and final sample; Conduct thorough piloting of instrument 4. Conduct assessment, enter individual item data (letters, words) for psychometric analysis 5. Conduct analysis and report and disseminate results	Mali Senegal Uganda Kenya Honduras Guyana
Program evaluation	Conduct baseline and monitor progress of ministry or donor programs that emphasize reading instruction. Use results to inform program improvements	Repeat as per National level, with the following additional steps: 1. Draw sample of treatment and control schools 2. Develop multiple, equated test forms for use over time 3. Conduct both baseline and follow on assessments to track progress 4. Assess degree of implementation through classroom observation and other complementary measures	Liberia Kenya Mali South Africa Egypt
Classroom-based continuous assessment	Develop teacher capacity to use regular classroom-based assessment measures to identify student needs and inform/ modify reading instruction	1. Review curriculum and existing approaches to initial reading instruction 2. Develop scope and sequence for instruction to operationalize existing curriculum goals and standards 3. Deliver professional development for teachers and provide continuous mentoring and support 4. Conduct analysis and report and disseminate results, providing feedback to teachers	Mali Kenya Liberia Niger

Source: Developed by the authors.

This research points to five skills that are necessary, but not sufficient, for learning how to read, which include *phonemic awareness* (ability to manipulate, break apart, put together sounds, which can be done orally), *phonics* (linking written letters to the sounds and spelling patterns), *fluency* (combination of speed, accuracy and expression), *vocabulary* (both oral and written), and *comprehension* (how students make meaning from what they read or hear). While the conceptual framework underpinning EGRA has its origins in the work of the National Reading Panel, results from more than 20 countries indicate that these key competencies are also important in other languages and contexts, but to a different degree. For example, students learning to read in Spanish still need to understand that when they see the letter "a" it makes an /a/ sound. But because, unlike English (which, depending on the dialect, has at least 11 sounds associated with the letter "a"), Spanish is (nearly) always consistent, students will not have to spend as much time learning how print maps to sound. The high correlations between these skills, as well as their predictive value for reading success, continue to justify their use in assessment across languages and contexts.

Third, colleagues fear that EGRA may encourage teachers to focus on speed reading or teaching of nonsense words. In each of the assessments we have conducted to date, we take great pains to communicate that the test components are indicators of student performance, but in many cases they are not designed to be explicitly taught. Just as a doctor would not encourage students to "practice" being healthy by taking their temperature on a regular basis, a diagnostic assessment is not always suited for direct instruction. We also emphasize that there is no "one" answer for meeting students' instructional needs. Rather, teachers need to use assessment as part of their reflective practice, couched within a continuous cycle of planning, teaching, and monitoring of instruction (Snow, Griffin, and Burns 2005).

Fourth, critics call into question the reliability and validity of the assessment, the limits to the level of rigor an individual oral assessment can have in comparison to a written test. For those purposes that require a high level of rigor, we have established procedures for calculating inter-rater reliability (IRR) among assessors. In a recent application in Kenya, IRR exceeded 95 percent for all language assessments (Piper 2009). Furthermore, in the more than two dozen EGRA applications conducted by RTI, tests of reliability exceed 0.8 (psychometric standards require an alpha of at least 0.7 to be considered of good quality). Nonetheless, the open source nature of EGRA has led to applications with varying degrees of technical rigor. For this reason we are in the process of establishing a peer review process, overseen by a community of practice, which would provide feedback to organizations interested in using the assessment. The review process would

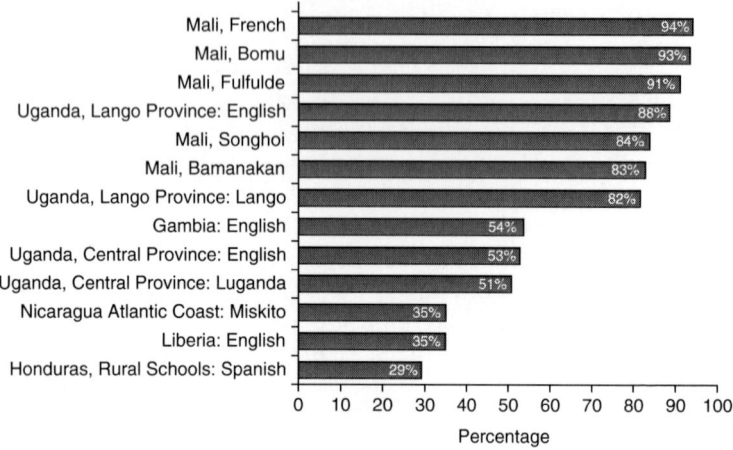

Figure 9.2 Percentage of Grade 2 Children Unable to Read Any Connected Text

Note: Honduras and Kenya are not nationally representative samples. All assessments were conducted in 2008 and 2009.

Source: Authors calculations, 2009, based on assessments conducted by RTI in each country.

be voluntary and the submitting organizations would receive professional input on their proposal to use EGRA, including suitability of the purpose and proposed use of the results.

Finally, the issue of comparability between languages is of concern given different word length and language structure across languages and dialect differences within languages. Our guidance documents have been explicit about the degree to which language results can be, and cannot be, compared. One common means of comparison is to report on the percentage of zero scores, or students who could not read a single word (see Figure 9.2). Ideally, as countries work to establish benchmarks and make progress toward improving learning outcomes, they will be able to report on the proportion of students meeting locally established goals for fluency and comprehension, as suggested by the Fast Track Initiative (FTI 2009).

The Case of South Africa

South African educators know that their system performs poorly compared to countries included in various international assessments. The basic facts can be summarized quickly. Figure 9.3 shows South Africa's performance

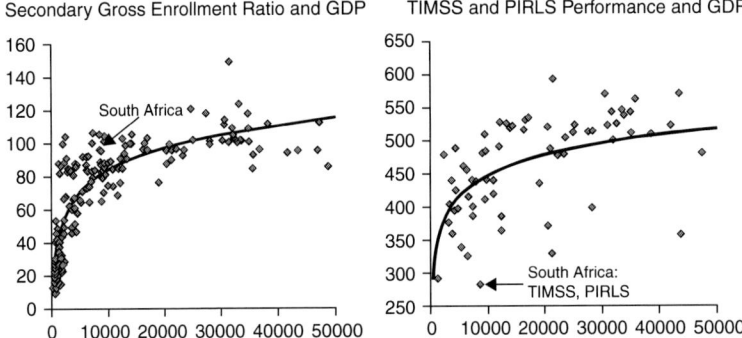

Figure 9.3   Relative Performance of South Africa on Access and Learning Outcomes

Source: World Bank Edstats query.

(relative to GDP per capita, relative to other countries) on both access and learning outcomes and makes it clear that South Africa "over-performs" on access and greatly under-performs on learning outcomes along with other countries with fast access expansion (see Crouch and Vinjevold 2006).[9]

South African educational researchers have spent a considerable amount of time, since the end of apartheid, attempting to solve the quality puzzle (see, e.g., Fleisch 2008; Taylor 2008). Reforms have emphasized the redistribution of funding (Crouch 2004), the democratization of management, and certain trends toward school autonomy (Sayed 1997, 1999; Beckman 2002; Karlsson 2003; Bush and Heystek 2003; Woolman and Fleisch 2008), and so on: more or less familiar recipes from a "reformist source book."

A favorite "usual suspect" for the quality crisis, for commentators on the South African scene, is the curricular reform introduced with democratization. Discussions on South African curricular reform and its implementation, which started almost immediately after it became a democracy, and on which perceptions in this paragraph are based, are intense and convoluted (see Taylor, Jansen 1998; Muller 2000; Cross, Mungadi, and Rouhani 2002; Muller and Vinjevold 2003; Rogan 2007). It is unlikely that the curricular reforms introduced with democracy are responsible for low quality in South African education, since most evidence would suggest quality, at least for the majority, has always been extremely poor, but it is also likely that the reforms have not helped.[10] Influential commentators and eventually the Department of Education itself have converged on the idea that the postapartheid curricula, and curricular execution, have

tended to be unclear and under-specified, and that classroom instruction is, in general, unplanned, poorly conceived in terms of scope and
sequence, lax in its use of time, unstructured and vague, and so on (South
Africa Department of Education 2009). There is also growing awareness
that the problems start in the earliest grades; or that schools fail to address
environmental poverty and lack of school readiness right from the beginning, particularly in issues such as reading. This growing perception has
led to a resurgence of interest in experimentation with instruction that
has clear goals, a tight and explicit scope and sequence, mandates the use
of time, and focuses on the most fundamental skills (reading) and in the
earliest grades. Thus, for example, in the government that was formed in
2009, the Office of the President itself took the unusual step of making
the education sector a pivotal example and challenged the education sector to choose two simple foci of improvement: learner performances on
literacy and on mathematics (The Presidency 2009). Though published
in 2009, the document reflects concerns that had been brewing for years.
Similarly, the Department of Education, to combat perceptions that core
skills such as reading need no longer be taught, had taken the unusual
step of publishing an open letter to principals in key newspapers, urging
principals to refocus on core skills (Tyobeka 2007). By 2008, a National
Reading Strategy had been put in place (South Africa Department
of Education 2008). A Department of Education conference in October
of 2008, on the Foundations of Learning, to which one of the authors of
this chapter (Crouch) along with reading specialist Sandra Hollingsworth
were invited, made it clear that specialist educators were still not coming
up with focused strategies—particularly strategies that weak and under-
trained classroom teachers could use with the confidence that the techniques would lead to results. During subsequent discussions, Department
of Education leaders explained that there was great interest on their part,
and political will and leadership, in attempting a reasonably rigorous controlled trial that would test the utility of well planned, quite scripted reading instruction, if not to bless a particular approach, at least to prove that
having an approach is useful. A particular highlight of the approach was
to test the utility of home language instruction in reading. South Africa
has 11 official languages—a matter of considerable cultural pride—yet
work on reading in the early grades traditionally does not recognize this
reality.

   In response to the above shortcomings, in late 2008 the Department,
with Hollingsworth's assistance, prepared a project to test a possible
approach. The approach tested was to be a mother-tongue adaptation for
South Africa of the Systematic Method for Reading Success (SMRS–see
Shefelbine 2000), an approach that was in turn informed by key literature

on reading (such as Chall 1985; Adams 1990; National Reading Panel 2000).

Given the importance of the home language issue in the attempt, three provinces where targeted: Northwest for Setswana; Limpopo for Sepedi; and Mpumalanga for isiZulu. Treatment and control schools were assigned at random but within an existing program of the Department's decision about which program would be intensified with the SMRS.

The approach designed is based on the notion that to read well in *any* language, learners should begin in their home languages, learn how to decode sounds into letters and words in those languages, and learn to read fluently with expression, with the goal of learning how to comprehend what they read. The approach starts with the notion that motivation is key, and that children can read successfully from the first day or two of reading instruction using their names as sight words, if they are motivated, and as a way to generate motivation. They quickly progress to small, simple stories that produce a feeling of progress. Children grow their skills with letter sounds and blending sounds into words. Sight words and comprehension are also worked on almost immediately. Words that are unfamiliar are presented as pictures at first.

Teacher guidance is quite prescriptive in this approach. The sequencing of letters and words to be taught is set out ahead, and each lesson plan introduces specific items to be covered. Furthermore, the plans fit into a logical overall structure that is also explained to the teachers. This is charted through an SMRS Program Progression Chart (PPC).

Two sets of materials are produced, totaling about 55 lessons. According to Sandra Hollingsworth and Paula Gains (2009, 7):

> In most languages, the first book uses only single-syllable words and the lessons take 30 minutes. The second book uses multisyllabic words and includes exercises to write brief stories; trade books are used as reading supplements. Because of the limited time period for the South Africa pilot, only 45 lessons were developed for isiZulu, Sepedi, and Setswana. Local teams developed progressively leveled stories for the first 25 lessons using the words introduced through the PPC. The teams also develop teacher read-aloud stories with comprehension and vocabulary questions. The stories are about learners' own cultures and environments, for familiarity, motivation, and pride. The program is designed in a scripted format in a teacher's manual so that teachers with little preparation in reading instruction can teach it. SMRS is meant to be a supplementary introduction to a full literacy program in learners' home languages.

The idea is that at the end of the 45 lessons, learners should ideally be able to read all of the *other* materials that the Department of Education felt was relevant to that grade—in a sense SMRS enables the learners to come up to speed so they can read materials that are otherwise too difficult, given their family background and teachers' skill, but which had traditionally been deemed appropriate. Hollingsworth and Gains then note (2009, 5): "Thereafter, the 30 minutes used for SMRS lessons should go to richer literacy instruction and informational reading. After a year of practice in their home languages, learners can begin to transition to other languages successfully (e.g., English or Afrikaans in South Africa)." As a measurement tool, the program used the EGRA, a measurement tool compatible with the instructional approach.

The results of the program, analyzed by Benjamin Piper (2009) using a differences-in-differences approach, show quite remarkable progress in a short time. One needs to recall that at the time of evaluation the program had been in operation for less than one-half of a school year, and that much of that time had been taken up by training, refining the approach, and so on. Nonetheless, according to Piper (2009, 2): "despite [the fact] that less than half of the intervention lessons were completed at the time of the post-assessment, the SMRS program dramatically increased the learning outcomes for South African learners across Limpopo, Mpumalanga and North West provinces." Since the program's baseline was taken at the beginning of Grade 1, naturally the children could be expected to read little. And since children in the course of Grade 1 would be expected to learn quite a bit even in an ineffective school, a differences-in-differences approach, designed to catch the difference between pretreatment and posttreatment, between control schools and treatment schools, was seen as important. The measurement instrument itself performed well, with a Cronbach's alpha of 0.95, and an inter-item correlation of 0.82. A Principal components analysis reveals a first component that captures most of the variance, much more variance than any other component, and which loads the original factors (such as letter-naming fluency, connected text fluency) in about equal proportions, sustaining the notion that there is an underlying "early skills" factor being captured.

Table 9.2 (culled and calculated from Piper 2009, Tables 8 to 11) shows the beginning-of-year to middle-of-year gain scores in both treatment and control schools.

Clearly, something focused and results-full seems to have been happening in the SMRS schools. Effect sizes in the range of 0.4 to 0.8, particularly in a differences-in-differences approach, in less than a year, are hard to come by. Now, does this endorse the particular approach taken? And, which specific components of the approach are responsible? Probably more research would have to be done to answer these questions. What does seem clear and relatively incontrovertible is that putting effort into specifying goals in a tightly sequenced basis, improving instructional technique, an approach that focuses on sounds and meaning from the beginning but

Table 9.2   SMRS Results

	SMRS Pretreatment to Posttreatment Gain scores				
	Treatment	Control	T	Pr	Effect size[11]
Letter-naming	22.93	8.79	−8.96	<.001	0.84
Familiar word fluency	7.14	2.53	−6.69	<.001	0.63
Connected text fluency	11.2	3.91	−6.16	<.001	0.58
Comprehension	0.13	0.04	−4.77	<.001	0.41

Source: Calculated by the authors from Piper (2009) data.

does it in a planned way, and the use of home language, or some mixture of all these, enable children to learn these basic skills two to three times faster than other children. Whether such a focused approach would sustain results for more complex skills later on would also have to be researched.

The Case of The Gambia

In contrast to South Africa, The Gambia is a small country of 1.6 million people located on the west coast of Africa and surrounded on three sides by French-speaking Senegal. A British colony until 1965 (Gambia's territory was demarcated by the distance a British naval cannon could target from the banks of its principal river), the Gambian education system follows the British structure of examinations at Grades 6 and 9 for selection to the next level. Some 43 percent of the population is under the age of 14, and more than 40 percent of students who enroll do not manage to complete the six-year primary education cycle (World Bank 2009a).

In early 2007, the World Bank was interested in piloting the newly developed EGRA in English. The government of The Gambia agreed to participate, with the goal of obtaining a rapid understanding of basic reading competencies in the first three grades of primary school. Following a week-long instrument refinement process, including adjustments to the word lists and oral reading fluency sections based on local curriculum materials, a team of 20 Education Department and Teacher Training college staff were trained over the course of six days before deploying to the field. Training included repeated role playing exercises, practice with the stop watch, and several pilot visits to schools before more than 1,200 copies of the final instruments were printed. The assessment, requiring approximately 15 minutes of administration time, included the following components:

- Text direction and orientation to print: students indicate where to begin reading and in what direction to read;
- Letter naming: timed reading of letters within one minute;
- Phonemic awareness: (a) recognition of the number of sounds in selected words and (b) phoneme segmentation of words;
- Familiar word identification: timed reading of words within one minute;
- Unfamiliar nonword decoding: timed reading of nonwords within one minute;
- Reading comprehension passage and comprehension questions: timed reading of a sixty-word passage followed by five comprehension questions;
- Listening comprehension: assessor reads passage and students respond to three comprehension questions;
- Dictation: assessor reads a ten-word sentence three times while students write; and
- Interviews on the educational and socioeconomic characteristics of the students.

The results were abysmal. Of the more 1,200 Grades 1–3 students tested in 40 schools randomly selected from across the country, nearly two-thirds of students could not read a single word of the reading passage. Among Grade 3 students, only 5 percent met the United States end of Grade 1 fluency benchmark of 50 words per minute or better (Hasbrouck and Tindal 2006). Notably only 14 children, or barely 1 percent of the sample, reported speaking English in the home, yet it was apparent that there was no particular strategy for teaching second-language learners. In fact the implementation team observed teachers struggling to complete the survey questionnaires in English. Other explanatory factors included the absence of learning materials (74 percent reported no books in the home), maternal illiteracy (66 percent), and high absenteeism (32 percent reported missing at least one day of school in the previous week). Despite the lack of instructional materials in their mother tongues, students who reported that their teacher spoke to them in their own language in the classroom performed significantly better on reading fluency (Sprenger-Charolles 2008).

As described in the *Handbook on Early Grade Reading Abilities*, these results spurred Gambian education officials to "embark on an immediate intervention to remedy the situation" (Department of State for Basic and Secondary Education 2007). The Permanent Secretary reported that he knew that quality was an issue, but it was not until he asked students to read aloud that he came to understand the severity of the problem (Bouy 2007). In addition to development of the handbook, complete with detailed lesson plans for teaching each of the five key competencies in reading, The Gambia conducted in-service training for all of the teachers in the early grades. The success of the new approach to teaching reading remains an open question. In terms of policy, The Gambia is reported to have a relatively inflexible curriculum with prescribed sequencing of topics and low expectations for teacher autonomy (Mulkeen and Higgins 2009). In practice, teachers are frequently isolated in their classroom and resources for instructional materials, supervisory visits, and pedagogical support are limited. Recognizing the importance of support for teachers in implementing the new approaches, supervisory visits were recently increased to at least twice a month (World Bank 2009b). Initial evaluation results are promising: a 2009 EGRA showed a significant, positive impact on students' overall reading scores, including improvement in every early reading skill tested. Comprehension results for Grade 2 students improved by more than 600 percent for girls (a 23.3 percentage point increase), while boys improved their performance by some 200 percent (a 10.6 percentage point increase).

Conclusion

The chapter has argued that reading practice in the early grades might be a useful entry-point into quality in various ways. It can provide a measurable goal that most stakeholders can agree is foundational in a pedagogical sense, and also as a marker or proxy for quality both at system level and individual school level (simply signaling the need for overall attention). Reading can be measured early and orally, in grades where interventions are relatively easy and can show quick success, and such measures appear to correlate well with later, more conventional pencil-and-paper tests. Incipient work with randomized trials and whole-country mobilizations both show that mobilization is possible, even without significant donor assistance, and that results can be delivered if there is sufficient focus on goals and clarity of procedure. It seems important for the developing countries, and the international community, to fix on some achievable goals that can provide a sense that quality improvement is possible. This can provide a sense of relief to systems under pressure to show progress. It can also provide models that can then be used to take on other skills at higher levels of the system, after the virtues of goal-oriented instruction have been demonstrated in large scale. Improving reading in the early grades might be the right entry-point goal.

Notes

1. As of writing this chapter, some of these trends were so fresh there was not much literature available on them.
2. http://stats.uis.unesco.org.
3. Author's calculations based on participating countries for TIMSS 1999 http://timss.bc.edu/timss1999i/participants.html and PISA 2000 http://nces.ed.gov/surveys/pisa/countries.asp. The countries are Argentina, Brazil (PISA only), Chile, Indonesia, Morocco, Philippines, and South Africa (both PISA and TIMSS).
4. See Ina V. S. Mullis, Michael O. Martin, Ann M. Kennedy, and Pierre Foy (2007, 311) and Ina V. S. Mullis and colleagues (2000, 110) and note that in spite of the advantages of the more sophisticated approaches used to score assessments such as TIMSS and PIRLS, the cross-country correlation between a simple measure such as percent correct and the more sophisticated scores is about 0.95. For our purposes the simpler measure will do.
5. The length of this chapter does not allow us to enter into any more detail on the derivation of these estimates. For relevant data, contact the first author at luis.crouch@gmail.com.
6. Explicit requests for simplified approaches to measuring learning outcomes include: Helen Abadzi (2006); Joel E. Cohen and David E. Bloom (2005), Colette Chabbott (2006), Center for Global Development (2006), and the World Bank: Independent Evaluation Group (2006).
7. In accordance with the joint standards issued by the American Educational Research Association, American Psychological Association, and National Council on Measurement in Education (1999, 17), "Standard 1.1: A rationale should be presented for each recommended interpretation and use of test scores, together with a comprehensive summary of the evidence and theory bearing on the intended use or interpretation."
8. All EGRA instruments developed to date are available at www.eddataglobal.org, where readers can also find a detailed toolkit with instructions for developing tests in English, French, and Spanish.
9. The secondary gross enrollment rate is chosen as an access indicator, because so many countries are at or near 100 percent on the primary ratio that it is difficult to tell a meaningful story around this issue. The average of all TIMSS and PIRLS assessments in the 2000s is used—these are all highly correlated with each other; the average is taken as an approximate index of the overall learning outcomes. Data for enrollment and GDP refer to 2005. Note that in Figure 9.3 the vertical axis is truncated so as to create the same absolute physical vertical spread of points for both graphics.
10. South Africa's tendency to perform at the bottom of international scales has existed at least since TIMSS 1995 (though the data were not published and might not be considered reliable), and the tendency to perform below much poorer African countries is obvious in the MLA assessments and SACMEQ II assessments, which came too soon after democratization for the poor results

to be blamed on the new curriculum. See SACMEQ (2005), J. P. Strauss and M. A. Burger (1999), and Vinayagum Chinapah and colleagues (2000).

11. This is the difference between treatment group gain and control group gain, divided by the pooled standard deviations of the treatment group gain and the control group gain.

References

Abadzi, Helen. 2006. *Efficient Learning for the Poor*. Washington, DC: The World Bank.

Abadzi, Helen, Luis Crouch, Marcela Echegaray, Consuelo Pasco, and Jessyca Sampe. 2005. "Monitoring Basic Skills Acquisition through Rapid Learning Assessments: A Case Study from Peru." *Prospects* 35 (2): 137–156.

Adams, Marylin Jager. 1990. *Beginning to Read: Thinking and Learning About Print*. Cambridge, MA: MIT Press.

American Educational Research Association, American Psychological Association, and National Council on Measurement in Education. 1999. *The Standards for Educational and Psychological Testing*. Washington, DC: American Psychological Association.

Beckman, Johan. 2002. "The Emergence of Self-Managing Schools in South Africa: Devolution of Authority or Disguised Centralization of Power." *Education and the Law* 14 (3): 153–166.

Bouy, Baboucarr. 2007. Personal communication to Amber Gove. The Gambia.

Brinkerhoff, Derick W., and Benjamin L. Crosby. 2002. *Managing Policy Reform: Concepts and Tools for Decision-Makers in Developing and Transition Countries*. Bloomfield, CT: Kumarian Press.

Bush, Tony, and Jan Heystek. 2003. "School Governance in the New South Africa." *Compare* 33 (2): 127–138.

Chabbott, Colette. 2006. *Accelerating Early Grades Reading in High Priority EFA Countries: A Desk Review*. Washington, DC: USAID.

Chall, Jeanne S. 1985. *Stages of Reading Development*. New York: McGraw-Hill.

Chinapah, Vinayagum, El Mustafa H'ddigui, Anil Kanjee, Wole Falayajo, Cheik Omar Fomba, Oumarou Hamissou, Albert Ramfalimana, and Albert Byamugisha. 2000. *With Africa for Africa: Towards Quality Education for All*. Pretoria: Human Sciences Research Council.

Cohen, Joel E., and David E. Bloom. 2005. "Cultivating Minds." *Finance and Development* 42 (2). Available online at: http://www.imf.org.

Cross, Micahel, Ratshi Mungadi, and Sepi Rouhani. 2002. "From Policy to Practice: curriculum reform in South African education." *Comparative Education* 38 (2): 171–187.

Crouch, Luis. 2004. "South Africa: Overcoming Past Injustice." In *Balancing Change and Tradition in Global Education Reform*, ed. I. Rotber. Lanham, MD: Scarecrow Education.

Crouch, Luis, and Penelope Vinjevold. 2006. "South Africa: Access Before Quality, and What to Do Now?" *Profesorado* 10 (1): 1–16.

EFA-FTI Secretariat. 2009. *A Fast Track to 2015: Educating the World's Children for a Better Future*. Washington, DC: The World Bank. Available online at: http://www.educationfasttrack.org.

Filmer, Deon, Amer Hasan, and Lant Pritchett. 2006. *A Millennium Learning Goal: Measuring Real Progress in Education*. Working Paper 97. Washington, DC: Center for Global Development and The World Bank. Available online at: http://www.cgdev.org.

Fleisch, Brahm. 2008. *Primary Education in Crisis*. Cape Town: Juta and Co, Ltd.

Fuchs, Lynn S., Douglas Fuchs, Michelle K. Hosp, and Joseph R. Jenkins. 2001. "Oral Reading Fluency as an Indicator of Reading Competence: A Theoretical, Empirical, and Historical Analysis." *Scientific Studies of Reading* 5 (3): 239–256.

Gove, Amber. 2009. *Early Grade Reading Assessment Toolkit*. Research Triangle Park, NC: RTI International, USAID and the World Bank. Available online at: https://www.eddataglobal.org.

Guszak, Frank J. 1985. *Diagnostic Reading Instruction in the Elementary School*. 3rd ed. New York: Harper and Row.

Hasbrouck, Jan, and Gerald A. Tindal. 2006. "Oral Reading Fluency Norms: A Valuable Assessment Tool for Reading Teachers." *The Reading Teacher* 59 (7): 636–644.

Hollingsworth, Sandra, and Paula Gains. 2009. *The Systematic Method for Reading Success (SMRS) in South Africa: A Literacy Intervention Between EGRA Pre- and Post-Assessments*. Research Triangle Park, NC: Integrated Education Programme, RTI International.

International Reading Association, and National Association for the Education of Young Children. 1998. *Learning to Read and Write: Developmentally Appropriate Practices for Young Children*. Newark, DE: International Reading Association and National Association for the Education of Young Children. Available online at: http://reading.org.

Jansen, Jonathan D. 1998. "Curriculum Reform in South Africa: A Critical Analysis of Outcomes-based Education." *Cambridge Journal of Education* 28 (3): 321–331.

Jiménez, Juan E., and Isabel O'Shanahan. 2008. "Enseñanza de la lectura: de la teoría y la investigación a la práctica educativa." *Revista Iberoamericana de Educación 45* (5): 1–22.

Karlsson, Jenni. 2002. "The Role of Governing Democratic Bodies in South African Schools." *Comparative Education* 38 (3): 327–336.

Linan-Thompson, Sylvia, and Sharon Vaughn. 2007. *Research-Based Methods of Reading Instruction for English Language Learners: Grades K-4*. Alexandria, VA: Association for Supervision and Curriculum Development.

Mulkeen, Aidan G., and Cathal Higgins. 2009. *Multigrade Teaching in Sub-Saharan Africa: Lessons from Uganda, Senegal and The Gambia*. Washington, DC: The World Bank.

Muller, Johan. 2000. *Reclaiming Knowledge: Social Theory, Curriculum and Education Policy*. London: Routledge/Falmer.

Mullis, Ina V. S, Michael O. Martin, Eugenio J. Gonzalez, Kelvin D. Gregory, Robert A. Garden, Kathleen M. O'Connor, Steven J. Chrostowski, and Teresa A. Smith. 2000. TIMSS 1999. *Findings from IEA's Repeat of the Third International Mathematics and Science Study at the Eighth Grade*. Boston: Boston College, Lynch School of Education.

Mullis, Ina V. S., Michael O. Martin, Ann M. Kennedy, and Pierre Foy. 2007. *PIRLS 2006 International Report*. Boston: TIMSS & PIRLS International Study Center, Lynch School of Education, Boston College.

National Reading Panel. 2000. *Report of the National Reading Panel. Teaching Children to Read: An Evidence-Based Assessment of the Scientific Research Literature on Reading and Its Implications for Reading Instruction* (NIH Publication No. 00-4769). Rockville, MD: National Reading Panel.

Organisation for Economic Co-operation and Development (OECD). 2008. *Review of National Policies on Education: South Africa*. Paris: OECD Centre for Cooperation with Non-Members.

———. 2004. *Review of National Policies on Education: Chile*. Paris: OECD Centre for Cooperation with Non-Members.

Piper, Benjamin. 2009. "Impact Study of SMRS Using Early Grade Reading Assessment in Three Provinces in South Africa." Research Triangle Park, NC: Integrated Education Programme, RTI International.

Presidency of the Republic of South Africa. 2009. *Improving Government Performance: Our Approach*. Pretoria: Presidency of the Republic of South Africa.

Rogan, John M. 2007. "An Uncertain Harvest: A Case Study of Implementation of Innovation." *Journal of Curriculum Studies* 39 (1): 97–121.

Savedoff, William D., Ruth Levine, and Nancy Birdsall, Co-chairs. 2006. *When Will We Ever Learn? Improving Lives through Impact Evaluation*. Washington, DC: Center for Global Development.

Sayed, Yusuf. 1997. "Understanding Educational Decentralization in Post-Apartheid South Africa." *The Journal of Negro Education* 66 (4): 354–365.

———. 1999. "Discourses of the Policy of Educational Decentralisation in South Africa since 1994: An Examination of the South African Schools Act." *Compare* 29 (2): 141–152.

Shefelbine, John. 2000. *Systematic Instruction in Phoneme Awareness, Phonics and Sight Words*. Oakland, CA: Developmental Studies Center.

Snow, Catherine E., M. Susan Burns, and Peg Griffin, eds. 1998. *Preventing Reading Difficulties in Young Children*. Washington, DC: Committee on Preventing of Reading Difficulties in Young Children and National Academy Press.

Snow, Catherine E., Peg Griffin, and M. Susan Burns, eds. 2005. *Knowledge to Support the Teaching of Reading: Preparing Teachers for a Changing World*. San Francisco, CA: Jossey-Bass.

South Africa Department of Education. 2008. *National Reading Strategy*. Pretoria: Department of Education.

South Africa Department of Education. 2009. *Report of the Task Team for the Review of the Implementation of the National Curriculum Statement.* Final Report Presented to the Minister of Education, Ms. Angela Motshekga. Pretoria: Department of Education.

Southern and Eastern Africa Consortium for Monitoring Educational Quality (SACMEQ). 2005. *SACMEQ Indicators.* Harare: SACMEQ. Available online at: http://www.sacmeq.org.

Sprenger-Charolles, Liliane. 2008. *The Gambia Early Grade Reading Assessment (EGRA): Results from 1,200 Gambian Primary Students Learning to Read in English.* Research Triangle Park, NC: RTI International. Available online at: http://www.eddataglobal.org.

Sprenger-Charolles, Liliane, Linda S. Siegel, Danielle Béchennec, and Willy Serniclaes. 2003. "Development of Phonological and Orthographic Processing in Reading Aloud, in Silent Reading and in Spelling: A Four Year Longitudinal Study." *Journal of Experimental Child Psychology* 84 (3): 194–217.

Strauss, J. P., and M. A. Burger. 1999. *Results of the Monitoring Learning Achievement (MLA) Project: Northern Cape.* Bloemfontein, South Africa: Research Institute for Education Planning, University of the Free State.

Taylor, Nick. 2008. "What's Wrong with South African Schools?" Presentation to the Conference What's Working in School Development, JET Education Service, 28–29 February 2008.

Taylor, Nick, Johan Muller, and Penny Vinjevold. 2003. *Getting Schools Working.* Cape Town: Pearson Education South Africa.

Tibi, Sana. 2005. "The Performance of Elementary Grades Students on Reading and Reading-related Measures in Arabic." *Journal of the College of Education, UAEU,* 22.

Tyobeka, P. 2007. "An Open Letter to All School Principals." *Mail and Guardian,* August 11, 17.

UNESCO. 2000. *Education for All: Meeting Our Collective Commitments.* Dakar: UNESCO. Available online at: http://www.unesco.org.

Wagner, Daniel A. 2003. "Smaller, Quicker, Cheaper: Alternative Strategies for Literacy Assessment in the UN Literacy Decade." *International Journal of Educational Research* 39 (3): 293–309.

Woolman, S. and B. Fleisch. 2008. "Democracy, Social Capital and School Governing Bodies in South Africa." *Education and the Law* 20 (1): 47–80.

World Bank. 2007. *Toward High-Quality Education in Peru: Standards, Accountability, and Capacity Building.* Washington, DC: World Bank.

———. 2009a. *EdStats Query.* Washington, DC: World Bank. Available online at: http://www.worldbank.org.

———. 2009b. *Status of Projects in Execution (SOPE) —FY09: The Gambia.* Washington, DC: World Bank. Available online at: http://www.worldbank.org.

World Bank: Independent Evaluation Group. 2006. *From Schooling Access to Learning Outcomes—An Unfinished Agenda: An Evaluation of World Bank Support to Primary Education.* Washington, DC: World Bank.

Chapter 10

Finessing Foreign Pressure in Education through Deliberate Policy Failure: Soviet Legacy, Foreign Prescriptions, and Democratic Accountability in Estonia

E. Doyle Stevick

Introduction

After a half century of foreign domination, Estonia relished the freedom and self-determination that it had reclaimed by declaring independence from the Soviet Union during the summer of 1991. That self-determination soon collided with the new geopolitical realities of Central and Eastern Europe in the post-cold war era. To secure its independence from Russia, which was perceived to be a hostile and menacing neighbor, Estonia would have to submit to a wide range of regulations and policies pushed by its allies and would-be protectors of the European Union and the North Atlantic Treaty Organization (NATO). Though many required changes were sensible importations of effective policies, others struck at the very core of cultural and historical divisions between Central and Eastern Europe and the West.[1] Rather than being able to look primarily to the strong policy preferences of its own people as a guide to policy—a premise of democratic governance in traditional

models of national sovereignty—Estonia had to navigate a new transnational policy environment that gave the European Union and NATO
extraordinary leverage over its domestic policies. At times, this pressure
would take unexpected directions.

In April 2002, the Baltic States (Estonia, Latvia, and Lithuania) gathered at
the Stockholm Security conference to learn how they were progressing toward
membership in NATO and—just seven months after September 11, 2001—
what would be expected of them in the unfolding conflicts in Afghanistan
and beyond. Primed to hear about troop deployments, equipment procure-
ments, and the like, the defense ministers of the Baltic States were almost
surely unprepared for the specific expectations that followed. Heather Conley,
U.S. Deputy Assistant Secretary of State for European and Eurasian Affairs,
complimented their progress to that point, and informed them,

> all the NATO aspirants need to do more to better prepare themselves for
> membership so that they are ready and able to contribute to European secu-
> rity in tangible ways. For the Baltic States, this means hard work—not just
> words but concrete action—on complex domestic issues like dealing with
> the history of the Holocaust. It means tackling the difficult task of fully
> integrating ethnic Russian-speakers into society—despite significant politi-
> cal cost. (Embassy 2002)

The very first criteria named involved the Holocaust and the Russian
minority, topics much more closely related than they would at first seem.
Why the United States used NATO as leverage to deal with Holocaust
issues in Estonia is beyond the scope of this chapter; the response of the
Estonian government, however, is a fascinating study in how governments
attempt to finesse the tension between intensive foreign pressure and policies that are deeply unpopular at home.

In no case were these tensions more evident than in the firestorm that
emerged over Estonia's adoption of a Holocaust education day for schools.
The Baltic states' national narratives of helpless victimization by the Soviets
were fundamentally incompatible with the West's interpretation of the history of the Holocaust, an interpretation that emphasized choice, agency,
individual responsibility, and the complicity of local actors in genocide.
As Anton Weiss-Wendt (2008, 475) notes, "in Western Europe and North
America the Holocaust is perceived as carrying a universalistic message, in
Estonia and other East European countries, it is ultimately linked to the
Jewish minority." To Estonian observers, this emphasis challenged fundamental tenets of Estonian national identity and history: victims were
redefined as collaborators, national war heroes became war criminals,
and culpability was foisted upon the powerless. Further, the struggle over

the meanings and legacy of the World War II hit at the heart of divisions between ethnic Estonians and the hundreds of thousands of ethnic Russians who settled—or were settled involuntarily—in Estonia during the Soviet period.

Strongly pressured to dedicate a day to commemoration of the Holocaust by American, European, and Israeli governments and nongovernmental organizations (NGOs), Estonia struggled to find a policy response that would deflect the foreign pressure without inviting punishment in the voting booth. Given the overwhelming domestic opposition to the policy, the risk was substantial. The Estonian government was placed in an untenable position between its own population and the memberships it felt were essential to its national security. Indeed, it understood that, in the words of one commentator, "Holocaust day is the entry-ticket for NATO" (mauri [sic] 2003).

For Estonia, no traditional policy approach could bridge the differences between foreign demands and domestic attitudes. A nimble policy dance between Estonia and the foreign advocates of this education policy ensued, one in which Estonia showed obeisance to the policy demands while subtly contesting their meaning. Estonia demonstrated a level of apparent compliance without admitting culpability for its citizens, a key premise behind the pressure to establish a Holocaust day. The compliance, however, was mostly illusory, a performance maintained for foreign audiences.

The government, trapped between its perception of national security needs on the one hand and its voters on the other, developed what may be a new policy form in free, democratic societies: deliberate policy failure. Estonia officially adopted a Holocaust education day policy and, through a variety of symbolic and practical steps, ensured that it would not be carried out in the way foreign governments intended and expected. Policy, in Thomas Dye's (1992, 2) famous and ironic formulation, is "whatever governments choose to do or not to do." The Estonian government wanted very much to do nothing, and it had to work very hard to do it. Estonia already knew from the Soviet era just how much effort is entailed in choosing not to do something that powerful interests very much wanted it to do; or, to adapt the title of Shakespeare's famous play, Estonia discovered there was "Much to Do, to Do Nothing."

Researching Education Policy and Its International Dynamics in Estonia

Holocaust Education in Estonia emerged as a special case in a larger project dedicated to understanding the policy and practice of civic education

in Estonia, from international influences to classroom practice. Between
September 2001 and December 2004, with a brief follow-up visit in 2006,
the author conducted a multisite ethnographic study (Marcus 1995) of
civic education in Estonia. To understand the nature and dynamics of
international influence in civic education, the author attended a wide range
of civic education–related events, including seminars for in-service civic
education teachers, teacher-training events, textbook approval meetings,
curriculum development sessions, national exam grading, international
conferences involving Estonians and foreigners, and county-level meetings
of social studies teachers, and observed hundreds of hours of classroom
instruction in a range of schools (elite, rural, urban) across the country.
Additional research was conducted at important sites of transnational
institutions, such as the European Union in Brussels and the Council of
Europe in Strasbourg. Interviews were conducted with important actors at
each of these levels—international, national, local/school—with particular attention to those who operated across multiple levels. Documents were
collected at every opportunity and tracked to see if they were incorporated
into the observed classrooms.

During this research, the specific issue of the Holocaust emerged as
an unexpected area of emphasis, particularly by foreign powers, while the
level of resistance to the issue was similarly unanticipated. The issue was
a good example of what Michael Agar (1994, 94–101) calls a "rich point,"
an issue in which the chasm of understanding between societies has the
potential to reveal a great deal about their different cultures. The apparent
richness and complexity of the issue was followed closely in the national
media, in the discourse of educators, and through interviews and participant observation.

The different histories, cultures, and resultant understandings in this
case played out in the policy arena, a new and complex one at that: not
only were European Union requirements complex and extensive, NATO's
requirements also impinged on traditionally national decision-making
powers, such as expenditures on the military. Add to this mix the attempt
to construct—or reconstruct—civil society after a half century in which
the state dominated all collective activity, and the policy environment
and its international dynamics become even more complex. With foreign
money available to support the activities of NGOs, the traditional forces
shaping the emergence of civil society were often subsumed to foreign agendas, policy entrepreneurs were often drawn into the more lucrative realm
of civil society, and the scarcity of English-language speakers resulted in
the elevation of a certain group of people more on the basis of their language skills than their particular expertise in an area (Wedel 2001; Stevick
2008a, 2008b; Stevick and Levinson 2008).

The anthropology of policy can make a special contribution to the study of policy in its many international manifestations. First, "anthropologists are able to take on the complexity, ambiguity and messiness of policy processes... [and a]nthropological analysis can disentangle the outcomes and help explain how and why they often contradict the stated intentions of policy-makers" (Wedel and Feldman 2005, 2). When a policy chain ranges from international powers, institutions, and forces, as in this case, to local classroom practice, a methodological approach that can explore a policy systematically as it unfolds across many levels is essential. In addition, many traditional policy tools operate at the macro level with a focus upon inputs and outcomes. Anthropology is well suited to help us appreciate the dynamics of policy processes, that is, the meanings it has for those who are charged with implementing it. Understanding these processes and meanings is critical not just because outcomes often deviate from stated policy goals—indeed, it is all but given that they will—but because "micro-level processes can in fact transform and even constitute the macro-level forces" (Burawoy and Verdery 1999, 3).

Because the anthropology of policy examines it as a sociocultural phenomenon, "a complex social practice, an ongoing process of normative cultural production, constituted by diverse actors across diverse social and institutional contexts" (Levinson and Sutton 2001, 1), its goals are more than simply instrumental. Understanding and explanation are goals of such inquiry, and these are considered prior to such practical considerations about whether the study has specific implications for "how to do" policy better. Indeed, recognizing that policy is also an act of power invites a critical perspective, one that asks how democratic a policy is.

The question of how democratic a given policy is has become considerably more difficult to answer in the emerging transnational policy context of the European Union because of the emergence of "overlapping majorities" (Thompson 1999). For example, if the majority of Europeans strongly support a Holocaust education day policy and a strong majority of Estonians oppose it, which majority should guide the country's policy? In other words, what does it mean to be democratic? Democratic theory has not worked out a compelling answer to this question. Amy Gutmann and Dennis Thompson (1996) have done groundbreaking work on the possibility that deliberation across moral disagreements could provide a basis for working through the problems of moral disagreements and of overlapping majorities. While inspiring in theory, in contexts of power and in highly charged issues such as the Holocaust, the responses to this new policy scenario unfold in very different ways (Stevick 2009). In such a context, instrumental goals—what the policy implications may be—are inseparable from the normative judgments about what should be done and the ethical dimension of what it means to be democratic in the first place.

This chapter will first provide the historical context that is essential for understanding the deliberate failure of the Holocaust education day policy. The chapter then discusses the elements of a deliberate policy failure, which will be followed by a review of some of the critical developments in the unfolding of the policy. These developments together reveal the extent of the effort and care taken to ensure that the policy would, in fact, do virtually nothing. Of particular note are the ways in which the different policy pronouncements contested meaning of the policy asserted by foreign powers, and how ambiguous language was used to communicate different meanings to different audiences.

The Historical Context

To understand why the issue of Holocaust education was so contentious, and how the issue relates to contemporary relations between ethnic Estonians and ethnic Russians in Estonia, an understanding of its historical context is essential. This section will review three critical aspects of such a context: the events and legacies of the Holocaust in the region; the broader history of Estonia and its relations to Russia and the Soviet Union; and resistance to Soviet power in Estonian education.

The Holocaust in the Baltic States and Neighboring Countries

Timothy Snyder (2009a) has eloquently drawn our attention to the "ignored reality" of the Holocaust in the regions east of Auschwitz-Birkenau, which so often symbolizes the Holocaust for Western readers. He notes that the Jewish victims of the Holocaust who were sent to Auschwitz were frequently assimilated Jews from West European countries, and that, unlike some camps to the east, some survived Auschwitz because it was a labor camp as well as death camp, and the stories best known to the world tend to be those of Jews who lived in or escaped to the free countries outside of the expanded Soviet bloc. Anne Frank's diary and Primo Levi's writings are cases in point. These texts, however, were not representative of the Holocaust as a whole. As Snyder (2009a) explains,

> By 1943 and 1944, when most of the killing of West European Jews took place, the Holocaust was in considerable measure complete. Two thirds of

the Jews who would be killed during the war were already dead by the end of 1942. The main victims, the Polish and Soviet Jews, had been killed by bullets fired over death pits or by carbon monoxide from internal combustion engines pumped into gas chambers at Treblinka, Be zec, and Sobibor in occupied Poland. Auschwitz as symbol of the Holocaust excludes those who were at the center of the historical event. The largest group of Holocaust victims—religiously Orthodox and Yiddish-speaking Jews of Poland...were culturally alien from West Europeans, including West European Jews. To some degree, they continue to be marginalized from the memory of the Holocaust. The death facility Auschwitz-Birkenau was constructed on territories that are today in Poland, although at the time they were part of the German Reich. Auschwitz is thus associated with today's Poland by anyone who visits, yet relatively few Polish Jews and almost no Soviet Jews died there. The two largest groups of victims are nearly missing from the memorial symbol.

As this chapter will show, the partial Western experience and history of the Holocaust continues to be an important dividing factor between the peoples of the former Soviet bloc and their Western counterparts.

There is some debate about whether, for example, the killings at Rom or Sinta should be regarded as a central aspect of the Holocaust or, as Snyder holds, that we should carefully distinguish between five major mass-killing policies conducted in the same period by the Soviet and Nazi regimes,[2] while reserving the term Holocaust exclusively for the annihilation of Jewry (Snyder 2009b). This distinction makes clear that there was no shortage of trauma to the peoples of the region. In Snyder's words (2009a),

> between 1933 and 1944, some 12 million victims of Nazi and Soviet mass killing policies perished in a particular region of Europe...the geographic, moral, and political center of the Europe of mass killing is the Europe of the East, above all Belarus, Ukraine, Poland, and the Baltic States, lands that were subject to sustained policies of atrocity by both regimes.

The scale of several atrocities in the region helps to explain why some nations are reluctant to look past their own suffering or to acknowledge the participation of some of its own people in the Holocaust. Three million Ukrainians died from starvation in 1932–1933; the peoples of the Baltic states felt they were victims of genocide; and full half the population of Belarus was killed or displaced between 1941 and 1944 (Snyder 2009a).

Issues of the Holocaust remain challenging and often contentious in this region for a number of other reasons. First, survivors from this region did not have the same opportunities to publicly share their experiences

(Gitelman 1990; Snyder 2009a). In addition, the ideological regimes of this region often suppressed historical inquiry efforts in these areas, so the historical happenings were never investigated in the same detail as in Western countries (Stevick 2009). Soviet propaganda tended to lump Holocaust victims into the broader category of Soviet citizens and those persecuted for political reasons (Gitelman 1990). To people in this region, foreign groups seem most interested only in the Jewish victims of the period, a fact that has generated considerable resentment in the region. These dynamics make the issue of Holocaust education throughout the countries of Central and Eastern Europe particularly important and trenchant; research results from across the region will soon be available in book form in the soon to be released "On This Ground: Education about the Holocaust in Central and Eastern Europe" (Stevick and Michaels, forthcoming).

Estonia, the Russian Empire, and the Soviet Union

Today a country of 1.4 million people, Estonia neighbors Russia and Latvia. A 50-mile span of the Baltic Sea separates Estonia from its close ally, Finland. In the nineteenth century, Estonians generally lived as farmers or serfs on Baltic German estates within the Russian empire. Estonian intellectuals sought to advance a sense of Estonian national identity and consciously emulated the class structure of the Germans, which was seen as a prerequisite for development of a national consciousness. However, Estonians often faced pressure to assimilate. Efforts to open the first Estonian-language school, for example, were stifled by Russification efforts, and when the funds were finally raised for the first such school to open in 1871, it did so as a Russian-language institution. Estonian national identity formed and developed in a dialectical relationship with the Russians, one that often included armed conflict and pressure to Russify.

Estonia first achieved its independence as a country by fighting off Russian and German units while Russia grappled internally with the effects of the Soviet revolution of 1917. Russia and the Soviet Union generally saw Estonia, part of the Russian empire since the eighteenth century, as a part of its legitimate sphere of influence, if not control. Estonia's first period of independence was short-lived. When Hitler and Stalin agreed to the secret protocols of the Molotov-Ribbentrop Pact, famously dividing Poland between the two powers, Estonia and the other Baltic States were ceded to the Soviet Union. Estonians, unaware that the Nazis were complicit in the Soviet invasion, were quickly overrun and experienced a terrible year of occupation. It is estimated that 60,000 out of Estonia's roughly 1 million people at the time were killed, deported, or conscripted into the military during the initial Soviet occupation, including 10 percent of its prewar Jewish population of roughly 4,000. On August 6, 1940, "the Supreme Council of the Soviet Union met the 'request of the Estonian people' incorporated Estonia into the Soviet Union" (Laur et al. 2002, 266). The anniversary of this date would become significant during the contemporary struggle over the meaning of World War II and the Holocaust.

Because Estonians were generally unaware of the Molotov-Ribbentrop Pact, and had suffered under Soviet occupation, the Germans were generally perceived as liberators a year later when they drove the Soviets out of Estonia. Many Estonian men, eager to fight the Soviets, enlisted in German units, including the Waffen-SS. Roughly two-thirds of Estonia's Jewish population retreated with the Soviet forces into the Soviet Union (Weiss-Wendt 2008, 476). Nazi control of Estonia lasted about three years, and by January 20, 1942 the Wannsee Conference declared Estonia *Judenrein*, free of Jews. While 963 Estonian Jews are known to have been killed, as many as 8,500 Jews from other parts of Europe were killed on Estonian soil (Weiss-Wendt 2008, 476–477). Estonia's remaining 2,600 Jews mostly withdrew with the Soviet forces, and due to limited access to archives, their fates are still unclear. The atrocities in Estonia were not confined to any one group, nor did the perpetrators come from a single background. The impact of World War II on Estonians as a whole was quite significant: "between 1940 and 1945," the original population of about one million "seems to have declined by a minimum of 200,000" (Raun 1991, 181).

Ethnic Estonians suffered under both regimes and were on opposite sides from the ethnic Russians of the Soviet Union throughout the conflict. Estonia's ethnic Russian and ethnic Estonian communities see each other as having been on the wrong side of the war. Russians sometimes still condemn Estonians as fascists, the preferred term of the Soviet Union to characterize their enemies in the "Great War."[3] Descendants of veterans and victims on each side see the other groups' soldiers as the enemy, the criminals, and the perpetrators. For these reasons, contemporary pressure to engage with the Holocaust engages directly with current ethnic tensions between the groups.

Although many Estonians do have negative memories of the German occupation, the return of the Soviets lasted a half century, and from the Estonian perspective, it is generally considered to have been even worse than German occupation. As historian Toivo Raun (1991, 181) documents, the "demographic consequences of Stalinism in peacetime proved even more devastating to the population of Estonia than the upheavals of World War II." For Estonians, memories of the major deportations to

Siberia or Kazakhstan in 1941 and 1949, experienced directly or passed down from victims, dominate the historical narrative. Russification efforts and the half century of Russian domination loom large for a group that felt itself threatened with cultural—if not physical—elimination by what was universally termed, across the Baltic States, as the Soviet genocide. As Budryte points out, the Baltic states' experiences of "the Stalinist deportations, planned immigration, and Russification policies were remembered as an attempt at nation killing, or genocide" (Budryte 2005, 8). The declaration of independence wasn't quite sufficient; as an Estonian civic educator explained to me, "For us, World War II didn't end until the last Russian troops left in 1994." This sentiment was repeated frequently in discussions and in public discourse, notably by two-time Prime Minister Mart Laar (2004) in the *Wall Street Journal*.

An ethnic transformation had taken place on its demography between 1939 and 1991. The interwar Estonia, a largely homogenous country of 90 percent ethnic Estonians, had become much more heterogeneous with less than two-third ethnic Estonians. As one civic education specialist noted disapprovingly in a trade magazine for educators, Estonia's restored constitution says that Estonia is a nation-state (that is, ethnically homogeneous), while in fact the country has become de facto multicultural (Valdmaa 2002). With a large proportion of ethnic Russians in the country, Estonia resisted giving blanket citizenship to all residents of the post-Soviet state, leaving hundreds of thousands of people without citizenship. Disenfranchised and uninterested in returning to a Russia in which their younger generations had never lived, the ethnic Russians became a political lever for Russia to apply pressure from the outside as well as a market for Russian media and schoolbooks.

Estonia and a Legacy of Quiet Noncompliance

The half century of Soviet domination created an environment in which people were unable to be openly critical of the regime, and yet the limits of the Soviet government's enforcement—particularly in the area of education and schools—became relatively clear. One of the first consequences was an indirect communication style in which listeners both expected surface statements to be empty lip service and believed that they were able to discern the real meaning under the surface. This sentiment recurred with great frequency, but perhaps no incident was more illustrative than an Estonian lawyer telling an anecdote at a civic education teacher-training seminar during November 2001 about a supposed office of Russian immigrants working above the 100th floor of New York's South Tower of the World Trade Center on September 11th.

> As soon as the voice came over the intercom saying that everything was all right, and telling everyone to return to their desks, they got the hell out. They knew, when the authorities tell you "Everything is okay," then there is something seriously wrong. (Fieldnotes, November 2001)

People often felt they could see the real meaning behind public pronouncements of authorities or individuals.

During the Soviet period in Estonia, the implementation of Soviet educational policy or directives often consisted of giving lip service to some new policy or rule, perhaps coupled with token if unenthusiastic compliance. In practice, particularly in schools, enforcement was difficult. Schools are dispersed across the country, and within each school the teachers are able to close their doors, which made monitoring quite difficult. While publicly-stated resistance was quite risky and quite rare, subtler forms of resistance were cited regularly during interviews. Enforcement was quite challenging. Very few foreigners were able to master Estonian to a degree that they could be mistaken for a native, and so they were easy to detect. The decrees often lacked legitimacy. As a result, it was not unusual for schools and educators to grant themselves a fair amount of latitude in doing the bare minimum necessary to follow regulations—but generally not to the extent that they would be openly critical of the Soviet government.

Examples of minimal compliance or even noncompliance abounded from my research: a rural school didn't even have a portrait of Khrushchev to be displayed and was cited by inspectors for the violation; a teacher rigged the public exam on Marxism/Leninism so students knew exactly which question they would get; a self-described true believer in Soviet ideology spoke of deportations openly in class and, though summoned to party offices to be rebuked, was nevertheless still requested to chair the party in the late 1980s. The practices and habits of lip service coupled with minimal compliance, learned during the Soviet period, became a resource on which Estonians could draw, a policy tool, when confronted with unpopular, externally imposed mandates. As we will see below, a similar approach was adopted not just by teachers but also, at the policy level, by the Estonian Ministry of Education itself.

Such a response may be unsurprising because Estonia felt compelled to embrace a policy that implicitly challenged its very sense of history. As Russia struggled to derive a positive heritage from the Soviet period, the one event that remains untarnished is the Great War, the defeat of the fascists, of Nazi Germany. For Estonians, who were often derided during the Soviet period as collaborators and fascists, having a grandfather who fought the Soviets is generally a point of pride. Pressure to adopt the meaning of Holocaust shared by the Americans, Western Europeans, and Israelis puts Estonians in the uncomfortable position of having to embrace Russia's narrative of World War II at the cost of their own. By aligning with Russia's version of history, these groups reveal themselves to be, essentially, anti-Estonian, ignorant of their history, naïve about both the crimes of the Soviets and the ongoing threat posed by Russia.

Deliberate Policy Failure: The Case of Holocaust Education Day in Estonia

Making education policy work can be difficult to accomplish in the best circumstances, but there are a number of tools in the policymaker's toolbox. Policymakers may, for example, use mandates with punishments, inducements, persuasion, provision of resources, capacity-building, system change, or development of an implementation plan (Fowler 2009, 250). The Holocaust education day policy in Estonia is notable not only for its stark absence of these tools but also for its proactive attempts to ensure that the policy failed.

Indeed, the policy approach in this case much more closely resembles the lip service and noncompliance pattern of the Soviet period. However, deliberate policy failure in this case included a different set of tools, and communication was the foremost of these tools. Timing, in both its practical and symbolic dimensions, played a role. Different messages were transmitted to different groups, in different languages, through different mediums, and for different purposes. Deliberate ambiguity was often employed, particularly the use of general or shifting signifiers, so that recipients could read their own meaning and context into the words of official statements. A policy was accepted while its premises and assumptions were subtly—or privately—challenged. Most critical, perhaps, was the selective deployment of a choice mechanism into a context in which it had become abundantly clear what "choice" would be made. In such cases, "choice" is little more than a policy fiat by those who frame the options.

The following section recounts the story of Holocaust education day policy and its meanings, beginning with the announcement of the policy itself on August 6, 2002.

The Adoption of Holocaust Education Day:
The Politics of Dates and Culpability

As a small country on the world stage, Estonia had become used to foreign interference, if not outright control, in its domestic affairs, though it deeply resented the perceived meddling. Estonians generally felt that they were not respected by foreign powers and their history not understood, which were sentiments they had to balance with their fear of Russian aggression and their frustration with the resident Russian minorities who seldom spoke the language well (Stevick 2007, 226–227). It was within this context that Estonia was expected to revamp its military, adopt 80,000 pages of European Union regulations and practices, and cede much of its independent authority over its foreign policy and financial practices to transnational institutions. Still, its memberships and security appeared to be contingent on an extremely unpopular policy: "[The] Estonian government... named January 27—the anniversary of the liberation of the Auschwitz-Birkenau Nazi concentration camp—as official Holocaust Day" (*City Paper's Baltics Worldwide* 2002).

Estonia officially adopted a Holocaust Education day policy on August 6, a day before August 7; the former is a date with profound meaning for Estonians, and the latter date held quite different meanings to foreign advocates and to Estonians. Announcing the policy in early August was shrewd for practical reasons, because many businesses in Estonia are closed down for the first half of the month for vacation. But the date's symbolic dimensions were powerful as well. August 6 is the anniversary of Estonia's involuntary annexation into the Soviet Union. While this fact is likely to escape the notice of all but the most attentive and informed foreigners, it has the potential to be broadly evocative for Estonians, who are reminded of a half century of foreign domination. While the evocation is itself ambiguous, it is not difficult to imagine some of the range of possible meanings that the anniversary would have for contextualizing this unpopular policy for Estonians who were concerned about potential Russian aggression: (1) this policy, while unpopular, is a small price to pay for security against Russia, whose 50-year occupation was so terrible; (2) the West is behaving like the Soviets in imposing an unwelcome policy upon us, and lacks legitimacy; and (3) we will outlast this foreign meddling, as we did Soviet rule.

The selection of January 27 for the Holocaust commemoration day constituted an implicit rejection of the reasoning behind the Simon Wiesenthal Center's (SWC) encouragement of the adoption of August 7. SWC had for years sought extradition of Nazi war criminal suspects from

Estonia, without success, and had given the Baltic states low grades for their cooperation with these efforts. In the negotiations behind the scenes over the Holocaust day policy, which were made public only years later, SWC officials advocated for August 7 as an appropriate date and were refuted:

> Estonian officials rejected a suggestion by the Simon Wiesenthal Center that they choose either 20 January, the date of the infamous Wannsee Conference in 1942, at which the implementation of the Final Solution was discussed and Estonia was declared Judenrein (free of Jews), or 7 August, the date on which the 36th Estonian Security Battalion murdered Jews in Nowogrudok, Belarus. (Zuroff 2005)

SWC officials promoted those two dates for their meaning: commemorating them would draw attention to Estonia's relation to the Holocaust, either in the complicity of other Estonians in the crimes (August 7) or at least in relation to the fate of Estonia's Jews (January 20). Just as Estonia refused to cooperate with the prosecution of Nazi war criminals, it rejected the premise that Estonians were complicit in crimes against Jews and other Holocaust victims by rejecting the proposed August 7 date. The politics of the date were manifestations of a larger struggle over the meaning of the Holocaust and World War II over Estonia's national historical narrative as a collective victim of the period. Two dates that could be taken to admit some culpability of Estonians were rejected, and January 27 was embraced instead.

What did January 27 mean? As the anniversary of the liberation of Auschwitz-Birkenau, the event had no connection to Estonia whatsoever. No Estonians worked at the camp, and no Estonian Jews perished there. Symbolically, the Estonian government chose this date to reject culpability and to assert that the country had nothing whatsoever to do with the crimes of the Holocaust. The selection of January 27, then, simultaneously allowed Estonia to represent itself as satisfying foreign pressure and joining the European mainstream, even as it permitted the country to distance itself both from acknowledgment of complicity in crimes of the Holocaust and from a connection to the Holocaust as a whole, since for Estonians Auschwitz-Birkenau was essentially a foreign site.

Further evidence of the Education Ministry's intent can be found in the rationale for adopting the Holocaust education day policy. It was not justified in terms of the universal importance of the Holocaust, in terms of its unprecedented status or unique nature, or relevance to people everywhere. Rather, the Ministry of Education asserted that it was "an important foreign policy factor, [showing] solidarity with the European and trans-Atlantic community" (City Paper's Baltics Worldwide 2002). To be part of the European and American community, it was important to adopt the policy—not for any intrinsic meaning of its own.

The Ministry of Education, however, did mention another rationale—that Holocaust education day would advance understanding of genocide (City Paper's Baltics Worldwide 2002). The choice of this word is significant, because genocide implies the destruction of a specific group as a general category—not representing the Holocaust exclusively—and Estonians felt that they had been victims of genocide at Soviet hands. Holocaust day would become an opportunity for Estonians to revisit their own historical suffering. The general signifier "genocide" is important here, because it allows Estonians to include themselves as victims of equal status to the Jewish victims of the Holocaust. This inclusive approach to genocide would recur and become a major point of contention between Estonians, who were subjected to scores of genocides, and those such as SWC officials, who argued for the unique nature and status of the Holocaust.

Through the negotiation over the date of Holocaust day and expressed justification for adopting it in the first place, the Estonian government signaled compliance while contesting the meaning of the policy to its foreign advocates and framing its adoption to domestic constituencies in terms of international geopolitical considerations rather than on its merits.

The Educators' Backlash

Estonia is a small country, and the headmasters of the country's most elite high schools are household names and akin to public intellectuals, known across the country. Within three weeks of the policy's announcement and just before school began for the year, two of the most famous headmasters publicly rejected the policy in the country's leading newspaper. One announced that he had no opposition to the notion but wouldn't be doing anything in his school to mark the day. The other condemned the policy outright, asserting that is was improper to put someone else's horrors above Estonia's own (*Baltic News Service*, August 26, 2002). This statement captures the common, if implicit, sentiment that the 4,000 Estonian Jews who fled or were killed or deported during this period were not Estonians. The exclusiveness of the Estonian identity has made it more difficult to craft an inclusive civic identity that transcends ethnicity.

The Ministry of Education had the opportunity to signal its commitment to the policy through traditional policy tools, such as a punishment to go with the mandate or simply by using its bully pulpit to condemn their statements and argue for the importance of the policy. No such public statement was ever issued from the Ministry of Education. The lack of response proved to be the first signal that deviation from the policy would not be punished.

As the day approached in January, there were newspaper interviews of teachers in Estonia's fourth largest city to hear their impressions about the policy. Their views were universally negative:

> "I think that Holocaust day is nothing but an activity for activity's sake, nothing more" [one said], adding that it brought the theme to the students on just one day.
>
> "The Soviet occupation interests students more, because they have more connections with this, more relatives were deported."
>
> "You shouldn't traumatize a child with description of this, how a baby was thrown into the air as target practice, the idea of history is not to shock youth. Rather on this day we should emphasize the danger of all types of violence."
>
> "This is foolish, I'm not going to make the students march or do something else on Holocaust day; with this I would perhaps destroy the history period."
>
> "The uprising on Juri's Night took more Estonian lives, that could be commemorated by the government. Let every nation commemorate its own day of mourning." (Nielson 2003)

These statements involve several typical strands of thinking about Holocaust education day. First, each nation should commemorate its own suffering, and not that of others. Second, as a corollary, nations are mutually exclusive. Third, the Holocaust does not merit special consideration but should be lumped together with violence and persecution of all sorts. This third sentiment was then found in a communication from the Ministry of Education.

The Ministry of Education Addresses Implementation: Choice Mechanisms as Policy Fiat

At issue in the negotiations between foreign powers and organizations and the Estonian government were two key issues: the question of the unique and unprecedented nature of the Holocaust and the complicity of some Estonians in those crimes. The Ministry used the date selected and the date of the announcement to counter rather than to embrace these meanings. These points were clear in a communication from the Ministry that was noted in the Estonian media:

> Education Minister Mailis Rand in a circular sent to the schools in the fall noted that not only the Nazi crimes against Jews but also all other victims

persecuted for ethnic, racial, religious, and political reasons should be remembered. The Ministry gave the schools a free hand in deciding how and in which classes the subject should be handled. (Baltic States Report 2003a)

With the circular, the Minister first affirmed the meaning of the Holocaust that most Estonians held, and thereby rejected the meaning attached to the day by its foreign advocates. The Holocaust should not be singled out as something unique but should be classed with all other victims (clearly including Estonian victims). This circular was another rejection of the uniqueness of the Holocaust. Most of all, however, it signaled that schools did not have to do anything to implement the policy.

The final method used to ensure that nothing would be done in schools was the inclusion of a "choice mechanism," in this case it was by not mandating how the day should be taught or acknowledged. The selective deployment of choice mechanisms need not be about granting additional freedom or choice to those granted the choice. Indeed, if those able to grant such choice know exactly how people would behave if given the choice, then the choice is simply a form of policy fiat. Knowing full well how educators and Estonians generally felt about the policy, the Ministry of Education effectively issued a policy fiat that Holocaust day would not be implemented.

The results bear out the effectiveness of the choice mechanism. A leading curriculum developer surveyed 30 school headmasters:

[O]ne of the homework [assignments] for 30 different school directors and headmasters was to examine the way the Holocaust Day was spent the first time in Estonia in 2003. We asked them to get the information from another school: to ask how it was spent and what people were thinking about the Holocaust Day. People were very bitter, most of the people in their responses, they were very direct and very honest, saying that this is not the day that is celebrated in Estonian school, and not in a nice way. But public opinion and the opinion of teachers and head directors was that this came from outside...and from these 30 answers that we got, we had zero responses that this was an important day that we need to have in our school system. (Interview, April 2004)

Holocaust education day was a successful failure.

The Denouement? Rejecting the Search for Nazi War Criminals

Any chance that a meaningful approach to the Holocaust education day might emerge was probably lost by events outside the schools during the same week when it was first to be implemented. The SWC launched its Operation Last Chance, an attempt to bring Nazi war criminals to justice before they died. An ad in Lithuania had declared that, "Jews of Lithuania did not disappear! They were mercilessly massacred in Vilnius, Kaunas, Siauliai and over 100 other places of mass murder; this text of the large black-and-white ad featured a photograph of Nazis beating Jews to death" (City Paper's Baltics Worldwide 2002). SWC's ad for Estonia read, "During the Holocaust, Estonians murdered Jews in Estonia as well as in other countries" (City Paper's Baltics Worldwide 2003). The response was unexpected:

> Chairwoman of the Estonian Jewish community Cilja Laud, Chairman of the Association of Former Prisoners of Ghettos and Concentration Camps Vladimir Perelman, and Rabbi Shmuel Kot sent a letter to the Media House advertising agency asking it not to publish the advertisements of the Simon Wiesenthal Center. (Baltic States Report 2003a)

Stunned that even the Jewish community of Estonia opposed the ad, SWC attempted to revise it to correct a problematic ambiguity in the translation of the original: since Estonian language has no definite or indefinite article, the "Estonians murdered Jews" line was easily read to mean that Estonians were collectively guilty. Peeter Torop, a prominent professor at Tartu University, "said that although the text of the advertisement does not call for violence, it instigates ethnic hatred and 'accuses Estonians as a nation of murdering Jews'" (City Paper's Baltics Worldwide 2003). The ad was revised to "Nazi henchmen" but was still rejected by the media outlets (Baltic States Report 2003b).

Keeping Up Appearances

During the spring of 2006, I had an opportunity to follow up on the issue, once Estonia had successfully been incorporated into NATO and the European Union and the controversy over the issue had given way. I followed up with the same curriculum developer, inquiring whether there had been any activity during 2006, the last time Holocaust education day would occur on a school day until 2009 (a gap, I suspected, which would be sufficient to eliminate most remaining practices). "Basically, Holocaust Day does not exist in Estonia," I was told.

By this time, Estonia had shifted strategy in its communication with foreigners and fully embraced the notion of complicity, at least in English. The strategy of contesting the foreign meaning of the Holocaust was no longer evident. The following statement, released in English by Estonia's Foreign Ministry, is remarkable for its shift in sentiment:

> During the Second World War, the Nazi regime systematically eliminated on the occupied Estonian territory both Estonian Jews, and those that had been brought here from elsewhere. There is no justification for the participation of anyone in these shameful and morally condemnable acts. Even if they have not directly shed the blood of anyone, they are nevertheless morally responsible. Knowing the past teaches tolerance and helps to achieve that the crimes of the last century will never be repeated. (Estonian Ministry of Foreign Affairs 2006)

At this point, the context of the Holocaust is clearly established in the statement. Capitalizing on that context, the Foreign Ministry continues the statement directly with a carefully selected quote from the Ministry of Education, and in so doing implies that the subject is still the Holocaust: "The Ministry of Education and Science called on all Estonian schools to explain to students the tragic events of the last century" (Estonian Ministry of Foreign Affairs 2006).

The Ministry of Education certainly did make such a call, but "the tragic events of the last century" constitute a shifting signifier. For English-language readers from the United States or Western Europe, the context clearly implies that "tragic events" is a synonym for the Holocaust. For Estonian recipients of the Education Ministry's message, however, absent the statement about the Holocaust, the tragic events of the last century were the tragedies that befell the Estonian nation, the occupations and the deportations.

A Path Forward?

Estonia's Holocaust education day policy is remarkable both for the extraordinary leverage brought to bear in order to get Estonia to adopt the policy, as well as for the lengths to which Estonia went to ensure its failure. For the foreign powers, it is a good example of the limits of policy to shape the attitudes and dispositions of citizens in another country. It also shows clearly the problems that can arise when outsiders try to promote an agenda with little understanding of a country's history and culture.

In the context of globalization and the emergence of new transnational governments such as the European Union, this case may ameliorate some concerns about the loss of national autonomy. Policies that lack domestic support may get unraveled in their implementation, no matter how much foreign pressure is applied—particularly in sectors such as education where the sites and implementation are dispersed. As a case in which foreign authorities and national democratic majorities are at odds, Estonia was able to achieve a deliberate policy failure, successfully finessing foreign pressure without incurring the wrath of the electorate.

Most intriguingly, perhaps, this case may force us to think in more complex terms about the Soviet legacy, often taken to be a wholly negative one to be shed. To the extent that Estonians drew upon practices and skills that they had developed while under Soviet authority in order to undercut the Holocaust education day policy, which it seems they did, we may have to regard the coupling of indirect and ambiguous communication styles with minimal or noncompliance as deliberate policy innovations drawn from the experience of resisting Russification efforts and Soviet authority generally. From one perspective, these tools, used so effectively to finesse foreign policy pressure in a complex geopolitical climate, enabled the Estonian government to accomplish a more democratic end by staying true to the majority will.

For those, including the author, who regard the Holocaust as more than simply one more history of national suffering among a hundred others, a different approach is surely necessary. While we can point to the suppression of historical inquiry during the Soviet period, to the fact that the Soviets did not criticize the Nazis for their anti-Semitism and the Holocaust as much as for their fascism, and to the fact that Estonians lacked access to the historical understanding developed in the West during their long occupation, it can be counterproductive to attribute others' attitudes and perspectives to ignorance, particularly absent an understanding of a group's history and culture.

Foreign powers committed to promoting understanding of the Holocaust have now lost much of the leverage that they once had, not that this leverage had, at the outset, been applied effectively. Beliefs are not easily changed, particularly in the contexts where painful histories are so deeply intertwined with questions of national identity. If such efforts are to bear fruit now, foreign advocates will have to navigate a new policy environment in Central and Eastern Europe without the carrots of EU and NATO accession on their side.

Notes

1. The West is certainly an imperfect term, and I use it here in short simply to encompass the United States and the countries of the European Union before it expanded to include Central and Eastern Europe.

2. Snyder (2009b) elaborates: "the five largest policies of mass killing of civilians carried out by Nazi Germany and the Stalinist Soviet Union: the German attempt to exterminate European Jews (circa 5.7 million deaths); German starvations of Soviet citizens (circa 4 million); German mass reprisals against civilians (at least 750,000); Soviet starvations of Soviet citizens (circa 5.5 million), and the shootings of the Soviet Great Terror (circa 700,000)."

3. These disputes are so familiar and circular that an Estonian commentator recently satirized them in the following way:

> E[stonian]: "Hey, you occupied and oppressed us for fifty years! You exiled half our population and sent your own people here to Russify us!"
>
> R[ussian]: "Stop crying, Nazi. You're just upset because we stopped you from killing Jews!"
>
> E: "The Nazis killed our people! We don't want to be occupied by anyone!"
>
> R: "So you can kill Jews!"
>
> E: "This has nothing to do with the Holocaust!"
>
> R: "Just what a Nazi would say!"

Available online at: http://www.tallinn-life.com.

References

Agar, Michael. 1994. *Language Shock: Understanding the Culture of Conversation.* New York: William Morrow.

Baltic States Report. 2003a. RFE/RL Reports 4, no. 5, February 10. Available online at: http://www.rferl.org.

———. 2003b. RFE/RL Reports 4, no. 8, March 4. Available online at: http://www.rferl.org.

Budryte, Dovile. 2005. *Taming Nationalism? Political Community Building in the Post-Soviet Baltic States.* Burlington, VT: Ashgate.

Burawoy, Michael, and Katherine Verdery, eds. 1999. *Uncertain Transitions: Ethnographies of Change in the Postsocialist World.* Lanham, MD: Rowman and Littlefield.

City Paper's Baltics Worldwide. 2002. "News Highlights from Lithuania, Latvia, and Estonia." November 18. Available online at: http://www.balticsww.com.

———. 2003. "News Highlights from Lithuania, Latvia, and Estonia." January 28. Available online at: http://www.balticsww.com.

Dye, Thomas R. 1992. *Understanding Public Policy.* 7th ed. Englewood Cliffs, NJ: Prentice Hall.

Embassy of the United States in Estonia. 2002. "Remarks by Heather Conley, U.S. Deputy Assistant Secretary of State for European and Eurasian Affairs at Stockholm Security Conference—The United States and Northern Europe: A Continuing Commitment." April 24. Available online at: http://www.usemb.ee.

196   E. DOYLE STEVICK

Estonian Ministry of Foreign Affairs. 2006. The Holocaust Day Was
Commemorated in Estonia. January 26. www.vm.ee/eng/kat_137/7304.html.
Fowler, Frances C. 2009. *Policy Studies for Educational Leaders.* 3rd ed. Boston:
Pearson.
Gitelman, Zvi. 1990. "History, Memory and Politics: The Holocaust in the Soviet
Union." *Holocaust and Genocide Studies* 5 (1): 23–37.
"Koolijuhid Taunivad Holokaustipaeva." Õhtuleht, August 26. Available online
at: http://www.sloleht.ee.
Laar, Mart. 2004. "When Will Russia Say Sorry?" *Wall Street Journal,* August
20, A12
Marcus, George E. 1995. "Ethnography in/of the World System: The Emergence
of Multi-Sited Ethnography." *Annual Review of Anthropology* 24: 95–117.
mauri [sic]. 2003. Holokaustipäev kui NATO pileti konts. April 10. Available
online at: http://www.minut.ee.
Nielson, I. 2003. "Holokaustipäev jätab koolid ükskõikseks." Pärnu Postimees,
January 25. Available online at: http://www.epl.ee.
Snyder, Timothy. 2009a. "The Holocaust: The Ignored Reality." *New York Review
of Books* 56 (12): July 16.
———. 2009b. " 'The Holocaust: The Ignored Reality': An Exchange." *New York
Review of Books* 56 (13): August 13.
Stevick, E. Doyle. 2007. "The Politics of the Holocaust in Estonia: Historical
Memory and Social Divisions in Estonian Education." In *Reimagining Civic
Education: How Diverse Societies Form Democratic Citizens,* ed. Stevick, E. D.,
and B. A. U. Levinson, 217–244. Lanham, MD: Rowman and Littlefield.
———. 2008a. "Education Policy, National Interests, and Advancing Democracy."
In *Advancing Democracy through Education? U.S. Influence Abroad and Domestic
Practices,* ed. E. D. Stevick and B. A. U. Levinson. Charlotte, NC: Information
Age Publishers.
———. 2008b. "Foreign Influence and Economic Insecurity in International
Partnerships for Civic Education: The Case of Estonia." In *Advancing
Democracy through Education? U.S. Influence Abroad and Domestic Practices,*
ed. E. D. Stevick and B. A. U. Levinson. Charlotte, NC: Information Age
Publishers.
———. 2009. "Overlapping Democracies, Europe's Democratic Deficit, and
National Education Policy: Estonia's School Leaders as Heirs to a Soviet Legacy
or as Agents of Democracy?" *European Education* 41 (3): 42–59.
Stevick, E. Doyle, and Bradley A.U. Levinson, eds. 2008. *Advancing Democracy
through Education? U.S. Influence Abroad and Domestic Practices,* Charlotte,
NC: Information Age Publishers.
Stevick, E. Doyle, and Deborah Michaels, eds. Forthcoming. On This Ground:
Holocaust Education in Central and Eastern Europe.
Thompson, Dennis. 1999. "Democratic Theory and Global Society." *The Journal
of Political Philosophy* 7 (2): 114–125.
Valdmaa, Suley. 2002, May. Ühiskonnaõpetus kui indikaator. *Haridus,* 22–24.
Wedel, Janine. 2001. *Collision and Collusion. The Strange Case of Western Aid to
Eastern Europe.* New York: Palgrave.

Wedel, Janine, and Gregory Feldman. 2005. "Why an Anthropology of Public Policy?" *Anthropology Today* 21 (1): 1–2

Weeks, Theodore R. 2008. "Remembering and Forgetting: Creating a Soviet Lithuanian Capital. Vilnius 1944–1949." *Journal of Baltic Studies* 39 (4): 517–533.

Weiss-Wendt, Anton. 2008. "Why the Holocaust Does not Matter to Estonians." *Journal of Baltic Studies* 39 (4): 475–497.

Zuroff, Efraim. 2005. "Eastern Europe: Anti-Semitism in the Wake of Holocaust-Related Issues." *Jewish Political Studies Review* 17 (1–2). Available online at: http://www.jcpa.org.

Chapter 11[1]

Australian Aid and the Development of Education Policy: Reframing Engagement in Papua New Guinea

Elizabeth A. Cassity

Introduction

A first glance at almost any policy document generated by a bilateral or multilateral donor agency reveals a familiar rhetoric of participation, partnership, aid effectiveness, good governance, and sustainable growth as key ingredients for a successful development program. A key policy debate is that while some critics of this rhetoric argue that this is merely a recasting of old aid agendas, there are others who confirm that recent rethinking of aid policies and agendas are sincere efforts to address poverty reduction and ensure aid effectiveness. Education has been proposed as an indispensable element to achieve the aforementioned goals of development policy rhetoric, not least in the eight UN Millennium Development Goals (MDGs).

Good policies have been heralded by many academics, researchers, and practitioners as indispensable elements in making donor countries' aid dollars more effective. While development has been a focus for a number of researchers and practitioners in international and comparative education, there has been little discussion as to how this new aid rhetoric is applied in a bilateral donor-recipient context. Many studies underscore the fact that bilateral relations that focus on negotiations between nation-states tend to develop in a more pragmatic manner. Certainly, recent international focus on the issues of security, terrorism, and international crime has influenced many bilateral programs' agendas. Alongside this argument has been recent discourse about partnership and donor harmonization, as well as the impact of global agendas generated by the international community, notably the MDGs, Education for All (EFA), and the World Bank's Poverty Reduction Strategy Paper (PRSP) process. International declarations such as the Rome Declaration on Harmonization (2003), the Paris Declaration on Aid Effectiveness (2005), and the Accra High Level Forum on Aid Effectiveness (2008) have also given shape to current donor agendas.

Education is central to many bilateral policies. Aid to education is claimed to have contributed to raising literacy rates, increased school enrollments, and improved girls' participation in schools. There have been numerous shifts in the rationale for funding aid programs to education since World War II and the advent of international thinking about development. The current rhetoric has placed many aid agencies—both bilateral and multilateral—backing a Sector Wide Approach (SWAp) to education. A commonly accepted definition of a SWAp—be it education, health, or other sectors—has the following elements: it supports a single sector policy and program, governments are the leaders of reform, common approaches are adopted by all funding parties, and recipient governments progress toward disbursing and accounting for all public expenditures (UNESCO 2007). SWAps are an approach to sector reform. Critics point to participation in SWAps as being suspect in that participation is limited to donors and national levels of government, therefore compromising exhaustive consideration of local educational issues.

The process of educational planning and policy development is being reconsidered at AusAID, as evidenced by major expansion and reorganization within the agency itself. But with the lessons learned from so many aid agendas in the past, experience suggests that local context and variations in the design and delivery of country aid programs should impact on the conceptualization of aid. Australian support to education in Papua New Guinea (PNG) since independence in 1975 has contributed to an expansion of the education system and improved access for many schoolchildren. At the same time, enrollments have increased but quality remains a concern, as evidenced by poor literacy outcomes, teacher shortages, and inadequate funding (AusAID 2008b). In recent policy documents, AusAID acknowledges this with proposals to improve quality through better management, teacher training, and curriculum reform.

Developing more effective aid policy is an important theme that occupies much of the current dialogue about donor aid to education. At the same time, effectiveness is a concept that needs to be explored. Is effectiveness determined by donors or is it determined by recipient governments?

There are numerous stakeholders involved in framing the future of education in PNG. AusAID, primarily because of its program size and historical links to the country, is an important donor. Recent policy prerogatives by government and donors are endorsing a SWAp to education in an attempt to rethink the system as a whole.

This chapter reviews scholarly debates about foreign aid, specifically bilateral aid, and education. Focus on the effectiveness of aid through partnership and donor coordination is prominent both in AusAID and international agencies. Education has been an element of international development plans since the post–World War II era, but ideas on what education is and how it contributes to growth have shifted to the center of many current policy debates. The education context in PNG is the most important consideration in developing aid programs there; however, historical documents, local commentary, and literary collections reveal that the issues present at independence in 1975 and those remaining 30 years later continue to be hauntingly similar. An examination of nonclassified policy documents confirm that AusAID's policy has shifted conceptually, and policy discourse over the past 10 years is convincingly coupled with international rhetoric. The documents also show that recent shifts in AusAID's internal policy have reframed the agency's approach to its PNG country program in an effort to address the country's educational disparities. Opinions of government and education experts were sought in relation to policy shifts and context in PNG. A few comments are included anonymously, which are individual reflections rather than agency or government policy. This chapter concludes by reconnecting fundamental debates on bilateral aid policy to AusAID's education development agenda in PNG.

Trends in Bilateral Aid and Education

To date, scholarly analysis on bilateral aid and education has not been extensive. Scholars have primarily focused on the pragmatic self-interest of donor states and how allocations of aid have impacted recipient governments (Alesina and Dollar 2000; Chauvet and Collier 2005b; Berthelemy 2006; Gyngell and Wesley 2007). Over the past 10 years, bilateral agencies have gradually assimilated global dialogue about development while remaining coupled with national foreign policy agendas. This is a significant shift when compared with the previous 50 years of a development assistance tradition. For example, using tied aid—the practice of ensuring that a donor's foreign aid utilizes its donor country resources—has been discouraged in recent bilateral policy agendas. A good example of this is the Australian government's recent *White Paper* that endorsed the untying of all aid in order to improve effectiveness, efficiency, and accountability (AusAID 2006, 23). Bilateral and multilateral agencies have aligned policies as part of a global development agenda particularly focused on effectiveness. Key frameworks for action have formed around the ideas of aid effectiveness, partnership, and donor coordination explicit in policy frameworks of a SWAp. Partnerships in aid and SWAp mechanisms are not new and have been addressed extensively from the 1990s in comparative and international educational policy literature (Ratcliffe and Macray 1999; Foster 2000; Brown et al. 2001; UNESCO 2007). While themes of ownership, participation, and power in partnerships and SWAps are consistent subjects of critique, they remain policy prerogatives of bilateral aid agencies. In fact, education SWAps have been increasing as a preferred mechanism for education reform and transfer of aid funds. It is worth examining research and rhetoric—often conflicting—that frame the current development paradigm.

Concepts and rhetoric carry considerable power in shaping the way aid policies are designed and implemented. Cornwall and Brock (2006) explore whether particular keywords carry cultural and political values of the time, and what these keywords do for development policy. For example, the mission statement "For a World Free of Poverty" is shared by the World Bank, ActionAid, and War on Want—three organizations with radically different views on development policy (47).

Participation is a key operational term in the idea of development partnerships. A sense of action or demand remains implicit in ideas about participation. In current usage, participation can mean simply recognizing and acting on one's interconnection with a larger society through a set of philosophical ideals (Patton 2005, 252). Participation can also be an ambiguous term as a means to gain political agency, maintain rule, neutralize political opposition, and tax the poorest, in other words, engaging communities in sharing the costs (Cornwall and Brock 2006). Importantly, lack of participation can imply the lack of resources to participate in a global society, where social exclusion is based on the inability to participate in the economy and democratic processes (Patton 2005, 253–254). Thinking about participation in this way has important implications for poverty. In terms of policy rhetoric, participation is a key working term in the World Bank's Poverty Reduction Strategy Papers (PRSPs)—plans for assistance to low-income countries. Guiding principles for PRSPs are that they are country-driven, long-term, sectoral, and a partnership involving civil society, government, and donor agencies. SWAps arguably operate on similar principles.

Participation is integral to partnership. The notion of partnership is a transformation that has dominated the literature on aid in the past ten years. Importantly, have a wide range of stakeholders and participants been able to contribute to aid programming and delivery? PRSPs, for example, were developed with the idea to include a wider range of stakeholders, and particularly include the voices of the poor (Narayan-Parker 2000). Policymakers and researchers consistently attempt to identify "best practice" models, yet these models emerge out of the particular and are unquestionably adapted to the universal. Freeman and Faure (2003) found that relevance of external support to local needs should be emphasized and tailored, while sector-wide approaches do not improve partnerships if they are implemented as a blueprint.

Klees (2002) provides a critical perspective on the notion of partnerships, particularly as formulated by the World Bank, and addresses the elusive ideal that multilateral and bilateral organizations, civil society and grassroots organizations, and nongovernmental organizations (NGOs) all collaborate with the rationale of representing participation. He writes, "This is partnering with a vengeance: no one is left out. At least, almost no one..." (Klees 2002, 455). The reality, Klees continues, is that groups such as teachers unions have been left out of the dialogue. Recent qualitative research on the effects of PRSPs suggest that they are creating different forms of power structures, and voices of the poor are still not being considered in any process other than rhetoric (Chambers and Pettit 2004; Kakande 2004; Higgins and Rwanyange 2005).

There is also skepticism about foreign aid in the new cooperative context (Knack 2004). On the one hand, current development rhetoric is perceived as an enabling factor that includes voices of the poor and civil society in order to frame effective development agendas. On the other hand, aid mechanisms like SWAps have been criticized as yet another exogenous tool to shape national policies that are tightly coupled with the donor countries' aid agendas. Added to this is critique that these mechanisms have, in fact, continued to marginalize the poor and local civil society organizations because of an administrative structure that does not encompass these sections of society. Coxon and Munce (2008) suggest that while partnership is an idea central to many aid agency agendas, in fact partnership has more to do with the management of projects rather than overcoming inequalities in the donor-recipient relationship. This has been particularly so in the education sector.

Ownership of development projects by recipient countries is a frequently cited objective of donor programs. This has emerged from the term partnership. In 1999, Kenneth King gave moderately positive assessment about the idea of ownership. "On its own, it may not always signify any change in the aid relationship except at the rhetorical level, but in the new partnership discourse, recognition of national ownership of projects and programs by the South is an important counterbalance to the admitted financial dominance of the North" (King 1999, 16). King suggests that the language of partnership may have been co-opted by bilateral and multilateral organizations from the aspirational language of NGOs. However, seven years later King was skeptical, writing that for all the rhetoric about country ownership and autonomy, aid dependency may actually have increased (King 2006).

In discussing current policy trends that promote SWAps as a development mechanism for better aid effectiveness, it is useful to revisit policy dialogue at the millennium. There was increased focus on accountability in domestic institutions that emphasized governance, participation, and reform through the PRSP process. This followed a shift in the 1990s of returning ownership to governments through sector programs, direct budget funding, and partnership rhetoric (Foster 2000, 7). Ratcliffe and Macray (1999) produced a commissioned report on sector-wide approaches in education for the United Kingdom's Department for International Development (DFID), arguing that the SWAp concept for education was the result of donor and recipient dissatisfaction with educational outcomes on poverty reduction. Better education standards were contingent on spending-effectiveness rather than spending-volumes (Ratcliffe and Macray 1999, 13–14). At the time of the study in 2000, a number of bilateral agencies were unconvinced about using a sector-wide approach in education as a reform mechanism.[2] At the same time, Ratcliffe and Macray predicted that the positions of bilateral agencies would change, and international trends suggest this is the case.

Brown, Foster, Norton, and Naschold (2001) suggest that SWAps have a clearer connection between policy and implementation than in the previous project world (Brown et al. 2001, 46). SWAps have worked best with fewer donors involved, as well as through a single ministry in the sector; multiple donors provide challenges for management and policy dialogue (10). Concerns have been raised about SWAps and conditionality in that recipient governments are unable to hold donors to their side of the bargain, making budget dependence on donors a significant risk, and civil society participation in policy formulation is generally low (46–47). To add to this, the diversity of development traditions among donor countries makes harmonization difficult; and as partnerships are formed, the amount of freedom for Southern partners to participate is reduced (King 1999, 22).

As much as the concept of donor coordination has been hailed by some scholars as a solution to solving aid-flow volatility and resolving equity issues (McGillivray 2005), it has been vehemently decried by other scholars as being another "aid cartel" by promoting Northern-developed policy frameworks (Guttal 2006). Numerous authors suggest that the power of the international community has the potential to displace fundamental recipient issues (Hinton 2004; Kakande 2004), while other contingents suggest that aid gets into the hands of corrupt officials, benefiting neither poor recipients nor donor taxpayers (Hughes 2004, 2003; Easterly 2006).

An issue that is often presented in the literature is the idea of power, specifically how it affects decision-making between donor and recipient. Robb (2004) makes the general observation that aid agency patterns of behavior are changing, with aid becoming untied, country offices being decentralized, and aid agencies becoming more critical of their programs. Alesina and Dollar (2000) suggest bilateral aid is given for political and strategic reasons of donors—as much as for economic and policy reasons of recipients. Several scholars have suggested that aid effectiveness in promoting growth is contingent on policy regimes in recipient countries (Burnside and Dollar 2001; McGillivray 2005). Chauvet and Collier (2005b), on the other hand, suggest that aid can expose governments to new ideas, and that reform should not be the only means of influencing policy and institutions. In fact, increasing the resource base of reform-minded governments can assist with good governance (Tavares 2003).

In terms of education, many scholars have noted the increased policy focus on education as a result of recent compacts to harmonize donor initiatives. Mundy suggests that the involvement and coordination of the international community has had the effect on bilateral donors of moving toward collective action through experimenting with pooled funding, direct budgetary support, and funding of recurrent costs of primary levels of education (Mundy 2007, 16). Mundy (2007) finds the focus on expanding resources and donor coordination as a positive move to funding of education as a basic social right.

Early research on motivation for giving aid concluded that bilateral allocations support donors' foreign, economic, political, and security interests (Maizels and Nissanke 1984, 891). While motivation for donor aid shifted from self-interest to recipient need in the 1970s, two major policy changes impacted shifts in aid in the early 1980s. The first shift was a cut in contributions by Development Assistance Committee (DAC) member countries to multilateral agencies. The second shift was the use of bilateral aid as an instrument of foreign policy (Maizels and Nissanke 1984, 892). Recent research reveals similar findings. Bilateral donors are motivated by self-interest, particularly from a geopolitical perspective; and a deepening of commercial linkages is also motivation for donors to contribute to a particular country (Berthelemy 2006, 183). Most bilateral donors give more aid to countries with better governance indicators and act as complements to multilateral financial institutions (Berthelemy 2006, 192).

Gounder (1999) studied aid motivation in the Australia-PNG relationship. PNG is dependent on aid from Australia, with Australia's emphasis on proximity and its special relationship with PNG as a former colony. Political and foreign policy concerns are not irrelevant to donors' behavior (Gounder 1999, 234). Even so, donors suggest there are multiple objectives and decisions about programs that depend on the complexity of objectives. The debate focuses on whether motivations of donors lead to effectiveness of aid for economic development (Gounder 1999, 236). In a 1990 critique of Australian educational aid, Maglen (1990) observed that Australia had managed "to retain within Australia and/or in Australian hands most of the aid it dispenses" (Maglen 1990, 91), concluding that Australia's educational aid program failed to support the quality of education in the South Pacific. Indeed, Maglen's analysis suggests aid effectiveness was compromised because of Australia's educational aid policies at the time.

In considering all of these studies, it is important to note the global context in which all aid actors—bilateral agencies, multilateral agencies, and NGOs—exist. A consistent argument about bilateral aid is its focus on self-interest; and certainly in tracing policy documents of AusAID, this is an explicit focus from the mid-1980s to the mid-1990s. However, while agency policy, as Mosse (2006) suggests,[3] may not be a true representation of aid in practice, the fact that bilateral organizations have become increasingly involved in international agendas, like the Paris Declaration on Aid Effectiveness, signals a shift to more collaborative and potentially less self-interested perspectives.

AusAID and Education Policy

Global agendas about development and the keywords that convey ideas are central to many policy documents. Australian aid priorities have ranged from the explicitly political and security-focused to those of education and basic needs. How does AusAID's education policy align with international goals for poverty reduction and sustainable development? How is AusAID reframing its education policy? In addressing the first question, AusAID's two education policies published over the past 11 years indicate a priority of funding education that leads to economic growth and sustainable development, and these objectives are synchronous with international policy and rhetoric. This section examines these questions as they apply to AusAID between 1996 and 2007. In addressing the second question, current AusAID policy indicates a general preference for a sector-wide approach in education. Sector-wide approaches, particularly in health and education, are "...better aligned with partner government systems, and adopt more responsive and flexible approaches" (AusAID 2006, 4). Similarly, AusAID has developed "new and sensible sectoral approaches to education" in the Pacific, which are also to be adapted in the Philippines, Indonesia, and PNG (AusAID 2006, 52).

In an effort to achieve better donor coordination and education-sector outcomes, AusAID is becoming increasingly involved as a key donor in supporting the sector-wide approaches and reform agendas of partner government recipients. Policy development in the organization indicates this approach is aligned with the 2005 *Paris Declaration on Aid Effectiveness*. AusAID's policy is increasingly aligned with multinational and bilateral agencies. Indeed, this is a significant policy shift within an agency that has traditionally focused on its involvement in the Asia Pacific region. While the Asia Pacific region remains primary in AusAID's policy agenda, AusAID has become more actively involved in global policy fora.

The 1997 *Simons Report* was a review of Australia's overseas aid priorities, objectives, and focus for its bilateral aid program. The report reiterated that the aid program was sound and that the program should remain geographically focused in East Asia and the Pacific (AusAID 1997). The report emphasized that overall policy imperatives should be a combination of humanitarian, foreign policy–focused, and commercial outcomes (AusAID 1997). For the agency, skills development and decentralization of AusAID management was a key recommendation of the Simons Committee (Cassity 2008, 255). The title itself—*One Clear Objective. Poverty Reduction through Sustainable Development*—signifies a shift in aid donor philosophy exemplified in numerous UN conferences in the 1990s, including the World Conference on EFA in 1990, the UN Conference on the Environment and Development in 1992 (also known as the Earth Summit), which established the UN Commission on Sustainable Development, and the Fourth World Conference on Women in 1995, leading to action plans focusing on the social, economic, and political empowerment of women. Poverty reduction, sustainable development, good governance, economic growth, and participation are guiding principles in the *Simons Report* and suggest a new direction in aid strategy.

Sustainable development and economic growth frame AusAID's first education policy statement released on August 20, 1996. By assessing individual countries' needs, a comprehensive education sector plan would be designed as a pathway to assisting with a country's human resource development. And this, among other things, emphasizes the policy rationale that education is a basic building block in alleviating poverty *through* the impact of economic growth and the development of quality human capital (AusAID 1996). AusAID notes that assessment of the global situation influenced its approach in funding education programs that recognize the gender gap, rural inequalities, high dropout rates, the need for relevance of curriculum content, and inefficiencies of school systems (AusAID 1996, 5–6). Finally, the policy affirms its commitment to basic education as a direct result of increased bilateral and multilateral funding of basic education following imperatives from the World Conference on EFA in 1990 (AusAID 1996, 7).

A shift in the late-1990s emphasized a significant clarification in regard to funding education subsectors. A July 1999 AusAID memo reviewed priorities in education sector interventions and found that a major challenge was in finding the right subsectoral balance in support for basic, vocational and technical, and higher education (AusAID 1999, 1). The memo reasserts AusAID's focus on the expansion of school systems, and its priorities are aligned with international agendas of expanding basic education, universal access, and helping vulnerable groups (especially girls) achieve access. While its emphasis on basic education and universal access are aligned with global trends, the continued emphasis on vocational and technical education and expansion of secondary education remained relatively specific to AusAID's program approach.

AusAID's 2006 *White Paper* reaffirmed sustainable development and economic growth as central policy objectives, and embraced some new terms. Indeed, more considered text is devoted to elaborating upon how participation will happen, why it is important to encourage good governance, why poverty is a challenge in the Asia-Pacific region, and how local AusAID offices need to have authority devolved to them. This is a shift, a significant one at that. The focus is on promoting growth and stability. Growth is important for poverty reduction, stability is important for effective aid.

The 2006 *White Paper* also recommends more aid to Asia and the Pacific, Australia's traditional areas of focus, but with increased attention paid to the efficacy of aid. In fact, it recommends the establishment of an Office of Development Effectiveness to evaluate the quality of aid projects (AusAID 2006). Regional security and Australia's political role in the region continue to be central themes, and the unifying objective of the program remains the same: "To advance Australia's national interest by assisting developing countries to reduce poverty and achieve sustainable development" (AusAID 2006, 8).

AusAID's most recent education policy was released in May 2007 and is fundamentally linked to the 2006 *White Paper* through the theme "Investing in People." At the outset, it highlights two priorities: the first, to improve functioning of national education systems to enable more girls and boys to complete primary school and progress to higher levels of education; and the second, to improve relevance and quality, including vocational and technical education, for students to acquire knowledge and skills necessary for life and productive employment (AusAID 2007a, 1–2). Education continues to be framed as a foundation for economic growth and self-reliance. Themes expanded upon in previous statements, such as improving access and equality, as well as supporting education that develops skills for productive employment, continue as central concepts. Added to these is security, with the recognition that lack of education may contribute to instability and violence.

The 2007 education policy also makes explicit links to global discourse about aid effectiveness. For education, this means strengthening performance (sector analysis, reporting, sector programs, and policy coherence), combating corruption, enhancing regional engagement, and strengthening partnerships (dialogue, harmonization, and whole-government approaches) (AusAID 2007a, 32–34)—all concepts linked to statements of multilateral and bilateral development agencies. Finally, the statement makes special emphasis that Australia will continue to integrate broader sector programs with partner governments and policies (AusAID 2007a, 33). Sector-wide programs in education are stated as a key approach to increasing the effectiveness of aid (AusAID 2007a).

In November 2007, a new Federal Government was elected in Australia. The swing from Liberal to Labor governments was predicted to have significant impact on the development of aid policy in PNG and the Pacific region. Prime Minister Kevin Rudd signed the *Port Moresby Declaration* in March 2008. This signaled a renewed commitment to partnerships in the Pacific region. The focus is on improving governance, increasing investment in economic infrastructure, and achieving better outcomes in education and health. Significantly, Australia has reiterated its commitment to improving cooperation with other donor countries, particularly New Zealand, which is another key Pacific donor, and has confirmed its commitment to the MDGs.[4]

Papua New Guinea Education Context

Policy infrequently elaborates about local context other than the rhetorical need to pay attention to schools and the societies that create them. This section discusses the context of the relationship between PNG and Australia. Since Independence, bilateral relations have swayed between tension and tolerance. For Australia, "PNG is deep in the Australian imaginary as well as our shared historical experience" (Modjeska 2003,

54). PNG has been dependent on donor aid since 1975. Australia continues to provide the majority of donor assistance, so much so that Australia-PNG relations are globally unique in terms of bilateral aid. The significance of a shared historical experience is not lost on AusAID. In a recent paper, Margaret Thomas, AusAID's former minister-counsellor in Port Moresby, acknowledged the special relationship between Australia and PNG (Thomas 2006, 2).[5]

In 1973, Australia granted PNG self-government, giving PNG leaders control of the education sector. In 1974 a *Proposed Five Year Plan for Education in Papua New Guinea* cited the need to consider alternative strategies for education focusing on relevance to the PNG context. At the time of independence in 1975, seminars and literary collections signified the beginning of a new era in Australia-PNG relations.[6] For the most part, they reflected optimism about the postcolonial future. However, there was also trepidation about the infrastructures of government, society, and the economy being neither well developed nor strong enough to meet the increasing demands placed upon them, and this state of affairs was the legacy of Australian rule (Davidson 1975, 229).[7]

In May 1974, the Eighth Waigani Seminar, *Education in Melanesia*, was held in Port Moresby. The tone of the conference was hope, with a dose of reality of the immense challenges facing educational development in PNG. In his opening address, Alkan Tololo, Director of the Department of Education, Port Moresby, noted the importance of relevance for the curriculum and teacher training. Reducing the costs of education, considering decentralization in education, and providing community education were issues Tololo cited as significant (Tololo 1974).[8]

More than 25 years later, issues surrounding the relevance of education continue to be salient. A PNG academic observed:

> In Papua New Guinea the desire to fulfill a national expectation is often the basis of half-baked educated bureaucrats and technocrats reluctantly writing off their cultures and dynamiting the earth, which holds the life of a people together. In the policy and planning oriented air conditioned offices countless hours are spent conferencing and discoursing every utterance in the most stoic and noncreative manner, only to find the implementation much more troublesome. (Winduo 2001, 102)

He concludes that, in formal education, culture should form the basic tenet of the education of a nation's youth. Winduo harshly critiques the perceived disconnectedness of government and policy in relation to the everyday realities of Papua New Guineans. Indeed, he implies that patterns of policy discourse make implementation problematic, and perhaps, for donors, ineffective. Education, in particular, is an opportunity to reconnect with culture.

The Papua New Guinean writer Regis Stella shares similar sentiments about relevance and development: "On many occasions, in recent times, outside financial institutions have reproached Papua New Guinea (and indeed Pacific Island States) on the failure of sustainable development because of its lack of policy shift towards one that is development and economic orientated" (Stella 2001, 12). He suggests that culture and development, or progress, have been perceived as being incompatible, and that the larger development project, specifically relations between Australia and PNG, have been framed through images of the other. Both Stella and Winduo provide persuasive comment about policy and context not often considered in major development frameworks.

The issue of relevance is a salient one. A recent report by the NGO World Vision emphasizes that despite education being valued by the population, the system is perceived by local citizens as being under-resourced, poor value for money, of poor quality, and irrelevant to many young Papua New Guineans (World Vision 2006, 7). School infrastructures are disintegrating, and there are few well-trained teachers and few teacher resources. There is little opportunity for children to read outside of school, and resources do not give skills learned at school concrete meaning in the everyday world (World Vision 2006, 15). Retention and completion rates have fallen, with the report citing that between 2000 and 2003 the primary school completion rate fell from 58 percent to 53 percent when school fees increased.[9]

Cleverly (2007) takes a critical stance on Australia's assistance to PNG, noting that it is debatable whether it can "hold the line in the provision of educational services" (248). He further includes a comment by Allan Patience, a professor of political science at the University of PNG:

The education system has all but disintegrated. Literacy rates are plummeting as schools close. Teachers are not being paid properly, or are not being paid at all. The higher education sector is fragmented and grotesquely under resourced. It has long ago ceased being the main builder of human capacity for PNG. (248)

National equity issues cited by PNG educators at the time of independence are no longer at the forefront of policymaking, and there needs to be renewed focus on the sector's social importance (Cleverly 2007, 250). As demonstrated, observers of PNG's education system relate a state of affairs far from the ideal hoped for in 1975. To be sure, the evidence suggests a dismal state of affairs where little in terms of educational development has contributed to a more equitable system. These data are certainly not lost on donors, but the number of policy shifts within PNG programming suggest that aid mechanisms in education have struggled to assist in better educational services for Papua New Guineans.

PNG is a long-term recipient of Australian aid, and it receives the largest sum of aid after AusAID's program in Indonesia.[10] Australia is also the largest donor by far in PNG, making it the most powerful donor. Yet, the argument follows that if AusAID has focused so much money and programming efforts on education in PNG, why are some indicators going backward? Certainly aid effectiveness is a concern.

Reframing Education Policy in PNG

The *Port Moresby Declaration* (2008) reaffirmed Australia's policy commitment to working with PNG and Pacific governments. This section discusses how AusAID is reframing its engagement in PNG through a SWAp in education. It begins with a discussion of major points of education reform in PNG in the 1990s that laid the groundwork for present policy engagement. It concludes with an analysis of key AusAID documents that outline the policy approach. A major organizational change in AusAID has been devolution of authority from Canberra to overseas posts. Currently, AusAID as an organization is developing a different skill set by shifting to policy engagement (personal communication).

As a diverse and politically decentralized country, the PNG context has presented numerous challenges to donor agendas. Until 1982, Australia accounted for 95 percent of foreign grants; however, by 1987–1988, only about 80 percent of PNG's donor aid still came from Australia. The Government of PNG invited the World Bank to establish a Consultative Group in May 1988, and this stimulated expansion of PNG's aid sources. In spite of this aid expansion, Australia continues to be the largest education donor, followed by the Japan International Cooperation Agency (JICA), the European Union (EU), New Zealand (NZAID), UNICEF, and the World Bank.

The general background of economic and social development in PNG from independence in 1975 through the 1990s included several issues considered by bilateral and multilateral aid agencies. PNG was perceived to have a weak institutional environment with poor control of government spending and a serious law and order problem (AusAID 2003b, viii). There was a dual economy (a formal mining sector and a large informal sector) combined with a series of external shocks, mineral boom, and structural adjustment in the 1990s that made for uncertain economic growth (World

Bank, 2000). Social indicators were reported to be either low (World Bank 2000) or improving marginally (AusAID 2003b).

Education Reforms in Papua New Guinea

A major reform in PNG's education system was the result of an *Education Sector Review* (Department of Education 1991). Results of the *Education Sector Review* included low transition rates to Grade 6 and Grade 10, an irrelevant curriculum, weak management and administration, declining resource allocations combined with high unit costs, and a severe imbalance in funding to higher education as compared with lower levels (Department of Education 1996, 1). The subsequent *National Education Plan 1995–2004* attempted to respond to the aforementioned issues.

The *Papua New Guinea Education Resources Study* (1995) analyzed costs related to the proposed reforms of the education system. A principal finding was that donor support would be a critical element in terms of feasibility of implementing reform (Government of PNG 1995, xiv). The study recommended that the government should take a lead role in policy, planning, and coordination to reduce unit cost of education at all levels. "Particular attention will have to be given to maximising the use of available resources and to acquiring the additional funds that will be required to implement and sustain the reform. Focused donor support will be critical" (Government of PNG 1995, xv). How donor support would sustain education reforms was a dominant policy theme.

The PNG Institute of National Affairs, a nonprofit policy research institute in Port Moresby, published research in 1997 on the role of the donor community, noting that aid had played and would continue to play a significant role in the socioeconomic development of PNG. However, the report cautioned about the adverse effects of donor assistance. These included government dependence on aid to fund recurrent costs of the budget, sustaining what has been left after donor assistance, the influence donors have on government policy, and the inability to absorb the level of finance (Institute of National Affairs 1997). At this time, the Institute promoted emerging ideas about development partnerships and coordination, cautioning about adverse effects on PNG's capacity in partnerships.

The *National Education Plan of 1995–2004* aims to increase access and participation at all levels of education in addition to supporting EFA goals, and revising the curriculum to be more relevant to village life. Successes of the previous *National Education Plan* included increased enrollments and increases in transition rates from Grade 6 to 7 and Grade 8 to 9 (Department of Education 2004, 23). The challenges, however, were borne out in statistics. Rapid expansion of the system in 1995 impacted upon school quality. Retention had fallen, delivery of services in rural and remote areas needed to be improved, and government support for reform to manage enrollment growth needed to be secured (Department of Education 2004, 23). Sustaining the reforms that began in 1995 has been a major policy challenge. The *National Education Plan 2005–2014* recognizes the challenges for education in PNG, the rights of all citizens to access education, and for all children to complete nine years of basic education (Department of Education 2004, 18–19).

PNG's *National Education Plan 2005–2014* is the document that donors, especially AusAID, refer to for policy decisions made by the Government of PNG. The *Medium Term Development Strategy 2005–2010* (MTDS) acts as a guide for AusAID funding, and aid effectiveness is measured against MTDS outcomes. The Strategy emphasizes strategic alliances with donor partners. The government recognizes that the HIV/AIDS epidemic, high population growth, unplanned urbanization, dysfunctional services delivery systems, and impediments to land utilization are challenges to education expansion and reform (Government of PNG 2004, 8–10). The MTDS recognizes the need for a relevant curriculum as expressed in the National Education Plans of 1995–2004 and 2005–2014. PNG's objective is to have Universal Basic Education by 2015, meaning that all children will be able to complete nine years of education (Government of PNG 2004, 38). While a SWAp for education is not mentioned as an objective in the MTDS, what the current pattern of donor support implies is that a SWAp is identified as a mechanism to achieve the reform required for Universal Basic Education.

UNESCO's *EFA 2000 Assessment of Papua New Guinea* focused on the country's progress toward EFA goals in the 1990s. In 1995, the Ministry of Education included four national EFA objectives in its *National Education Plan*: the education system should meet the needs of PNG people; provide basic schooling for all; help people understand changes in society through nonformal education and literacy; and identify manpower development needs in public and private sectors (UNESCO 2000). UNESCO recommended that the achievement of these goals meant that donor and government attention needed to focus on policies and effective legislation, capacity building, coordinated planning and implementation, efficient staff deployment, and community involvement (UNESCO 2000). Education access has improved but quality and equity are still concerns: education level of workforce and general population is low; there is low gross enrollments, especially of females; high attrition rates prevail; and 40 percent of PNG aged above 14 years (49 percent women) have never attended school (World Bank 2005, 10–11).

The contribution of Australian aid to PNG's development between 1975 and 2000 is framed as part of AusAID's focus on improved learning and accountability and a general strengthening of AusAID's policy research and analysis capacity. Education has consistently accounted for at least 25 percent of the Australian aid budget, and the report notes a number of achievements in the sector (AusAID 2003b, 34–35), although there are ongoing issues with quality, equity, and retention and progression rates, as well as lack of access to secondary schools. Governance became a priority in 1997 following the recommendations of the *Simons Review*. Since the early 1990s, there have been a number of shifts in AusAID's funding strategy to PNG.

A recent AusAID report on PNG and the Pacific recognizes the disparities within PNG, noting that many Highland provinces have little access to safe water, have low literacy rates, and low school enrollments compared with coastal and island provinces (AusAID 2003a, 2). Weak economic growth and rapid population growth—approximately half of PNG's population is under the age of 19 years—mean negative rates of per capita growth. The 2003 report argues that the quality of governance significantly impacts development and growth. The Report addresses aid effectiveness as well as the potential deleterious effects of aid (AusAID 2003a, 14–15). AusAID is specific on the need to coordinate to be effective.

Through an Enhanced Cooperation Program (ECP) with the Government of PNG, Australia has altered the aid paradigm to a "whole-of-government" approach with a key objective of building capacity and strengthening institutions (World Bank 2005; AusAID 2007b). The ECP is aligned with both AusAID's 2006 *White Paper* and its 2007 *Education Policy*. The *PNG-Australia Development Cooperation Strategy 2006-2010* (AusAID 2007b) recommends improved donor coordination to reduce the administrative burdens on the PNG government. It is also suggested that improved donor coordination will improve aid efficiency (AusAID 2006, 30). A former AusAID Port Moresby minister-counsellor described the agency's current strategy as working with existing PNG systems (Thomas 2006, 3).[11] AusAID strategy in PNG will move away from three-year project approaches to five- to ten-year program approaches.

The *Annual Program Performance Updates* were developed by AusAID's Office of Development Effectiveness in 2006–2007 to enable critical assessment of country programs. In PNG, school completion rates have fallen and net enrollment is much lower than gross enrollment. Service delivery is a challenge because of decentralization and expectations on poorly resourced and supported local governments (AusAID 2007c, 2). The PNG *Annual Program Performance Update 2006-2007* acknowledges expansion of the education system and negative impacts on quality with falling completion rates, increasing class sizes, and declining gender parity in classrooms. However, the performance update claims that AusAID has supported better quality through assisting with the completion of a national curriculum and supporting materials, as well as funding of better school facilities. The performance update emphasizes that AusAID seeks to progress on donor coordination to work toward the creation of an education SWAp. Practically, donor coordination is underdeveloped in PNG: "Of the 46 AusAID missions to PNG in 2006, only three were conducted jointly with other donors" (AusAID 2007c, 18).

AusAID currently recognizes that SWAps are led by partner governments, that inputs from donors are prioritized against costed education sector plans, and that donors will rely on partner government systems to deliver programs (AusAID 2008a, 18). In PNG, AusAID is leading the efforts to improve donor coordination and has played an important part in generating support of a sectoral program in education (AusAID 2008a, 18). AusAID views sectoral programs as "the most effective means for supporting public education systems in partner countries since aid is aligned with partner government plans, coordinated with other foreign assistance, and efficiently targeted" (AusAID 2008a, 20). The PNG Department of Education has stated support of the SWAp, but both donors and government recognize that the process of aligning systems is slow. In the face of declining human development indicators, perhaps the notion of such a partnership and the notion of shared credit will help identify past and current failures (personal communication). There remains the concern that aid will be ineffective because capacity building and sustainability are not practically interpreted by donors, with ownership and cultural differences being crucial issues. The point is that if and when consultants leave, the gains of the project would collapse if local Papua New Guineans have not bought into the project.

Conclusion

This chapter has examined the extent to which AusAID has aligned itself with international aid trends and provided analysis of trends in AusAID's education program in PNG. It has examined both scholarly debate and significant policy papers of AusAID in order to examine the meta-narrative of shifts in global aid policy. Exploring policy debates at an international level enables an examination of the level of diffusion of rhetoric and ideals in donor agendas. Viewed this way, AusAID's bilateral statements that focus on partnerships, donor coordination, capacity building, participation, and aid effectiveness are substantially influenced by global dialogue. In the 2005 Paris Declaration on Aid Effectiveness, targets were agreed upon for twelve indicators of progress. One of these targets was that by 2010 two-thirds of aid flows would be provided through program-based approaches (UNESCO 2007). As a policy guideline, this is significant. The literature on trends in bilateral aid to education suggests that ideas about partnership, participation, and coordination have emerged as important in discourse about aid policy. These elements are combined in the program-based concept of a SWAp—whether it be named a sector-wide approach, a reform agenda, or whole-of-sector strategy. A SWAp is emphasized as an approach to educational reform and a means to achieve policy coherence. While definitions of SWAps may vary depending on relevance to context, several concepts remain consistent. These concepts include that there is a focus on a single sector policy or program, that governments are the leaders of reform, that all funding parties adopt common approaches, and that recipient governments work toward the responsibility of disbursing and accounting for all public expenditures. In theory, dialogue, partnership, participation, and coordination are important in establishing such an approach.

At the same time, several scholars have noted the need to view such partnerships with caution. For example, the rhetoric of participation is a fundamental element of partnerships, but participation as practice has the potential to be ambiguous and exclusive, thereby posing the challenge of exactly who will be included. From this perspective, power and ownership become important elements in influencing who will determine policy planning and who will participate in policy dialogue. Brown et al. (2001) acknowledge that SWAps can place an element of dependence on donors by recipient governments whether for expertise or funds, and civil society participation is often low.

In the case of PNG, locale may play the complex factor in policy translation at a local level. This has an impact on implementing a SWAp in education and how policy is bound to practice. Scholarly literature notes that SWAps give policy power to recipient governments by encouraging donors to work through government systems and departments. However, practical implications of ownership and the depth of partnership and participation signal a need to be cautious, a need to not implement a blueprint policy approach. Freeman and Faure (2003) found that sector-wide approaches do not improve partnerships if they are implemented as a blueprint. Certainly the linking of context and realigned rhetoric of policy present complex challenges for bilateral agencies.

A difficult aspect of measuring policy impacts on aid effectiveness seems to be entrenched in the very complexity of the aid process itself. In this sense, identifying the exact input(s) that can contribute to improved educational outcomes is difficult because the very nature of context and community make reliable conclusions challenging. Over two decades ago, Bray (1984) studied decentralization in PNG's education system. Noting the various shifts in philosophy on the rationale for decentralization in development settings, Bray suggested that tracing the causality of decentralization on improved outcomes in education systems was difficult. Improved outcomes could be the result of numerous other factors, decentralization being only one of these factors.

We need to be careful that complexity itself does not become a cliché. While complexity offers an explanation for a number of parallel social, political, and economic processes that occur in context at any given time, it can likewise be used in proposing that something is too difficult to deal with or is unexplainable. Change in schools takes time. Perhaps the pursuit of aid effectiveness and clear outcomes after annual progress reviews may place too much pressure on making rapid change, particularly in education, where change takes up to a generation at a minimum.

Education arguably contributes to the implied benefits of enabling communities, encouraging good governance, and developing civil society. Some scholars are now making explicit ties between the expansion of secondary education and the development of good governance (Chauvet and Collier 2005a), while others emphasize that secondary education can provide capabilities for students hoping to achieve personal and social freedom (Sen 1999; Walker 2006). Presumably, if secondary education systems are well planned, citizens are endowed with critical thinking skills and schooling literacy that result from quality education beyond the primary years. This statement alone implies the need to engage in some serious discussion about educational expansion and aid efficiency.

It is worth recalling Tyack and Cuban's work on public school reform in the United States. Importantly, a few dedicated practitioners will get extraordinary results in isolated settings (Tyack and Cuban 1995). While this may lend a spurious sense to the work of development agencies in their attempts to encourage sustainable, long-term development, it also gives credence to the fact that context may be one of the key indicators for aid success. In all of this, the local actors continue to be crucial in any aid project or program implementation and success. Notably, states are not passive actors (Clayton 1998). Interpretation of aid policies is no doubt affected by local conditions and the ability or inability of local and civic institutions to enact those policies. Resources and political will are common factors in lack of policy collusion, while partnership and levels of participation may be exogenously determined factors based on pragmatic outcomes of bilateral aid programs.

The introduction to this chapter outlined a commonly accepted definition of SWAps outlined from research compiled by UNESCO (2007). It is significant, then, that UNESCO highlights two considerations in determining what roles should be created for SWAp participants: first, that policymaking organs are not donor constructs, and second, that the prevailing political economy of a country—or its context—will determine the viability of SWAp committees or steering groups (2007, 16). Bilateral donors are becoming more influential in a global dialogue on education policy development, and with histories of giving aid motivated by geopolitical interest or commercial linkages, this is a significant policy shift. Arguably, these histories continue to inform bilateral foreign policy frameworks. Current indications, as evident in recent AusAID policy development in the PNG education sector and the agency itself, are that bilateral agencies are becoming key actors in working with governments and other donors in framing context-relevant sector-wide approaches as part of the aid effectiveness agenda. But the processes of implementing sector-wide approaches in the Asia-Pacific region are still in relatively early stages. Outcomes seem far from predictable. This emerging policy architecture will depend on the quality of engagement that combines the perspectives of multiple donor and recipient actors to potentially improve development indicators.

Notes

1. This research was funded by Australian Research Council and AusAID through an Australian Research Council Linkage Project Grant. I would like to thank my colleagues at the University of Sydney and AusAID's Education Thematic Group for their ongoing support.
2. Ratcliffe and Macray (1999, 47) suggest this was due to an adherence to familiar processes, the need for policy control, and a lack of understanding about fungibility issues. The cited bilateral agencies (Canada, Germany, and Japan) preferred funding education reform through projects. AusAID policy in the late 1990s basically adhered to a similar philosophy.
3. The anthropologist David Mosse has conducted extensive ethnographic research on his long-term experience as a consultant for the United Kingdom's Department for International Development (DFID). He examines relationships in the forming of policy and the potential for dissonance between policy and practice. See also David Mosse (2005).
4. To view the *Port Moresby Declaration*, visit http://www.ausaid.gov.au.

5. The State Society and Governance in Melanesia program at the Australian National University publishes discussion papers and monographs from a range of informed contributors. See http://rspas.anu.edu.au/melanesia/.

6. The Australian literary journal *Meanjin Quarterly* published two issues—one in 1975 and one in 2003—commemorating the significance of Australia-PNG relationship. Contributors were from a range of disciplines, both scholarly and professional, and were both Papua New Guinean and Australian. See *Meanjin Quarterly* 34 (September 1975) and *Meanjin Quarterly* 62 (September 2003).

7. For further commentary on the pre-independence relationship between Australia and PNG, see A. M. Healy (1975).

8. The Eighth Waigani Seminar was called *Education in Melanesia*. From May 5 to 10, 1974, "those concerned in and with education from all parts of Papua New Guinea and the Pacific, and a handful of visitors from further afield" (1974, v) discussed education in Melanesia (see J. Brammall and Ronald J. May's [1974] *Education in Melanesia*).

9. World Vision (2006) gathered data from the *World Bank Global Data Monitoring Information System*.

10. For current and recent comparative data produced by the OECD's Development Assistance Committee (DAC) for donor countries that are DAC members and for recipient countries, see http://www.oecd.org.

11. Margaret Thomas, AusAID's former Minister-Counsellor in Port Moresby, outlined AusAID's PNG policy approach in a position paper published in 2006. The State Society and Governance in Melanesia program at the Australian National University publishes discussion papers and monographs from a range of informed contributors (see http://rspas.anu.edu.au/melanesia/).

References

Alesina, Alberto, and David Dollar. 2000. "Who Gives Foreign Aid to Whom and Why?" *Journal of Economic Growth*, 5 (March): 33–63.

AusAID. 2008a. *Education: Annual Thematic Performance Report 2006–2007*. Canberra: AusAID.

———. 2008b. *Annual Program Performance Report for Papua New Guinea 2007*. Canberra: AusAID.

———. 2007a. *Better Education. A Policy for Australian Development Assistance in Education*. Canberra: AusAID.

———. 2007b. *PNG–Australia Development Cooperation Strategy 2006–2010*. Canberra: AusAID.

———. 2007c. *Papua New Guinea: Annual Program Performance Update 2006–2007*. Canberra: AusAID.

———. 2006. *Australian Aid: Promoting Growth and Stability. White Paper on the Australian Government's Overseas Aid Program*. Canberra: AusAID.

————. 2003a. *Papua New Guinea and the Pacific: A Development Perspective.* Canberra: AusAID.

————. 2003b. "The Contribution of Australian Aid to Papua New Guinea's Development 1975–2000: Provisional Conclusions from a Rapid Assessment." *Evaluation and Review Series* 34 (June). Canberra: AusAID.

————. 1999. *AusAID's Education Sector Interventions.* Internal paper by the Gender and Education Group (July). Canberra: AusAID.

————. 1997. *One Clear Objective. Poverty Reduction through Sustainable Development: Overview and Recommendations.* Canberra: AusAID.

————. 1996. *Education and training in Australia's aid program.* Policy Statement announced by The Hon Alexander Downer, MP, Minister for Foreign Affairs (June 20). Canberra: AusAID.

Berthelemy, Jean-Claude. 2006. "Bilateral Donors' Interest vs. Recipients' Development Motives in Aid Allocation: Do All Donors Behave the Same?" *Review of Development Economics* 10 (May): 179–194.

Brammall, J., and R. J. May. 1974. "Preface." In *Education in Melanesia*, ed. J. Brammall, J., and R. J. May. Proceedings of the Eighth Waigaini Seminar, University of Papua New Guinea, Port Moresby, Papua New Guinea (May 5–10): v–vii.

Bray, Mark. 1984. *Educational Planning in a Decentralised System. The Papua New Guinean Experience.* Sydney: Sydney University Press.

Brown, Adrienne, Mick Foster, Andy Norton, and Felix Naschold. 2001. "The Status of Sector Wide Approaches." Working Paper 142. London: Overseas Development Institute.

Burnside, Craig, and David Dollar. 2001. "Aid, Policies and Growth." *American Economic Review* 90: 847–868.

Cassity, Elizabeth Anne. 2008. "Cast the Net a Little Wider: Australian Aid in the South Pacific." *International Journal of Educational Development* 28 (May): 246–258.

Chambers, Robert, and Jethro Pettit. 2004. "Shifting Power to Make a Difference." In *Inclusive aid. Changing power and relationships in international development*, ed. L. Groves and R. Hinton. London: Earthscan.

Chauvet, Lisa, and David Collier. 2005a. "Alternatives to Godot: Inducing Turnarounds in Failing States." Paper presented at the Conference on Badly Governed and Collapsed States, Yale Center for the Study of Globalization, Yale University, May 13–14.

————. 2005b. "Development Effectiveness in Fragile States: Spillovers and Turnarounds." Background paper for the Senior Level Forum on Development Effectiveness in Fragile States, Lancaster House, London, England, January 13–14.

Clayton, Thomas. 1998. "Beyond Mystification: Reconnecting World-System Theory for Comparative Education." *Comparative Education Review* 42 (November): 479–496.

Cleverly, John. 2007. "Schooling in Papua New Guinea." In *Going to School in Oceania*, ed. C. Campbell and G. Sherington. Westport, CT: Greenwood Press.

Cornwall, Andrea, and Karen Brock. 2006. "The New Buzzwords." In *Reclaiming Development Agendas. Knowledge, Power and International Policy Making*, ed. P. Utting. New York: Palgrave Macmillan.

Coxon, Eve, and Karen Munce. 2008. "The Global Education Agenda and the Delivery of Aid to Pacific Education." *Comparative Education* 44 (2): 147–165.

Davidson, J. H. 1975. "Introduction." *Meanjin Quarterly* 34 (September): 229–230.

Department of Education, Papua New Guinea. 2004. *Achieving a Better Future: A National Plan for Education 2005–2014*. Port Moresby: Department of Education.

———. 1996. *Papua New Guinea National Education Plan, 1995–2004, Volume A*. Port Moresby: Department of Education.

———. 1991. *Education Sector Review, Volume 1, Executive Summary and Principal Recommendations*. Port Moresby: Government of Papua New Guinea.

Easterly, William. 2006. *The White Man's Burden. Why the West's Efforts to Aid the Rest Have Done So Much Ill and So Little Good*. New York: The Penguin Press.

Foster, Mick. 2000. "New Approaches to Development Cooperation: What Can We Learn from Experience with Implementing Sector Wide Approaches?" Working Paper 140. London: Overseas Development Institute.

Freeman, Ted, and Sheila Dohoo Faure. 2003. *Local Solutions to Global Challenges: Towards Effective Partnership in Basic Education*. The Hague: Netherlands Ministry of Foreign Affairs.

Gounder, Rukmani. 1999. Modelling of Aid Motivation Using Time Series Data: The Case of Papua New Guinea. *Oxford Development Studies* 27 (2): 233–250.

Government of Papua New Guinea. 2004. *Medium Term Development Strategy 2005–2010*. Port Moresby: Government of Papua New Guinea.

Government of Papua New Guinea, Australian Agency for International Development, Asian Development Bank. 1995. *Papua New Guinea Education Sector Resources Study. Final Report*. Port Moresby: Papua New Guinea.

Guttal, Shalmali. 2006. "Challenging the Knowledge Business." In *Reclaiming Development Agendas. Knowledge, Power and International Policy Making*, ed. P. Utting. New York: Palgrave Macmillan.

Gyngell, Allan, and Wesley, Michael. 2007. *Making Australian Foreign Policy*. Melbourne: Cambridge University Press.

Healy, A. M. 1975. "Australia's Essay in Colonialism." *Meanjin Quarterly* 34 (September): 231–239.

Higgins, Liz, and Rosemary Rwanyange. 2005. "Ownership in the Education Reform Process in Uganda." *Compare* 35 (1): 7–26.

Hinton, Rachel. 2004. "Enabling Inclusive Aid: Changing Power and Relationships in International Development." In *Inclusive aid. Changing Power and Relationships in International Development*, ed. L. Groves and R. Hinton. London: Earthscan.

Hughes, Helen. 2004. "Australian Pacific Aid Supports Bankrupt Regimes." *On Line Opinion*. Available online at: http://www.onlineopinion.com.au.

————. 2003. "Aid Has Failed the Pacific." *Issue Analysis* 33: 1–32. Available online at: http://www.cis.org.au.

Institute of National Affairs. 1997. *Papua New Guinea: Country Case Study.* Port Moresby: Papua New Guinea Institute of National Affairs.

Kakande, Margaret. 2004. "The Donor-Government-Citizen Frame As Seen by A Government Participant." In *Inclusive aid. Changing Power and Relationships in International Development,* ed. L. Groves and R. Hinton. London: Earthscan.

King, Kenneth. 2006. "Knowledge Management and the Global Agenda for Education." In *Reclaiming Development Agendas. Knowledge, Power and International Policy Making,* ed. P. Utting. New York: Palgrave Macmillan.

————. 1999. "Introduction: New Challenges to International Development Cooperation in Education." In *Changing International Aid to Education,* ed. K. King and L. Buchert. Paris: UNESCO Publishing/NORRAG.

Klees, Stephen J. 2004. "World Bank Education Policy: New Rhetoric, Old Ideology." *International Journal of Educational Development* 22 (September): 451–474.

Knack, Stephen. 2004. "Does Foreign Aid Promote Democracy?" *International Studies Quarterly* 48 (March): 251–266.

Maglen, Leo. 1990. "The Impact of Bilateral Aid on Educational Development: The Case of Australia and the South Pacific." *Comparative Education* 26 (1): 83–93.

Maizels, Alfred, and Machiko K. Nissanke. 1984. "Motivations for Aid to Developing Countries." *World Development* 12 (September): 879–900.

Makuwira, Jonathan. 2006. "Aid Partnership in the Bougainville Conflict: The Case of a Local Women's NGO and Its Donors." *Development in Practice* 16 (3&4): 322–333.

McGillivray, Mark. 2005. "Aid Allocation and Fragile States." Background Paper for the Senior Level Forum on Development Effectiveness in Fragile States, Lancaster House, London, England, January 13–14, 2005.

Modjeska, Drusilla. 2003. "PNG Writing, Writing PNG." *Meanjin Quarterly* 62 (September): 47–54.

Mosse, David. 2006. "Anti-Social Anthropology? Objectivity, Objection, and the Ethnography of Public Policy and Professional Communities." *Journal of the Royal Anthropological Institute* 12: 935–956.

————. 2005. *Cultivating Development: An Ethnography of Aid Policy and Practice.* London and Ann Arbor: Pluto Press.

Mundy, Karen. 2007. "Education for All: Global Promises, National Challenges." In *International Perspectives on Education and Society,* ed. D. P. Baker and A. W. Wiseman. Oxford: JAI Press.

Narayan-Parker, Deepa. 2000. *Can Anyone Hear Us?* New York: Oxford University Press.

Patience, Allan. 2006. "The Other Disaster on Our Doorstop." *Sydney Morning Herald,* June 1, 19.

Patton, C. 2005. "Participation." In *New Keywords: A Revised Vocabulary of Culture and Society,* ed. T. Bennett, L. Grossberg, and M. Morris. Oxford: Blackwell Publishing Ltd.

Ratcliffe, Mike, and Murray Macray. 1999. *Sector Wide Approaches to Education: A Strategic Analysis*. Number 32. London: Department for International Development.

Robb, Caroline. 2004. "Changing Power Relations in the History of Aid." In *Inclusive Aid. Changing Power and Relationships in International Development*, ed. L. Groves and R. Hinton. London: Earthscan.

Sen, Amartya K. 1999. *Development as Freedom*. New York, Oxford: Oxford University Press.

Stella, Regis. 2001. "'Heart of Blankness': Artists in Unquiet Waters." *Savannah Flames: A Papua New Guinean Journal of Literature, Language and Culture* 4 (1): 12–22.

Tavares, Jose. 2003. "Does Foreign Aid Corrupt?" *Economics Letters* 79 (April): 99–106.

Thomas, Margaret. 2006. "The Role of Donors in Papua New Guinea's Development." *State, Society and Governance in Melanesia. Discussion Paper Series* (6). Canberra: Australian National University. Available online at: http://rspas.anu.edu.au.

Tololo, Alkan. 1975. "Opening Address." In *Education in Melanesia*, ed. J. Brammall and R. J. May. Papers delivered at the Eighth Annual Waigani Seminar sponsored jointly by the University of Papua New Guinea, The Australian National University, and The Council on New Guinea Affairs, held at Port Moresby, May 5–10, 1975.

Tyack, David B., and Larry Cuban. 1995. *Tinkering Toward Utopia: A Century of Public School Reform*. Cambridge, MA: Harvard University Press.

UNESCO. 2007. *Education Sector-Wide Approaches (SWAps). Background, Guide and Lessons*. Paris: Division of Education Strategies and Field Support, UNESCO. Available online at: http://unesdoc.unesco.org.

———. 2000. *Education for All Assessment 2000. PNG Country Report*. Paris: UNESCO. Available online at: http://www.unesco.org.

Walker, Melanie. 2006. "Towards a Capability-Based Theory of Social Justice for Education Policymaking." *Journal of Educational Policy* 21 (2): 163–185.

Winduo, Steven. 2001. "Literary Culture as Intellectual Capital for Nation Building." *Savannah Flames: A Papua New Guinean Journal of Literature, Language and Culture* 4 (1): 97–106.

World Bank. 2005. *International Bank for Reconstruction and Development International Development Association Interim Strategy Note for PNG*. Washington, DC: Pacific and Timor-Leste Country Unit, East Asia and Pacific Region, World Bank.

———. 2000. "PNG Country Assistance Evaluation." Operations Evaluation Department, Report No. 20183. Washington, DC: World Bank.

World Vision. 2006. *Gutpela Tingting na Sindaun: Papua New Guinean Perspectives on a Good Life*. Burwood East, Victoria: World Vision Australia.

Chapter 12

The Challenges of Universal Primary Education Policy in Sub-Saharan Africa

Mikiko Nishimura and Albert Byamugisha

Introduction

Universal Primary Education (UPE) policy in the form of fee abolition has become popular in many countries in Sub-Saharan Africa (SSA) for achieving Education for All (EFA) since the mid-1990s (Avenstrup et al. 2004; UNESCO 2008). Among 54 low-income countries, 15 countries have already introduced fee abolition policies and 10 countries are either at the planning stage or have shown interest in adopting fee abolition, among which 11 and seven of the latter countries are in SSA (see table 12.1). Despite its recent rapid expansion, UPE policy has a long history in SSA. Existing literatures indicate that previous attempts to achieve UPE in developing countries faced problems in its supply-driven policies, unclear mechanisms, and low quality of education (Allison 1983; Bray 1986; Prince 1997; Sifuna 2007). The past experiences in countries such as Nigeria and Kenya also show that UPE policy implementation was prone to be affected by economic crisis (Obasi 2000; Sifuna 2007). A number of lessons exist from the past; however, the current UPE policy severely lacks analytical studies on its impacts and challenges beyond school enrollment (Nishimura et al. 2008). Furthermore, some researchers have indicated the recent uniformity of the educational policies that prevail in SSA countries and suggested that there should be studies to examine how these seemingly similar policies are responding to the

Table 12.1 Primary Education and Fee Abolition in 54 Low-Income Countries

Region	Country	Net Enrollment Rate		Survival Rate to Grade 5		Year of Fee Abolition
		(1991)	(2005)	(1991)	(2004)	
Middle East and North Africa (1)	Yemen	51	75	–	73	2006
Central Asia (3)	Kyrgyz	92	87	–	–	–
	Tajikistan	77	97	–	–	–
	Uzbekistan	78	–	–	–	–
East Asia and the Pacific (9)	Cambodia	69	99	–	63	2001
	North Korea	–	–	–	–	–
	Laos	63	84	–	63	–
	Mongolia	90	84	–	–	–
	Myanmar	98	90	–	70	–
	Papua New Guinea	–	–	69	68	Interested
	Samoa	–	90	88	–	–
	East Timor	–	98	–	–	2001
	Viet Nam	90	88	–	87	2004
Latin America and Caribbean (1)	Haiti	22	–	–	–	Interested
South Asia (6)	Afghanistan	–	–	–	–	–
	Bangladesh	–	94	–	65	Interested
	Bhutan	–	–	–	–	–
	India	–	89	–	–	–
	Nepal	–	79	51	79	–
	Pakistan	33	68	–	70	–
Sub-Saharan Africa (34)	Benin	41	78	55	52	2004
	Burkina Faso	29	45	70	76	Interested
	Burundi	53	60	62	67	2005
	Central Africa Rep.	52	–	23	–	–
	Chad	35	61	51	33	–
	Comoro	57	–	–	80	–
	Congo DRC	54	–	55	–	Planned
	Cote Devoir	45	56	73	–	–
	Eritrea	16	47	–	79	–
	Ethiopia	22	68	18	–	1994

Continued

Table 12.1 Continued

Region	Country	Net Enrollment Rate (1991)	Net Enrollment Rate (2005)	Survival Rate to Grade 5 (1991)	Survival Rate to Grade 5 (2004)	Year of Fee Abolition
Sub-Saharan	Gambia	48	77	–	–	–
Africa (34)	Ghana	54	69	80	63	2005
	Guinea	27	66	59	76	–
	Guinea Bissau	38	–	–	–	–
	Kenya	–	79	77	83	2003
	Liberia	–	–	–	–	Interested
	Madagascar	64	92	21	43	2003
	Malawi	48	95	64	42	1994
	Mali	21	51	70	87	Interested
	Mauritania	35	–	75	–	–
	Mozambique	43	77	34	62	2004
	Niger	22	40	62	65	–
	Nigeria	–	68	89	73	–
	Rwanda	66	74	60	46	–
	Sao Tome Principe	–	97	–	76	–
	Senegal	43	69	85	73	Interested
	Sierra Leone	43	–	–	–	Planned
	Somalia	9	–	–	–	–
	Sudan	40	–	94	–	–
	Tanzania	49	98	81	85	2001
	Togo	64	78	48	75	Interested
	Uganda	–	–	36	49	1997
	Zambia	–	89	–	–	2002
	Zimbabwe	–	82	76	70	–
Developing Countries*		79	86	–	81	–
Low Income Countries**		48	79	62	63	–

Notes: Definition of low-income countries and regional classification are adopted from the World Bank. Low-income countries denote countries with Gross National Income per capita of 875 US dollars or less in 2005.

*Net enrollment rate is the weighted mean and survival rate is the median.

**All numbers denote median.

Sources: The Association for the Development of Education in Africa (ADEA), UNICEF and the World Bank (2007), UNICEF and the World Bank (2006), and UNESCO (2008).

capacity and needs of each country (Samoff 1999; Foster 2000; Brown et al. 2001; Klees 2001).

Under such a situation, this chapter attempts to analyze how UPE policies have been formulated, implemented, and evaluated in each country and what kind of administrative and financial issues should be raised from comparative perspectives. As the first attempt to create a comparative analytical lens, four countries were chosen, namely, Ghana, Kenya, Malawi, and Uganda. Malawi (1994) and Uganda (1997) have initiated the UPE policies relatively earlier than other countries, while Kenya (2003) and Ghana (2005) are among the more recent implementers.[1] The next section illustrates the historical background of UPE policy development in the case countries. Based on the results obtained from our field study in these four countries (Nishimura and Ogawa 2008), the third section of this chapter demonstrates some common and unique themes that emerged with regard to policy impact, educational administration, finance, and stakeholders' perception. The chapter further attempts to analyze perception gaps among stakeholders and difficulty facing UPE implementation. We then present a tentative conclusion in the final section of this chapter.

UPE Policy Revisited

The ideal that education is everyone's right was articulated in the United Nations *Universal Declaration of Human Rights* in 1948. However, a real turning point in the development of education came about in 1990 when, for the first time in history, the Jomtien Conference demonstrated that education for all could be transformed from a vision into a reality by the beginning of the new millennium. It was recognized, though, that achieving this goal was not going to be easy for those nations that faced the many intractable challenges of underdevelopment, particularly those countries in SSA. Whereas the world's nations reaffirmed their commitment to EFA in 2000 in Dakar, the expanded EFA vision articulated in Jomtien has remained the basis of all national and international action.

Provision of primary education for all children has long been seen as of great importance, at least in policy discussions, in all the four countries. In Ghana, an Accelerated Development Plan, declared in 1961, sought to expand "access to education," and the Education Act made education free and compulsory at the basic level. In Kenya, it was in the 1970s that the country introduced free primary education for the first time, which brought a dramatic rise of gross enrollment rate from 47 percent in 1963 to 115 percent in 1980. Similarly, UPE has been an important part of the political agenda since the 1960s in Malawi and Uganda. In Uganda, an Education Review Commission was appointed soon after the country's independence in 1962, which stated that expansion of primary education is an essential precondition for producing highly educated human resources to build and develop a new nation.

Such promising policy direction in the four countries, however, faced serious economic and political predicaments in the late 1970s and throughout the 1980s. In Ghana, the real value of government financing for education fell sharply from 6.4 percent of GDP in 1976 to 1.4 percent in 1983. In Kenya, due to a stagnated economy since the early 1980s, a cost sharing policy altered the free primary education policy in 1989 whereby the cost of textbooks, school activities, additional tuition, and examination fees became parents' responsibility, and communities were to construct physical facilities and ensure their maintenance as the government paid teachers' salaries. This policy change resulted in a drop in enrollment by approximately 20 percent between 1989 and 1995 due to the inability of parents to bear the economic burden of education. In Malawi, political intervention of the Malawi Congress Party abolished any strategies to achieve the goal of UPE in the late 1960s, and high priority was placed on secondary and tertiary education up until the 1980s. Likewise, in Uganda, the political turmoil that persisted over two decades damaged educational expansion and made UPE a mere slogan until 1986 when the National Resistance Movement took power.

Implementation of fee abolition regained its prominence in the 1990s after the Jomtien Conference on EFA, but the policy environment and the way policy was implemented varied in the four countries. While national political pledges in the presidential campaigns were the driving force for the implementation of fee abolition in Uganda and Kenya, the cases of Malawi and Ghana were driven more by the education reform process mainly initiated by the external donors. In Ghana, the Free Primary Education Policy was placed at the heart of the Free Compulsory Universal Basic Education (FCUBE) Programme initiated in 1996 with support from the World Bank and other international donors. However, it was not until 2005 that the Education Strategic Plan (ESP) 2003–2015 introduced capitation grant to schools nationwide, which put UPE in effect. The characteristics of fee abolition in Ghana, therefore, are that the implementation slowly took place while the idea of fee abolition stayed in the policy documents throughout the country's history of education policymaking, and that enrollment did not rise sharply due to delay in its full implementation. The net enrollment rate at primary school level for children in the age group 6–11 years increased from 59.1 percent in 2004/2005 to 81.1 percent in 2006/2007, an unprecedented increase attributed to the introduction of capitation grant (Ministry of Education, Science and Sports [MOESS] 2007). The challenges of UPE in Ghana lie in acute shortages of teachers persisting in the rural areas and worsening teacher/pupil ratios and academic perfor- mance as well as regional disparity (Ampiah and Yamada 2008).

The case of Malawi exhibits a more tragic reality of fee abolition policy. With the support of the World Bank, the abolition of school fees began from Grade 1 for the 1991/1992 school year and was pursued in Grades 2 and 3 in the ensuing years. In the 1992/1993 school year, the Girls' Attainment in Basic Literacy and Education (GABLE) Programme, funded by USAID, was established, which abolished school fees for non-repeating primary school girls from Grades 2 to 8. The complete fee abolition for all grades was then introduced in 1994 as the Free Primary Education (FPE) Programme. However, in Malawi, no direct financial support (e.g., capita- tion grant) was made to schools to replace the abolished tuition collection at school level until very recently in 2008 when a capitation grant began to be piloted in all schools by the World Bank. The enrollment jumped from 1.9 million in 1993/1994 to 2.9 million after the fee abolition was introduced, but the gross enrollment rate (GER) sharply declined from 137 percent in 2002 to 106 percent in 2004. The shortage of qualified teachers is also a serious matter. The ratio of pupil to qualified teacher in 2005 remained high at 83:1, which was worse than 81:1 before FPE in 1993/1994. This decreasing trend indicates the low efficiency that sur- faced after the implementation of FPE.

The cases of Kenya and Uganda signify rapid implementation of fee abolition and alternative funding scheme for schools. In Kenya, the Free Primary Education (FPE) policy was implemented in January 2003 as a result of one of the presidential campaign pledges by the National Rainbow Coalition (NARC) Party. In November 2003, the Ministry of Education, Science, and Technology (MOEST)[2] held a national conference on educa- tion and training to address various challenges arising from the abolition of fees and levies. The conference outcomes were then used to develop the Sessional Paper of 2005 and the Kenya Education Sector Support Programme (KESSP) 2005–2010. Although the administrative struc- ture is still centralized in Kenya, finance has been decentralized, whereby funding from the government is provided directly through the Ministry of Education to each primary school. The capitation grant is equivalent of 1,020 Kenyan Shillings per pupil to finance the purchase of textbooks and other teaching and learning materials, as well as to support other school operation activities. Not only public schools but also registered nonpub- lic ones are entitled to receive the capitation grant after meeting certain requirements. Each school must spend the grant in accordance with the instructions given by the Ministry and not utilize it based on actual needs.

As a result of implementation of the FPE program, the GER increased rapidly in a year, from 88.2 percent in 2002 to 104.8 percent in 2003. One of the key achievements of the FPE policy in Kenya is the provision of learning materials. The textbook-pupil ratio tended to be toward 1:3 for core subjects in lower primary and 1:2 for those in upper primary in 2003, as compared to 1:15 before the FPE. A serious challenge that FPE has not yet been able to solve lies in regional and gender disparities in enrollment and educational achievement.

In Uganda before 1986, the education system was severely disrupted prior to the introduction of UPE. The status of the primary education subsector in Uganda was extremely poor, whereby budgetary allocations had declined from 3.4 percent to 1.4 percent between 1971 and 1985, and the burden of this poverty was borne by parents of students. While expansion of primary education attracted both international and domestic attention in the 1990s, presidential candidate Yoweri Kaguta Museveni pledged for UPE implementation during presidential campaigns in 1996. The UPE policy started to be implemented in January 1997 after his election as president. The components of the UPE policy initially included five major fields of policy intervention. The first component was abolition of school fees, which initially applied to only four children per family and was later changed to all children in 2003. The second component was to increase the government expenditure on primary education. The education expenditure as percentage of GDP increased from 1.6 percent to 4.0 percent and the share of primary education in the total education expenditure rose from 40 percent to 65–70 percent. The third component was to introduce double shift for Grades 1 and 2. The fourth component defined the parental responsibilities as provision of lunch, uniform, and shelter while the government provides school fees, textbooks, teachers, and infrastructure. The fifth component was to abolish the Parent Teacher Association (PTA) fees, with an exception for the urban areas where voluntary labor is hard to obtain and cost of utilities is high. Moreover, the government initiated administrative and financial decentralization and implemented advocacy campaigns for girls' education. The Ministry of Education and Sports developed a Gender and Education Policy to provide a framework for planning and implementation of gender responsive education sector programs. In the policy, gender equality has been recognized as central to the achievement of universal primary education. Key gender concerns in education highlighted in the policy included disparities in enrolment, retention and transition rates, negative sociocultural practices and attitudes that inhibit girls' access, learning environments that are not conducive to girls, stereotyping in learning materials and in class teaching, and drop out of girls due to pregnancy and early marriages. The UPE education policy succeeded in reaching the poorest region and children since it reduced the burden of education costs from parents' shoulders, and its impact was especially large on girls from poor families (Nishimura et al. 2008).

Since 1997 the government of Uganda has been disbursing the UPE capitation grant from the Ministry of Finance, Planning, and Economic Development (MFPED) to schools via districts. The grant is calculated based on a variable cost of about 4,000 Ugandan shillings per pupil per year for all government primary schools, and a threshold cost for each school of 100,000 Ugandan shillings per month for nine months a year.[3] The UPE has brought a sharp increase in primary school enrollment. The total primary school enrollment has risen from almost 3 million in 1996 to 5.3 million in 1997 and to a phenomenal 7.5 million in 2007. The net enrollment rate jumped from 60 percent before UPE to 92 percent in 2007. The most serious challenges under UPE have been low internal efficiency and quality of education. The available statistics show that only 22 percent of the children that enrolled in Primary 1 in 1997 managed to survive to Primary 7 in 2003 (Byamugisha 2006). The majority of the remaining 78 percent repeated classes and 5 percent dropped out of school. Results from the National Assessment Progress in Education (NAPE) have indicated that the percentages of pupils who reached defined competency levels in literacy and numeracy was approximately half the original enrolments or lower in 2007, albeit with substantial improvement between 2003 and 2007.[4]

As such, the idea of fee abolition policy under the UPE or the FPE programs in four countries have long been reflected in their policy agendas since independence, but these have been abruptly implemented owing to both national and international pressure over the past decade or so. When the policy gained momentum for implementation, politicians and external donors have basically forced it on the countries. However, the implementation of such bold policy in the real sense represents a complex reality. While many agree to the policy direction, as primary education is largely appreciated by the population and fee abolition is regarded as being beneficial for the poor, it seems implementation schemes and procedures had not been carefully thought through by policymakers and external donors prior to policy implementation. There are numerous disparities in educational access and quality, for which fee abolition alone would not be a simple solution, and the new financial flow of education budget does not cater for pupils with specific needs (e.g., children in the disadvantaged areas and disabled children). Thus, this seemingly simple policy of fee abolition requires thorough investigation that reflects the reality on the ground and stakeholders' reaction to the policy implementation.

Similarly, with the help from donor funds and debt relief in 2002, Tanzania was able to make primary education free for all children. Almost overnight, an estimated 1.6 million children enrolled in school, and by 2003 about 3.1 million additional children were attending primary education. In Zambia, the abolition of school fees and the possibility of establishing community schools to receive school grants have helped improve data on community schools. The number of community schools increased from 55 in 1996 to over 2,700 in 2006, and the enrollment increased from 6,600 in 1996 to 470,000 in 2006 in these schools. Like in other developing countries, which started FPE, the top-level dynamic political initiative triggered FPE implementation in SSA, leaving little time for detailed planning before start up.

Common and Unique Themes

General Impact of UPE Policy

The development of a UPE policy signifies a strong governmental commitment and donor contribution toward EFA goals by enabling children who would not have enrolled in school to come to school. The most apparent impact of UPE is seen in increased enrollments in all the four countries. In Kenya, Uganda, and Ghana, UPE interventions also included provision of teaching and learning materials and additional classroom construction.

However, UPE implementation also had drawbacks at the school level. When school fees were abolished, overage and underage children flocked into schools. The most notable challenge was overcrowded classrooms, which in some schools led to low teacher motivation. The leverage between strong commitment of governments and donors and available resources was another issue. Schools suffered from lack of funds and were not able to ask parents for fees. Parents also became passive in every form of participation in school activities and decision-making. A common attitude illustrated by parents and community members is that now that the government is responsible for *everything*, they have no stake in school governance (Nishimura and Ogawa 2008). In such an environment, dropout of students became another challenge under UPE.

Some unique themes are seen in Kenya and Malawi. In Kenya, examination results declined after the introduction of the UPE policy, while experiencing increased repetition in contrast to a decrease in dropouts. In Malawi, quality indicators of schools also declined. However, some parents in Malawi have changed their passive attitudes and become more

cooperative with schools after years of witnessing the lack of additional
public resources available to schools. The case of Malawi shows that
quality of education still depends on how parents[5] support education,
and hence there is much diversity in the quality of education among
schools.

Administrative Challenges

Common themes that cut across administrative issues of UPE policy is
mainly rooted in its top-down policy implementation and the unprepared-
ness of the system for changes envisaged. Since the inception of UPE policy in the four case countries, no clear policy on roles and responsibilities
has been shared by stakeholders. Ad hoc training opportunities given to
head teachers on accounting and school management under UPE were not
enough for head teachers and School Management Committees (SMCs) to
obtain confidence in daily school management.

UPE also creates some conflicts that make administration and implementation of the policy fairly difficult. For instance, an automatic promotion policy adopted under UPE policy in Ghana, Kenya, and Uganda
and a simultaneous increase in enrollments—which brought overcrowded
classrooms—inevitably placed teachers in an extremely difficult situation.
Fee abolition and an inadequate amount of UPE capitation grants are also
contradictory scenarios and give head teachers' significant challenges and
sometimes push themselves into debt. In fact, our field study revealed that
the amount of capitation grants are much lower than what schools used
to collect from parents as fees (Nishimura and Ogawa 2008). As a consequence of these conflicts, schools are compelled to hold larger classes with
more limited resources.

Some unique themes exist in each of our case countries. For instance,
in Uganda some of the local politicians interfere in school affairs when
schools ask parents to offset some of the financial costs. This interference only furthered confusion on the roles and responsibilities of parents and community members under Uganda's UPE policy. In Ghana,
SMCs responsibilities are weak compared to the relatively strong position
assumed by district officials' tasks under UPE. In Kenya, the low participation of parents and SMCs seems to create mutual mistrust and poor
relationships in schools, especially between teachers and the community.
Finally, in Uganda, Ghana, and Malawi, decentralization policies devolve
a significant amount of power over education planning and budgeting to
district councils. As a consequence of this decentralization effort, district-
level education officers are left with less autonomy over sectoral planning,

which in some cases causes decisions made at the district level to compromise with the national policy.

Financial Challenges

Under the UPE policy, disbursement of capitation grants are done through the central government directly to schools in Kenya, and via district offices in Uganda and Ghana. Interview respondents indicated that capitation grant disbursement amounts are not necessarily determined by a baseline survey that highlights needs[6] but by whatever is available within the national account. Furthermore, the aggregated capitation grant amount at the school level is lower than the amount schools used to collect from parents and communities prior to the implementation of UPE (Nishimura and Ogawa 2008). In addition to the insufficient amount of the capitation grants, delay in fund disbursement is an all too common experience in each country. Disbursement delays can range from a period of one month to an entire term. Late payments generally have a negative effect on school planning, schedules, and other activities. Mismanagement of school funds at the school level was another oft-reported challenge by respondents.

Since the introduction of UPE, the primary education subsector budget has become heavily dependent on the central government. Although districts may offer some additional resources, only minimal resources (often none at all) are available at the district level. Parents often cater to the schooling costs, in excess of what is available, through capitation grants, which cover the costs of school uniforms, development fees, examination fees, lunches, transportation needs, and extra tutoring. The insufficient budget allocation toward primary education at the district level seems to most negatively affect the monitoring of schools. Thus, regular monitoring of quality of education and the quality assurance system are yet to be put in place in many schools.

One unique theme exists in Malawi where there has been no capitation grant scheme for more than ten years under the UPE policy. Much of the education budget goes toward such items as grants for teachers on leave, teacher deaths, and transfer of teachers, leaving a negligible amount of the budget for teaching and learning materials. In addition, the case of Uganda also uniquely revealed notable variability of primary education financing at the household, school, and district levels under the UPE policy (Byamugisha and Nishimura 2008). Under a decentralized system, district resources are minimal, and resources contained in the central budget on education can be diverted to other sectors according to decisions made by the district council. School finance and household expenditures on education vary based on the capacity of the SMC and parents' ability to contribute to schools. Under such circumstances, rural schools with a weak resource base are more prone to suffer from insufficient and unpredictable budgets to implement planned activities.

Perceptive Issues

UPE was an education policy agreed upon through democratic elections and a domestic decision-making process in each of the countries described in this chapter. The majority of the stakeholders interviewed in our study felt the current UPE policy was good overall and that they viewed primary schooling as either important or very important for both boys and girls (see table 12.2). Parents of students in Kenya, Uganda, and Ghana also report that although they are bearing the private cost of schooling under the UPE policy, the amount is lower than what it used to be. The UPE policy is greatly appreciated by parents and community members for its equitable nature of benefit to the poor. The cases of Uganda and Kenya also showed that parents appreciate the provision of teaching and learning materials to their children under the UPE policy.

Despite the positives associated with UPE in Ghana, Kenya, Malawi, and Uganda, the majority view that the implementation of the policy also has a number of challenges. In particular, the automatic promotion policy is contested by all stakeholders at the district and school levels. Promoting students to the next grade level when they have not yet met the proficiency set by each grade will actually do more harm to the unqualified students in the long run. These students will not attain the knowledge they need after completing their primary level education, ultimately compromising the quality of education. How to improve internal efficiency of education in large classrooms without sacrificing student learning is a critical challenge that persists in the four case countries.

There are some unique themes revealed in the data from respondents in Uganda, Kenya, and Malawi. In Kenya and Uganda, there was a gap between what parents perceive and what they actually do. Although interviewed parents claimed that they made substantial contributions to school by attending meetings and so on, interviews with district officials, head teachers, and teachers contradict these responses. There is a possibility of our sampling bias whereby the interviewed parents are those who are relatively cooperative with schools, but through a series of general school observations we recognized that parents generally hold more negative and passive attitudes in most schools (see table 12.2). In Malawi, fee abolition was not complied with due to lack of any other

Table 12.2   Perception Gap between Teachers and Parents on Parental Passive Attitudes

	Number and percentage of teachers and head teachers who perceive passive attitude of parents as a serious problem after fee abolition (%)	Number and percentage of parents who perceive schooling as important or very important (%)	Number and percentage of parents who perceive their contribution to schools as important or very important (%)
Kenya	All focus group discussion interviews raised the issue (48 teachers)	For Boys: 52 out of 52 parents (100%) For Girls: 46 out of 52 parents (89%)	52 out of 52 parents (100%)
Uganda	55 out of 60 teachers and head teachers (92%)	For Boys: 59 out of 60 parents (98%) For Girls: 59 out of 60 parents (98%)	58 out of 60 parents (97%)
Ghana	12 out of 20 teachers and head teachers (60%)	For Boys: 120 out of 120 parents (100%) For Girls: 119 out of 120 parents (99%)	114 out of 120 parents (95%)
Malawi	29 out of 53 teachers and head teachers (55%)	For Boys: 83 out of 83 parents (100%) For Girls: 81 out of 83 parents (98%)	80 out of 83 parents (96%)

Note: We conducted semi-structured interviews, which followed same interview protocols, in four countries, in two districts per country. The basic sampling methodology was purposive sampling based on school location and performance. We also shared the minimum number of sample schools. However, since the countries differ in terms of the population and diversity within the region, the decision on the total number of samples was devolved to each country study team, which caused variability in the number of respondents.

Source: Created by authors with reference to Nishimura and Ogawa, eds. 2008.

resource base, and hence parents responded that the cost of schooling was higher than before the introduction of the UPE policy (Chimombo et al. 2008). Malawian parents also hold negative views on nonexistence of the provision of teaching and learning materials, unlike parents in the other three countries. The case of Malawi, therefore, indicates that the lack of financial and administrative preparedness can lead to noncompliance of the UPE policy.

Linkages among Factors

All four countries showed that administrative and financial constraints have strong links and mutual effects at both the district and school levels. The limited resources and lack of administrative capacity constrain the capacity of the schools to fully and adequately implement UPE and maintain a high level of school performance. However, the overall perception of parents and SMC members of UPE was positive and did not reflect the administrative and financial constraints and school performance in Kenya, Uganda, and Ghana. In Malawi, where there are no capitation grants to replace school fees, stakeholder reactions varied indicating that the stakeholders are capable of introducing positive or negative changes to the way schools perform. The linkage among factors seems to cut across rural and urban schools, and there was no clear regional difference within any of the case countries.

Popular Policy, Responsibility Deficit?

The popularity of UPE cannot be sustained unless it is supported by a strong commitment of stakeholders in the implementation of the policy. In this context, it is important to inquire who is responsible for UPE policy implementation and in what manner should UPE be implemented. This section analyzes stakeholders' perception gap under the UPE policy, illustrated partially in the earlier section, and assesses how UPE suffers from responsibility deficit on the ground.

As noted in table 12.2, there exists perception gaps on parental attitudes between teacher and parent respondents. According to our study conducted in two districts in each of the four countries, more than half of the participating teachers and head teachers reported an increasing passive attitudinal change among parents toward participation in school activities and management and perceived this change as a serious challenge after UPE policy implementation. In Uganda, over 90 percent of teachers and head teachers interviewed were concerned with the passive attitude of parents after the introduction of UPE. In Kenya we conducted focus group interviews with 48 teachers in the Central and Western Regions, and the issue of passive parental attitudes was mentioned in most interviews. Also noted in Kenya was that many SMCs have become inactive to the extent that they are regarded as mere "book committees" that simply choose and purchase a textbook using the capitation grants given by the government (Sifuna et al. 2008, 44). The shared view of most teachers in the four case countries was that parents and community members interpret fee abolition as a message from the government that the government is in a position to take care of *everything*.

In contrast, parents and SMC members do not reveal their passive attitudes, at least when interviewed during this study. As reflected in table 12.2, almost all parents regard schooling for boys and girls as either important or very important, and the majority regard their contribution to schools as important. Here we cannot infer that their attitude is "the government should take care of everything." It sometimes occurs in social research that perceptions do not necessarily match with realities and in some cases may contradict with each other (Schneider and Buckley 2002). Nevertheless, why is there such an evident gap?

Let us look more closely at how parents perceive quality of education under the UPE/FPE policy. Except in Malawi, over half the participating parents from the other three countries in this study perceived quality of education as either good or very good. In Malawi, only 22 percent of participating parents perceived the quality of education as either good or very good, while 35 percent responded that the quality of education is either bad or very bad. This implies parental dissatisfaction and disappointment with a UPE policy implementation that was not accompanied by additional public expenses to replace withdrawn fees, which was the case for 13 years in Malawi.

How are perceptions of parents and community members on policy implementation established and how do they relate to their perceptions on the quality of education? The majority of education administrators, teachers, and head teachers responded that "fee abolition policy is good but not well implemented."[7] Many education administrators and teachers are confused and unhappy with the way the policy was implemented, especially in that it was implemented in a top-down manner without prior consultation or preparation for administrative and financial mechanisms. Such perception is well represented by the following statement by one education administrator in Uganda:

> UPE was a top-bottom policy without any consultation with people. The only option we had was "to adjust ourselves to accommodate it." People own things [when] they have made decisions themselves. People do not see it as their program because there was no consultation. People should have been consulted. (Interview, July 2007)

While administrative officers and teachers have negative views on policy implementation, parents of students and SMC members do not necessarily hold such views. Less than half of all participating parents and SMC members indicated that "the UPE policy could have been implemented differently." Malawi participants were different, however, where the majority of parents held negative views on the quality of education. Parents seem to hold some negative views on the quality of education but do not necessarily have alternative suggestions.

Parental reaction can also reveal a complex nature. In Kenya, for instance, a substantial number of parents who feared a decline in the quality of education after the implementation of the FPE policy in 2003 transferred their children into private schools. In fact, the number of private primary schools increased by approximately 30 percent in 2003/2004 alone, and the disparity in quality of education between public and private primary schools became a significant concern (Sawamura 2006). A panel data taken from over 700 rural households in Central and Western Kenya in 2004 and 2007 shows that the percentage of those who chose private schools rose from 5.5 percent for boys and 4.4 percent for girls in 2004 to 12.0 percent and 12.2 percent, respectively, in 2007 (Nishimura and Yamano 2008). When disaggregated at the household asset level, it was found that households at all asset levels followed this trend. It is worth noting that even the lowest quartile of the asset level witnessed a rise in selection of private schools from 1.6 percent to 6.2 percent during this same time period. Many of the poorest children who were to be among those who most benefited from the FPE policy chose to attend private schools by paying school fees. Parents are not necessarily willing to participate in school activities in order to reveal their perceptions on education reform programs, rather they show their perceptions by choosing private schools or exiting public schools. More detailed statistical analyses are presented in Nishimura and Yamano (2008).

Although limited by small case studies, these empirical data identify two critical issues. First, substantial parental participation is hard to obtain unless their perceptions are clearly noted. If parents do not recognize the significance of their participation, it is hard to obtain their participation in meetings or school activities. Even if invited, parents do not always have suggestions for improving education or the schooling process.

Second, even if parents have some perceptions on the quality of education, their acts are not necessarily consistent with their perceptions. Although interviewed parents mentioned that they regarded their contribution to schools as important, there remained a gap between their perceptions and their behaviors that teachers witnessed at schools. In addition, as the case of Kenya indicates, anxiety and dissatisfaction often led parents to "exit" from the public school system altogether. In sum, mere promotion of parental participation in school activities and governance may not change parental behavior, as parents tend to espouse wait-and-see attitudes or enroll their children in private options rather than participate in public school operations.

It seems clear that positive or passive attitudes of parents and community members are rooted in a more complex phenomenon than a mere equation of "not paying school fees equals termination of their roles." Existing literatures also note that when communities are supported without local participation, human capacity, understanding, and willingness to form a new school operation and learning environment, school operations are weakened and do not improve the quality of education (Chapman 1998; Chapman et al. 2002; Rivarola and Fuller 1999; Sasaoka and Nishimura 2007). Fee abolition policies in the four case countries had common features of a rapid top-down implementation and divisions among stakeholders' perceptions and their behaviors. Even among education administrators, confusion on their roles and responsibilities was evident and their dissatisfaction with actual implementation was widely noted. This is because fee abolition policies did not accompany proper and wide consultation with stakeholders in these four countries; there were no upfront detailed plans of administration and finance to enable a clear implementation process and accompanying monitoring and evaluation of the program's overall impact. Parents did not seem able to voice their perceptions about the fee abolition policies, which ultimately led to a responsibility deficit of the local public. This further induced neglect of downward accountability of the overall education system and caused a negative spiral of accountability absence in UPE implementation.

Conclusion

This chapter has helped highlight the importance of including widespread consultations with all stakeholders as a key ingredient of effective education policy implementation. Who owns UPE in the four case countries discussed in this chapter is an important question to be posed. Our study revealed that the relationship between school administrators and parents and community members has weakened since the inception of UPE implementation in Ghana, Kenya, Malawi, and Uganda. We are not arguing that parents must pay in order for their voices to be heard at schools. On the contrary, how parents voice their opinions when fees are no longer required is a key question to be pursued in order to make UPE sustainable.

Regardless of good intentions, top-down policy implementation tends to overlook stakeholders' attitudes and behaviors that eventually determine policy outcomes. Without a baseline survey, any systematic implementation of the policy may not be feasible. Although governments and donors have organized a series of advocacy campaigns on their respective UPE policies, continuous and untiring sensitization and commitment toward these policies may be required to avoid confusion at the local level. In particular, there is a need for an effective system of monitoring and tightening accountability of UPE policies and implementation effectiveness. Faced with increased enrollments, each country now needs to make cost-effective strategies to raise the quality of primary school education with limited resources in order to tackle the ongoing challenge of maintaining both quantity and quality of education.

Who owns UPE in each country and who is accountable and responsible for UPE policy implementation? Ultimately, it is not just the government that should comply with the policy and is accountable to the public, the public should also be responsible for the policies they support through democratic voting processes. Sustainability of UPE policies can be ensured only with this mutual-accountability model. The attainment of UPE by 2015 will necessitate an even stronger combination of political will, deep-rooted and sustained reform, faster dissemination of best practices, and intensified financial effort than has been marshaled to date.

Notes

1. This chapter includes findings of Kobe University's project entitled "A Comparative Analysis of Universal Primary Education Policy and Administrative Financial Systems in Sub-Saharan Africa," supported by the Africa-Asia University Dialogue project and International Cooperation Initiative by the Ministry of Education, Culture, Sports, Science, and Technology of Japan (MEXT).
2. The Ministry was divided into the Ministry of Education (MOE) and the Ministry of Science and Technology (MOST) in 2005.
3. From 1997 to 2002, schools received 5,000 shillings per year for each child in Grades 1–3 and 8,100 shillings per child in Grades 4–7. A threshold for each school was adopted in 2003/2004. As is the case of Kenya, schools had to comply with the detailed guidelines for the usage of the capitation grants.
4. The proportions of students who reached defined competency levels in literacy were 43 percent for Primary 3 and 20 percent for Primary 6 in 2003, which improved to 45 percent and 41 percent, respectively, in 2007. For numeracy, the percentages were 34 percent for Primary 3 and 20 percent for Primary 6 in 2003 and it increased to 46 percent and 50 percent, respectively, in 2007.
5. From this point forward, the term *parents* refers primarily to parents of students.

6. In Uganda, allocation was amended based on a study in 2003.

7. Four options were given as a response: "UPE policy is good and well implemented," "UPE policy is good but not well implemented," "UPE policy has problems but well implemented," and "UPE policy has problems and not well implemented."

References

Allison, Christine. 1983. "Constrains to UPE: More than a Question of Supply?" *International Journal of Educational Development* 3 (3): 263–276.

Ampiah, Joseph G., and Shoko Yamada. 2008. "Chapter 1: The Case of Ghana." In *A Comparative Analysis on Universal Primary Education Policy, Finance, and Administrative Systems in Sub-Saharan Africa: Findings from the Field Work in Ghana, Kenya, Malawi, and Uganda*, ed. Mikiko Nishimura and Keiichi Ogawa, 9–32. Kobe: Kobe University.

Association for the Development of Education in Africa (ADEA), UNICEF, and World Bank. 2007. International Conference: School Fee Abolition: Planning for Quality and for Financial Sustainability. Bamako, Mali: ADEA, UNICEF, and World Bank.

Avenstrup, Roger, Xiaoyan Liang, and Søren Nellemann. 2004. "Kenya, Lesotho, Malawi and Uganda: Universal Primary Education and Poverty Reduction." A paper presented at the Scaling up Poverty Reduction; A Global Learning Process and Conference in Shanghai, May 25–27, 2004.

Bray, Mark. 1986. "If UPE is the Answer, What is the Question? A Comment on Weakness in the Rationale for Universal Primary Education in Less Developed Countries." *International Journal of Educational Development* 6 (3): 147–158.

Brown, Adrienne, Mick Foster, Andy Norton, and Felix Naschold. 2001. *The Status of Sector Wide Approaches*. Working Paper No. 142. London: Overseas Development Institute.

Byamugisha, Albert. 2006. *Overall Performance of Districts and Constraints towards Attainment of Sector Targets Using the District League Table (basing on Education Performance Index: EPI)*. Kampala: Government of Uganda.

Byamugisha, Albert, and Mikiko Nishimura. 2008. "Chapter 5: The Case of Uganda." In *A Comparative Analysis on Universal Primary Education Policy, Finance, and Administrative Systems in Sub-Saharan Africa: Findings from the Field Work in Ghana, Kenya, Malawi, and Uganda*, ed. Mikiko Nishimura and Keiichi Ogawa, 99–125. Kobe: Kobe University.

Chapman, David W. 1998. "The Management and Administration of Education across Asia: Changing Challenges." *International Journal of Educational Research* 29: 603–626.

Chapman, David, Elizabeth Barcikowski, Michael Sowah, Emma Gyamera, and George Woode. 2002. "Do Communities Know Best? Testing a Premise of Educational Decentralization. Community Members' Perception of Their

Local Schools in Ghana." *International Journal of Educational Development* 22 (2): 181–189.

Chimombo, Joseph, Demis Kunje, and Keiichi Ogawa. 2008. "Chapter 4: The Case of Malawi." In *A Comparative Analysis on Universal Primary Education Policy, Finance, and Administrative Systems in Sub-Saharan Africa: Findings from the Field Work in Ghana, Kenya, Malawi, and Uganda*, ed. Mikiko Nishimura and Keiichi Ogawa, 61–97. Kobe: Kobe University.

Foster, Mick. 2000. *New Approaches to Development Cooperation: What Can We Learn from Experience with Implementing Sector Wide Approaches?* Working Paper No. 140. London: Overseas Development Institute.

Klees, Steven J. 2001. "World Bank Development Policy: A SAP in SWAPs Clothing." *Current Issues in Comparative Education* 3 (2): 1–11.

Ministry of Education Science and Sports (MOESS). 2007. *Education Sector Performance Report 2007.* Accra: MOESS.

Nishimura, Mikiko, ed. 2007. *Country Status Report for the International Cooperation Initiative on A Comparative Analysis on Universal Primary Education Policy and Administrative and Financial Systems in Sub-Saharan Africa.* Kobe: Kobe University.

Nishimura, Mikiko, and Keiichi Ogawa, eds. 2008. *A Comparative Analysis on Universal Primary Education Policy, Finance, and Administrative Systems in Sub-Saharan Africa: Findings from the Field Work in Ghana, Kenya, Malawi, and Uganda.* Kobe: Kobe University.

Nishimura, Mikiko, Takashi Yamano, and Yuichi Sasaoka. 2008. "Impacts of the universal Primary Education Policy on Educational Attainment and Private Costs in Rural Uganda." *International Journal of Educational Development* 28 (2): 161–175.

Obasi, Emma. 2000. "The Impact of Economic Recession on UPE in Nigeria." *International Journal of Educational Development* 20 (3): 189–207.

Prince, Asagwara. 1997. "Quality of Learning in Nigeria's Universal Primary Education Scheme-1976–1986." *Urban Review* 29: 189–203.

Rivarola, Magdalena, and Bruce Fuller. 1999. "Nicaragua's Experiment to Decentralize Schools: Constraining Views of Parents, Teachers, and Directors." *Comparative Education Review* 43 (4): 489–521.

Samoff, Joel. 1999. "Education Sector Analysis in Africa: Limited National Control and Even Less National Ownership." *International Journal of Educational Development* 19 (4): 249–272.

Sasaoka, Yuichi, and Mikiko Nishimura. 2007. "Educational Decentralization in Low Income Countries: Contradiction with Universal Primary Education (UPE) Policy." *Journal of International Development Studies* 16 (2): 21–33. In Japanese.

Sawamura, Nobuhide. 2006. "Exam-oriented school education: Current situation in primary education in Kenya." *Journal of International Cooperation in Education* 9 (2): 97–111. In Japanese.

Schneider, Mark, and Jack Buckley. 2002. *What Do Parents Want from Schools? Evidence from Internet.* NCSPE Occasional Paper 21. New York: National Center for the Study on Privatization in Education, Columbia University.

Sifuna, Daniel N. 2007. "The Challenge of Increasing Access and Improving Quality: An Analysis of Universal Primary Education Interventions in Kenya and Tanzania since the 1970s." *International Review of Education* 53: 687–699.

Sifuna, Daniel N., Ibrahim O. Oanda, and Nobuhide Sawamura. 2008. "Chapter 3: The Case of Kenya." In *A Comparative Analysis on Universal Primary Education Policy, Finance, and Administrative Systems in Sub-Saharan Africa: Findings from the Field Work in Ghana, Kenya, Malawi, and Uganda*, ed. Mikiko Nishimura and Keiichi Ogawa, 33–60. Kobe: Kobe University.

UNESCO. 2008. *Education for All Global Monitoring Report 2008*. Paris: UNESCO.

UNICEF and World Bank. 2006. School Fee Abolition Initiative (SFAI) Workshop: Building on What We Know and Defining Sustained Support. Nairobi: UNICEF and the World Bank.

Chapter 13

Time Misspent, Opportunities Lost: Use of Time in School and Learning[1]

Audrey-Marie Schuh Moore, Joseph DeStefano, and Elizabeth Adelman

Introduction

Instructional time is a multifaceted concept (Berliner 1990). While the importance of sufficient instructional time and its impact on student achievement is well documented in literature (Aronsen et al. 1998; Berliner 1990; Abadzi 2007a, 2007b, 2009), the length, type, and focus of time for improving student learning remains unclear. How much instructional time is lost in schools? Should educators extend the school day/year to add instructional time? Or, should the focus be on improving the use of existing instructional time? If existing time is increased, will it impact student achievement? These questions form the core of the policy debate surrounding investments in instructional time.

This chapter documents the loss of "effective allocated and engaged" instructional time and argues that it is more effective and cost-effective to improve the use of existing time. The analysis from four cases in Ethiopia, Guatemala, Honduras, and Nepal provides useful insights into the relationship between schools, instruction, and learning, and the cost-effective interventions that improve the use of time in schools. The chapter lays out the arguments in the time-use debate, discusses the methodology for the study, and presents findings. The conclusion offers policy recommendations for improvements and interventions that will assist schools in improving time-use.

The Debate

The idea of adding time to school calendars to increase instructional time has been debated in the United States for over three decades. Literature on the relationship between time and learning extends back to the 1970s and has typically fallen into one of the following categories: (1) empirical, data-based research and reviews or syntheses of existing research; (2) policy reports that combine educational theory with empirical research; and (3) anecdotal, experientially-based periodical publications, usually explaining one school's experience implementing a certain time-related policy (Aronson et al. 1998).

The literature (Stallings 1973; Aronson et al. 1998; Abadzi 2007a) further defines instructional time in three ways:

(1) *Allocated Time*: The total number of days or hours that students are expected to attend school. The allocated time is usually set by the Ministry/Department of Education.
(2) *Engaged Time*: The time within a class period when students are involved in learning activities. Engaged time is also referred to as "time-on-task."
(3) *Academic Time*: The precise period in a class when a learning activity aligns with a student's readiness and ability to learn.

The majority of studies dealing with instructional time focus on allocated time since it is easier to measure and more readily understood by policymakers. Over the past several decades, school districts throughout the United States have studied options for extending the school day and year in an effort to provide more allocated time to students.

A study conducted by the Virginia Department of Education (1992) found that lengthening the school day did not significantly impact student learning. The study focused on moving to year-round schooling and stated that higher gains in student achievement would be made by focusing on teacher training, appropriate class sizes, and summer programs for at-risk youth.

The *Massachusetts 2020* report maintained that extending allocated time in schools is not sufficient and that educators must also focus on learning. However, allowing for more allocated time naturally increased engaged and academic time as well through longer class periods. The report cited evidence of students who took two periods of math in a previous year performing better on standardized tests than their counterparts who only took one period. Teachers argued that longer class periods allow them to both introduce new material and conduct remediation as needed (*Massachusetts 2020* 2005).

While the review of research conducted in US school districts indicates mixed findings about the degree to which allocated and engaged time influences student learning (Holsinger 1982; Nelson 1990; Aronson et al. 1998), it reveals a fairly consistent pattern: there is little or no relationship between allocated time and student achievement; some relationship between engaged time and achievement; and a larger relationship between academic time and achievement (Aronson et al. 1998). In short, time does matter and is predictive of academic achievement if properly used for engaged academic activities (Latham 1985 as cited in Hollowood et al. 1994; Good and Brophy 1986; Greenwood 1991). Research also shows that the amount of allocated and engaged time is greatly reduced by time spent on nonacademic activities, transition to classes or topics, poor classroom management, and disciplinary activities (Stallings 1973; Aronson et al. 1998; Abadzi 2007a, 2009).

The remaining portion of this chapter presents data on allocated and engaged time, on classroom practices, and on student performance in reading from four countries. The data demonstrate the amount of time that can be gained for instruction in the existing school day and explain low levels of literacy acquisition among Grade 3 students.

Methodology

A case study approach was used for this study, with four country cases selected based on the presence of NGO-supported work related to school improvement. Data for each case study were collected through field research made possible through collaboration with CARE and Save the Children USA. Field teams visited each school and conducted interviews with the school director and with teachers from Grades 1, 2, and 3. Observations using the Stallings methodology (1980) were conducted in Grade 1, 2, and 3 classrooms for one hour each. A random sample of students was drawn from Grade 3 to be interviewed, take a ten-item assessment based on Concepts About Print ([Clay, 2000] a pre-literacy evaluation of students' familiarity with printed materials), and Early Grade Reading Assessments (EGRA) including letter recognition, word recognition, and text reading.[2]

The study drew samples of 24 schools in Ethiopia, 26 in Guatemala, 33 in Honduras, and 23 in Nepal. In Ethiopia, 15 of the schools were community schools, and nine were government schools, of which six control schools received no support from Save the Children. In Guatemala, the sample included 26 schools. In Honduras, the sample included 33 schools. In Nepal, the study included 23 schools.

Findings

How well do schools provide allocated and engaged time?

To measure and compare allocated and engaged time, we used a set of ten factors. Allocated time is captured by the first factor: the percentage of days school is open. This factor is based on the official length of the school year and accounts for days a school is closed when it should be open. Teacher and student attendance (factors two and three) allow us to account for time available on only those days when teachers and students are present. The fourth factor accounts for time lost in the management of the school day: school starting late, recess, interruptions, and other time when students and teachers are not in classrooms together. The fifth factor is the percentage of time students are on task during observed classroom lessons. All five of these factors are then combined to estimate the equivalent percentage of allocated time that students are engaged in instructional activities with their teachers (factor six).

The other factors include measures that indicate how time is used, including the percentage of students with access to a language textbook (factor seven), the percentage of classroom observations during which students were seen using a textbook (factor eight), and the percentage of students observed to be engaged in any reading activity (factor nine).

Oral fluency of Grade 3 students is the final factor. Table 13.1 summarizes the average values of each of the ten factors for the sample schools in each country. Sample schools in all cases were open on average over 90 percent of the time, and teacher and student attendance rates are fairly high. Only a small portion of allocated time is lost due to factors one through three. However, other factors do lower the provision of instructional time. In Guatemala, sample schools on average used only 72 percent of the available day for instruction. Additional time is lost when student time-on-task (engaged time) in class is taken into account. In Nepal and Guatemala, students are on-task only 60 and 59 percent of the time, respectively. In Honduras, students were on-task 56

Table 13.1 Sample School Averages for Time, Time-Use, and Reading-Related Factors

Factor	1	2	3	4	5	6	7	8	9	10
	% Days school is open	teacher attend. rate	student attend. rate	% of day used	% time-on-task	% equiv days for instruct.	% students w/ text	% students obs using text	% time students obs read	oral reading fluency (wpm)
Nepal	90%	91%		92%	60%	45%	84%	14%	12%	26
Ethiopia	93%	89%	97%		41%	33%	83%	4%	3%	18
Guatemala	97%	88%	92%	72%	59%	33%	63%	3%	11%	46
Honduras	93%	94%	97%	82%	56%	30%	63%	20%	15%	66

Note[1]: 63 percent reflects Grade 3 only.

percent of the time while in Ethiopia they were on-task only 41 percent of the time.

When time loss due to factors of school closure, teacher and student absence, time lost during the day, and off-task students during lessons are combined, schools on average used less than 50 percent of the equivalent available time (in days) for instruction. Ethiopia and Nepal were better than Honduras or Guatemala at ensuring that schools had language textbooks. However, students were observed using those books for a very small percentage of the time. Students were also observed reading in class only for 15 percent or less of the observation time in all the countries. Oral reading fluency scores in the languages of instruction in Ethiopia, Guatemala, and Nepal were low, while students were clearly better oral readers (in Spanish) in Honduras.

How Does Allocated Time Compare to Engaged Time?

To answer this question, this study compares the combined effect of factors one through five to determine the equivalent number of days of engaged instruction as compared to the total number of days officially allocated in the school year. The official school year in Guatemala is 180 days, in Nepal, 192 days, in Honduras, 200 days, and in Ethiopia, 203 days. All four countries have above average total allocated hours of instruction when compared to the regional averages of 789 (Latin America and the Caribbean), 665 (South and West Asia), and 809 (Sub-Saharan Africa) for Grades 1 through 3 (Benavot 2004).

In all four countries, no school in the sample was open on every day that it should have been. Figure 13.1 summarizes the ways by which time is lost during the school year and shows how it erodes the potential time available for opportunity to learn.

In Guatemala, instruction occurs on only the equivalent of 56 out of 180 possible days. In Honduras, an equivalent of 78 out of the possible 200 days of instruction are being used. In Ethiopia, the equivalent of 69 out of 203 days are being used for instruction (which would be lower if on-time lost data during the school day were available). In Nepal, the equivalent of 87 out of 192 days are being used for instruction (which would be lower if student attendance data were available).

In addition to comparing the time-related factors to the total potential time for instruction, data on the percentage of observations during which children were seen to be reading also sheds light on the actual versus allocated instructional time. In all cases, the percentage of observations that included students reading any written materials (including from the blackboard) was less than 15 percent.

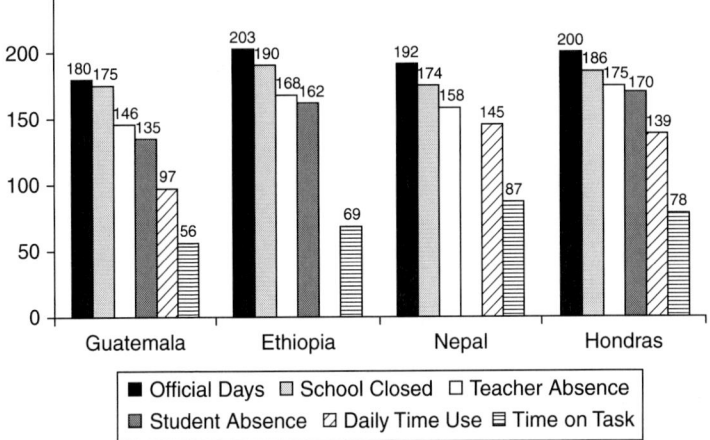

Figure 13.1   Equivalent Days of Schooling Available for Teaching and Learning

How Do Time Factors Vary Across Schools?

More significant than the average values is the variation in time availability and use across schools in each country. The factors impacting time
availability and the observed patterns of time-use vary considerably, as
shown in figure 13.2.

Factor One: The Percentage of Days School is Open

In Ethiopia, no school in the sample was open every day. Many schools
initiated the school year after the official start date, and most were also
closed for additional days during the year. At least two of the 26 schools
were open less than 90 percent of the days available for instruction. One
school had been closed for almost all of the first three months.

Guatemala has the lowest range of variation. Some schools were
open every day, and one was open on only 90 percent of the days. In
Guatemala, schools were most often closed due to training days for teachers or unplanned holidays. School closures in Guatemala tended to follow
a similar pattern to other countries in the region, where days lost to school
closings ranged from a high of 6.3 in Paraguay to a low of 1.3 in Uruguay[3]
(Zhang et al. 2008).

In Honduras, 50 percent of principals interviewed reported beginning
the school year, on average, five days after the official start date. Schools
most often reported being closed around teachers' pay day, for strikes, and

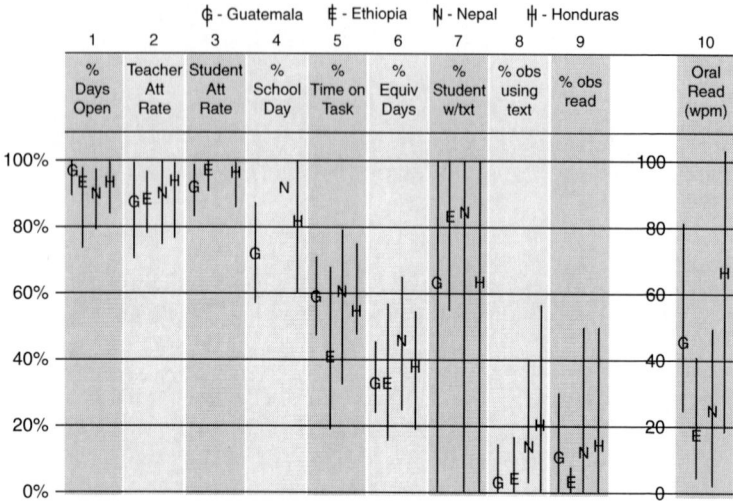

Figure 13.2 Time, Use of Time, and Reading: Variation Across Sample Schools

for teacher training. On the day of the observations, 40 percent of the schools in Honduras reported that they had already lost over two weeks of school due to unofficial closings.

Similar to the other cases, no school in Nepal was open every day, and the number of days schools were closed ranged from as few as four to as many as 39 days. At least eight of the 23 schools were open less than 90 percent of the days available for instruction.

Factor Two: Teacher Attendance

In Ethiopia, teachers had an average attendance rate of 89 percent on days school was open. Three schools had teacher attendance of 70 to 80 percent, nine had teacher attendance of 80 to 90 percent, and nine had attendance rates above 90 percent.

In Guatemala, teacher attendance data were difficult to obtain. Generally, average absenteeism rates had to be estimated based on the principal log books and student absenteeism logs. On average, across the 26 schools in Guatemala, teachers were absent two days per month, which equates to an average attendance rate of roughly 88 percent. Some schools had perfect teacher attendance (at least based on the available records), while some had attendance rates as low as 68 to 80 percent.

In Honduras, teacher attendance data were obtained from official school records maintained by the principals and cross-referenced with data obtained from student attendance books maintained by teachers. On average, across the 33 schools, teachers were absent 12 days per year. Only two schools had attendance rates below 90 percent while 15 had teacher attendance of 95 percent and higher.

In Nepal, we were unable to obtain official records for teacher attendance. However, principals were asked to report on teacher attendance during the previous week, which was used to calculate a rough estimate of what teacher attendance rates would be for the entire school year. On average, these estimates showed that teachers had an attendance rate of 91 percent. Two schools had teacher attendance rates below 80 percent, and five others had rates between 80 and 90 percent.

Factor Three: Student Attendance

In Ethiopia, students in most schools were present more than 90 percent of the time. Only one school had an official record of attendance lower than 90 percent. However, during classroom observations the attendance was spot-checked and it often revealed a higher rate of absenteeism than recorded in the official register.

In Guatemala there is considerably more variation in student attendance rates. The data collected indicate that, across the sample schools, students were present an average of 92 percent of the time. The relatively high average student attendance rate could be due to the schools' close proximity to students' homes. Most students traveled only 15 to 18 minutes to school.

Student attendance rates in Honduras were similar to those found in Ethiopia. On average, students were present 97 percent of the school year. Only two schools had attendance rates lower than 90 percent and 14 schools had attendance rates between 99 and 100 percent. The adjusted school schedule in rural areas may account for such high attendance rates.

Factor Four: Percentage of the School Day Available for Instruction

The percentage of the school day available for instruction takes into account the noninstructional components of the school day, such as recess. It also explicitly recognizes that often school does not start on time, may close early, or has instructional time interrupted for a variety of reasons (e.g., the teacher or students are outside the classroom). This study was only able to systematically collect data on the loss of instructional time during the school day in Guatemala, Honduras, and Nepal.

In Guatemala, students and teachers were regularly observed arriving late to school. Additionally, recess often ran longer than the time allocated. On average, schools in the study made use of only 72 percent of the school day, with wide variation across schools. One school made use of only 57 percent of the day, and eight others used only about two-thirds of the available time. These numbers represent huge losses in effective engaged time.

In Honduras, schools often began on time but then took multiple breaks during the day, including both a recess and a lunch break, the timing and length of which varied from 30 minutes to two hours. A number of schools did not give a lunch break because the government had not yet distributed the provisions needed to prepare student lunches. Schools also ended the day at varying times, with classes often being cut short to accommodate parent meetings, bus schedules, or lack of material. On average, Honduran schools in the study used only 80 percent of the available day, with a wide amount of variation. One school made use of 100 percent of the day, compensating for recess with an extra 30 minutes of class, while seven only used 70 percent of available time. Data on this factor for Nepal only accounts for the programmed time for recess (30 minutes each day), leaving 92 percent of the day available for instruction.

Factor Five: Percentage of Student Time-on-Task

Measured time-on-task refers to the engaged time that students pay attention to materials with instructional goals. In all cases, the overall equivalent time lost due to any other factors is small compared to the loss of time when students are off task. The variation in the percentage of time-on-task in all four countries is broad, but the range is widest in Ethiopia and Nepal. One school in Ethiopia averaged almost 70 percent of student time-on-task during a lesson, while others were below 20 percent. In Nepal, two schools were almost at 80 percent of student time-on-task, but one had as little as 33 percent. Time-on-task in Honduras ranged from 47 to 75 percent. In Guatemala, the range was much smaller—between 47 and 71 percent.

Students were on average more likely to be engaged in noninstructional activities than any single on-task activity. In all four countries, students were off-task between 40 and 58 percent of the time. Ethiopia had the largest percentage of students observed in off-task activities. Most often these students socialized with others or simply did not participate in the learning activity. In Ethiopia, on-task students were mainly engaged in activities involving demonstration and practice and drill, while in Guatemala and Honduras more students were observed doing seat-work. In Nepal, students, on average, were observed copying or doing seatwork. In addition to calculating the overall percentage of students observed to be on-task, the study also looked at patterns in students' behavior when the teacher was on-task or off-task. When the teacher was involved in a learning activity, greater percentages of students were on-task as well. When teachers were observed to be off-task, students were much less likely to be engaged in learning activities.

Factor Six: Equivalent Percentage of Days Available for Instruction

This study revealed that, on average, only the equivalent of 69 out of 203 days are used for instruction in Ethiopia, 56 out of 180 in Guatemala, 78 out of 200 in Honduras, and 87 out of 190 in Nepal (although the days used in Ethiopia and Nepal would be fewer if data were available for time lost during the day and student attendance, respectively). This study also uncovered considerable variation across schools in how the time-related factors combine to determine an equivalent percentage of days each school makes available for instruction. In Nepal and Guatemala, some schools had as much as double the equivalent number of days available for instruction compared to others. In Ethiopia, the schools that best ensure time is available for instruction have three times the equivalent available days than those that do not. In Honduras, some schools provide up to four times the number of equivalent instructional days than other schools.

Factor Seven: Percentage of Students with a Textbook

Language textbooks are readily available for students in Grades 1, 2, and 3 in most schools. On average, eight to ten schools provide over 75 percent of students with a language textbook, and five to six schools in each of the countries have textbooks for every student. In Guatemala, six schools in the sample have no language textbooks for students in Grades 1 through 3, and one school in both Honduras and Nepal similarly lack this important resource. Although most classrooms in Honduras had some textbooks available, less than 50 percent of students had exercise books, which are an integral part of the national curriculum teachers are supposed to follow.

Factor Eight: Percentage of Observed Use of Textbooks

A higher percentage of students were observed using textbooks in Honduras than in Ethiopia, Guatemala, or Nepal. Figure 13.3 combines factors seven and eight to show how textbook availability and textbook use interrelate in the schools studied. The vertical axis plots the percentage of observations during which textbook use was noted and the horizontal axis plots

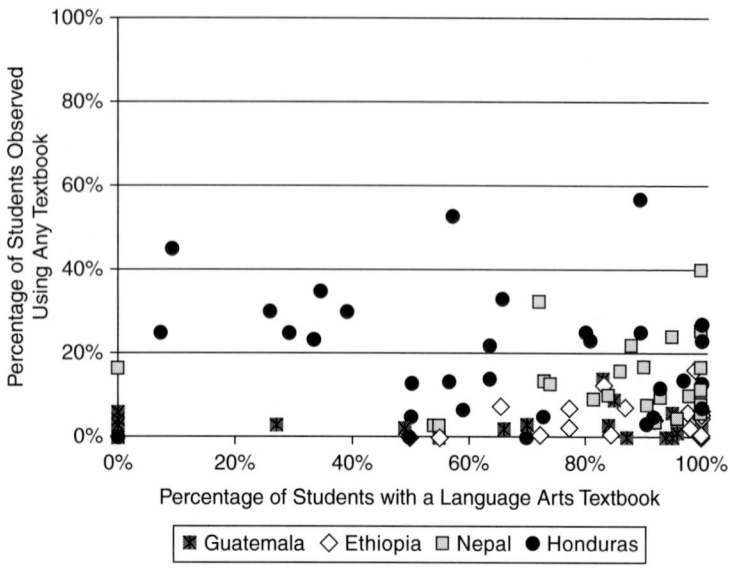

Figure 13.3   Percentage of Students Observed Using a Textbook for a Given Level of Textbook Availability

the percentage of students with a language arts textbook. Each data point represents a school.

Most data points cluster in the lower right-hand portion of the graph. This indicates that high language arts textbook availability in a school is associated with relatively low observed textbook use. All of the outliers (i.e., schools with higher than average textbook use for a given level of textbook availability) are schools in Honduras.

Factor Nine: Percentage of Time Spent Reading

Classroom observations revealed that reading instruction is almost nonexistent. Students were rarely observed reading aloud, reading silently, or interpreting text. In addition, no country had an official curriculum for teaching reading and there were no observations of a structured approach to reading. Ethiopian schools provided the least amount of engaged class time for reading activities on average. Honduras and Nepal were much better, averaging about 40 minutes per day for different reading activities. Obviously, students cannot be reading or engaged in academic content 100 percent of the time (Stallings 1980), but the potential opportunity to practice reading is part of academic learning time and should include more than such a small fraction of each school day. In Ethiopia, for example, in a four-hour school day, 3 percent of the time equates to about seven minutes of reading per day. Achieving automatized reading processes requires extensive practice with books and phonics (Abadzi 2009). Such low amounts of daily practice therefore may explain the low levels of fluency in Ethiopia.

Factor Ten: Reading Fluency

Reading ability is both an outcome of opportunity to learn and a critical factor determining whether students can continue to learn and advance through school.

Given the lack of focus on engaged time and more specifically on reading and reading instruction, it was not surprising to find low reading performance among Grade 3 students. In Honduras, where the highest percentage of reading activities were observed, students' overall reading performance surpassed that of students in the other three countries. While each country's average number of words read per minute by students provides a general idea of reading levels, this number masks the enormously wide range of reading abilities. Students in all four countries were reading at many different rates.

In Nepal, the majority of students either could not read at all (44 percent) or were able to read more than 40 wpm (38 percent). In Ethiopia, very few students read more than 40 wpm, the largest percentage (36 percent) could not read at all, and not a single student was able to read more than 70 wpm. The reading scores of students in Guatemala were more evenly distributed. Very few children could not read (4 percent), there were only 8 percent who could read only 1 to 20 wpm, and almost half the sample (46 percent) could read more than 50 wpm. Guatemalan students in the study averaged 47 wpm, but school averages ranged from 25 wpm to 82 wpm.

Students in Honduras were, on average, the strongest readers in the sample: the average reading score for the sample was 66 wpm. Similar to Guatemala, there were few children (8 percent) who could not read, and only 3 percent more could read only 1 to 20 wpm. The largest share of students, over 48 percent, was able to read at least 70 wpm, and 27 percent could read above 90 wpm.

Neurocognitive research conducted by Abadzi (2008) suggests that all students should be able to decode by the end of Grade 1; all Grade 2 students should be able to read at least 60 wpm; and by Grade 6 all students should be able to easily read 120 to 150 wpm and provide summaries of the passage. In the Arabic script languages, all students should be able to read effectively within one to two years of beginning instruction.

Conclusions and Policy Implications:Relationships among Time Variables and Student Outcomes

Numerous studies suggest that, across developing countries, a great deal of existing allocated and engaged time is lost due to nonacademic activities that take place in the classroom (Hollowood et al. 1994; Benavot and Amadio 2004; Abadzi, 2007a; 2007b; 2009). The literature further supports improvements in the use of existing time as a more effective, and cost-effective, way to improve time-use within the existing allocation (Aronsen et al. 1998; Berliner 1990; Abadzi 2007a; 2007b; 2009).

The analysis of cases from these countries provides useful insights into the relationship between schools, instruction, and learning: namely, that unless there is a minimum amount of engaged instruction, then we should not expect to find a relationship between engaged time and learning. Moreover, there is a great deal of engaged time to be gained from improving the use of existing time in classrooms rather than adding more time to the school day. Across all four studies, schools vary in how regularly teachers attend, how regularly students attend, whether there are enough textbooks, more importantly, whether the textbooks are used, and how much time children spend reading in class.

Schools in Ethiopia, Guatemala, Honduras, and Nepal used, on average, less than half the available allocated and engaged time. This loss of time was due primarily to students and teachers being off-task for significant amounts of time during classroom lessons. The study further finds that students being off-task is directly tied to teachers being off-task. In all cases, when teachers were on-task, greater percentages of students were also on-task. In addition, students lost between 30 and 75 days of instruction due to school closures, teacher and student absenteeism, and time lost to late start and extended recess.

Policymakers need to distinguish between the relatively easy-to-address factors and those that require more complicated policy interventions. Factors such as school closures, absenteeism, and daily time loss are more easily corrected than time-on-task, teacher training, and quality support services. Based on the results of this study, ensuring that schools were open 100 percent of the allocated time and that teachers were present on those days would add the equivalent of an additional 35 days of instruction in Ethiopia, 34 days in Guatemala, 25 days in Honduras, and 34 days in Nepal. In Guatemala, ensuring that the schools open on time and that recess is kept to 30 minutes would add an additional 50 days of instructional time that students and teachers could use on learning activities. Even if the quality of instruction were held constant, it is likely that this increase in time for learning would help improve student outcomes.

While there are trade-offs and political challenges to these implications, it is important that we as educators look at concrete ways to increase the amount of time that teachers and students spend engaged and learning in the classroom. As cited above, much time can be gained by simply ensuring that schools take advantage of all the allocated time. Beyond full use of the allocated time, teachers need to be monitored and supported to ensure that students spend more time within the allocated time engaged and focused on learning and in practicing reading.

Notes

1. These case studies were made possible by the generous support of the American people through the United States Agency for International Development (USAID) under Cooperative Agreement No. GDG-A-00-03-00008-00. The contents are the responsibility of the Academy for Educational Development through the Educational Quality Improvement Program 2 (EQUIP2) and do not necessarily reflect the views of USAID or the United States Government.

    In addition to the authors, contributors include Amy Jo Dowd (Save the Children USA), Margaret Meagher (CARE), Dr. Conrad Wesley Snyder, Nawsheen Elaheebocus, Elliott Freidlander, Eva Grajeda, and the Save the Children field offices in Ethiopia, Guatemala, and Nepal, as well as the CARE Honduras office. We would like to thank the CARE and the Save the Children field offices for their support in the development and completion of these case studies.

2. EGRA provides a methodology for quickly assessing a variety of early literacy skills. It uses oral reading fluency as a measure of overall literacy. The EdData II project in particular has been instrumental in promoting and improving the use of EGRA and has its application in more than 20 countries. See Jukes, Banu Vagh, and Kim (2006) for research on the reliability of EGRA as a tool for evaluating literacy acquisition.

3. Zhang (2008) provides data that shows days lost for Grade 4 pupils in public schools on average: Argentina (6 days); Brazil (2.6 days); Paraguay (6.3 days); Peru (4.5 days); and Uruguay (1.3 days).

References

Abadzi, Helen. 2007a. "Absenteeism and Beyond: Instructional Time Loss and Consequences." Policy Research Working Paper No. 4376. Washington, DC: World Bank.

————. 2007b. "Instructional Time Loss and Local-Level Governance." *Prospects* 37 (1): 13–16.

Abadzi, Helen. 2009. "Instructional Time Loss in Developing Countries: Concepts, Measurement, and Implications." *World Bank Research Observer* 24 (2): 267–290.

Anderson, Maria Elena. 2001. "Guatemala the Education Sector." Guatemala Poverty Assessment (GUAPA) Program, Technical Paper No. 2. Washington, DC: World Bank.

Aronson, Julia, Joy Zimmerman, and Lisa Carlos. 1998. *Improving Student Achievement by Extending School: Is It Just a Matter of Time?* Paper presented at the PACE Media/ Education Writers Seminar, San Francisco, April 20, 1998.

Benavot, Aaron, and Massimo Amadio. 2005. "A Global Study of Intended Instructional Time and Official School Curricula, 1980–2000." Paper commissioned for the *Education for All Global Monitoring Report 2005, The Quality Imperative.* Geneva: UNESCO International Bureau of Education.

Berliner, David. 1990. "What's All the Fuss About Instructional Time?" In The *Nature of Time in Schools. Theoretical Concepts, Practitioner Perceptions,* ed. M. Ben-Peretz and R. Bromme. New York: Teachers College Press.

Bloom, Benjamin. 1968. "Learning for Mastery." *UCLA Evaluation Comment* 1 (2): 1–8.

Brophy, Jere, and Thomas Good. 1986. "Teacher Behavior and Student Achievement." In *The Handbook of Research on Teaching* (3rd ed.), ed. M. C. Wittrock. New York: Macmillan.

CARE. 2009. *Care's Work in Guatemala.* Atlanta: CARE. Available online at: http://www.care.org.

Carrol, John B. 1963. "A Model of School Learning." *Teachers College Record* 64 (8): 723–733.

CIA. 2009. *The World Factbook: Guatemala.* Washington, DC: CIA. Available online at: https://www.cia.gov.

Clay, Mary. 2000. *Concepts about Print: What Have Children Learned about the Way We Print Language?* Portsmouth, NH: Heinemann.

Edwards, John. 2002. "Education and Poverty in Guatemala." Guatemala Poverty Assessment (GUAPA) Program, Technical Paper No. 3. Washington, DC: World Bank.

EQUIP2. 2008. *Framework for School Effectiveness Research.* Washington, DC: EQUIP2, AED, and USAID.

Fisher, Douglas. 2009. "The Use of Instructional Time in the Typical High School Classroom." *The Education Forum* 73 (2): 168–176.

Gettinger, Maribeth. 1984. "Individual Differences in Time Needed for Learning: A Review of the Literature." *Education Psychologist* 19 (1): 15–19.

Gillies, John, and Jessica Jester-Quijada. 2008. *Opportunity to Learn: A High Impact Strategy for Improving Educational Outcomes in Developing Countries.* Washington DC: EQUIP2, AED, and USAID.

Greenwood, Charles. 1991. "Longitudinal Analysis of Time, Engagement, and Academic Achievement in At-risk and Non-risk Students." *Exceptional Children* 57 (6): 521–535.

Hollowood, Tia, Christine Salisbury, Beverly Rainforth, and Mary Palombaro. 1995. "Use of Instructional Time in Classrooms Serving Students With and Without Severe Disabilities." *Exceptional Children* 61 (3): 242–253.

Holsinger, Donald B. 1982. "Time, Content and Expectations as Predictors of School Achievement in the US and other Developing Countries: A Review of IEA Evidence." Paper presented at a Meeting of the National Commission on Excellence in Education, New York, September 28, 1982.

Hossler, Carol-Anne, Frances Stage, and Karen Gallagher. 1988. "The Relationship of Increased Instructional Time to Student Achievement." Policy Bulletin No. 1. Bloomington, IN: Consortium on Educational Policy Studies.

Jukes, Matthew, Shaher Banu Vagh, and Young-Suk Kim. 2006. *Developing Measures of Reading Ability and Classroom Behaviour for Use in Multi-country Evaluations*. Washington, DC: World Bank.

Karweit, Nancy. 1985. "Should We Lengthen the School Term?" *Educational Researcher* 14 (6): 9–15.

Levin, Henry M. 1984. *Clocking Instruction: A Reform Whose Time Has Come?* Palo Alto: The California Institute for Research on Educational Finance and Governance, quoted in Joshua Aronson. 1995. *Stop the Clock: Ending the Tyranny of Time in Education*. San Francisco: Far West Laboratory.

Lowe, Robert, and Robert Gervais. 1988. "Increasing Instructional Time in Today's Classroom." *NASSP Bulletin* 72 (19): 19–22.

Massachusetts 2020. 2005. *Time for a Change: The Promise of Extended-Time Schools for Promoting Student Achievement*. Boston: Massachusetts 2020.

Moore, Mary, and Janie Funkhouser. 1990. *More Time to Learn: Extended Time Strategies for Chapter 1 Students*. Washington, DC: Decision Resources Corp.

Nelson, Steve. 1990. *Instructional Time as a Factor in Increasing Student Achievement*. Washington, DC: Office of Educational Research and Improvement.

Quartarola, Bob. 1984. *A Research Paper on Time on Task and the Extended School Day/Year and Their Relationship to Improving Student Achievement*. Burlingame, CA: Association of California School Administrators.

Save the Children. 2006. *Metodología del Programa de Educación*. Guatemala City: Save the Children USA.

———. 2009. *Guatemala*. Westport, CT: Save the Children. Available online at: http://www.savethechildren.org.

Stallings, Jane. 1978. "The Development of the Contextual Observation System." Paper presented at the Annual Meeting of the American Educational Research Association, Ontario, March 27–31, 1978.

———. 1980. "Allocated Academic Learning Time Revisited, or Beyond Time on Task." *Educational Researcher* 9 (11): 11–16.

Stallings, Jane, and David Kaskowitz. 1974. *Follow Through Classroom Observation Evaluation*. Washington, DC: Office of Education.

Stallings, Jane, and H. Jerome Freiberg. 1991. "Observation for the Improvement of Teaching." In *Effective Teaching: Current Research*, ed. H. Waxman and H. Walberg. Berkeley, CA: McCutchan Publishing Corporation.

UNESCO. 2006. *Education Counts: Benchmarking Progress in 19 WEI Countries*. Montreal: UNSECO.

264   SCHUH MOORE, DESTEFANO, AND ADELMAN

UNESCO. 2009. *Overcoming Inequality: Why Governance Matters. EFA Global Monitoring Report.* Paris: UNESCO.

UNESCO, and LLECE. 2008. *Los aprendizajes de los estudiantes de América Latina y el Caribe. Resumen Ejecutivo del Primer Reporte de Resultados del Segundo Estudio Regional Comparativo y Explicativo.* Santiago: UNESCO and LLECE.

Virginia Department of Education. 1992. *Instructional Time and Student Learning: A Study of the School Calendar and Instructional Time.* Richmond: Virginia Department of Education.

Zhang, Yanhong, Neville Postlehwaite, and Aletta Grisay, eds. 2008. *A View Inside Primary Schools.* Montreal: UNESCO.

Contributors

Elizabeth Adelman is a Research and Program Officer at the Academy for Educational Development (AED). She has more than eight years of experience working in the area of international education and development and has spent considerable time working throughout Latin America. In her current research, she is a collaborating partner on a study of the opportunities to learn and school-effectiveness in Guatemala, Honduras, Nepal, and Ethiopia for the Education Quality Improvement Program 2 (EQUIP2). Adelman coled the EQUIP2 field research in Guatemala as well as the research team in Honduras. Before joining AED, Adelman lived in Chile for eight years, where she founded and ran her own independent English language training program. She obtained her MA in International Education Policy from the Harvard University School of Education, and her BA in Comparative Literature and Spanish from Haverford College.

Albert Byamugisha is Commissioner of Monitoring and Evaluation in the Uganda Office of the Prime Minister. Prior to this position, he served as the Assistant Commissioner in charge of Statistics, Research, Monitoring, and Evaluation in the Education Planning and Policy Department of the Uganda Ministry of Education and Sports, as well as the Uganda National Southern and Eastern Africa Consortium for Monitoring Education Quality (SACMEQ) Research Coordinator, National EFA Coordinator, and as a Lecturer of Statistical Methods at the Makerere University Institute of Statistics and Applied Economics (from 1993 to 2000). He has excellent planning skills in designing and implementing the Education Management Information System. He is the coauthor of the book titled *With Africa for Africa: Towards Quality Education for All*, which was a 1999 MLA Project. He holds a Postgraduate Diploma in Pure Science and Master's of Science (Statistics) obtained from Sheffield University, United Kingdom. He is currently a PhD Candidate at the Graduate School of International Cooperation Studies (GSICS), Kobe University, Japan.

Elizabeth A. Cassity is a Lecturer and Research Fellow in the Faculty of Education and Social Work, University of Sydney. Since 2007, she has conducted research on the major Australian Research Council Linkage grant "AusAID at Work: The Design, Delivery and Impact of Australian Aid to Education in Asia and the Pacific." She graduated with a PhD in Comparative and International Education from Columbia University, New York, in 2001, and shortly afterward moved to Sydney. Her PhD focused on Australia's impact on the development of higher education in the Pacific in the latter part of the twentieth century. She has published in the fields of foreign aid and international educational development, policy studies, and youth transition. She was a researcher at the Centre for Cultural Research, University of Western Sydney. She has also worked as a Research Analyst on public school reform with the Academy for Educational Development in New York, and prior to commencing graduate studies she was a teacher in northern Namibia.

Luis Crouch, who earned his PhD at the University of California, Berkeley, in 1981, is Vice President of RTI's International Development Group. His areas of specialization include social sector finance, policy reform, and the political economy of social sector development. Crouch has worked on all aspects of policy analysis research and implementation—from field surveys to quantitative and qualitative analysis, to policy dialogue presentations at the Cabinet level. His interests include educational economics and planning, research and information use, and the presentation of research results for policy debate, including the importance of early grade reading (EGRA), Education Reform Support, and the use of quality indicators to supplement access indicators. He has experience in more than 15 countries, focusing especially on Latin America, South Africa, and Southeast Asia. From 1996 to 1998, he served as resident advisor to the Department of Education, South Africa, on financial reforms in the education sector. Prior to working at RTI he was a Lead Education Economist at the World Bank.

Joseph DeStefano is a Senior Education Research Analyst with the Research Triangle Institute (RTI International). He has 25 years of experience working on education improvement and reform internationally and in urban school districts in the United States. Joe currently does research and supports projects in numerous countries in Africa, Asia, and the Middle East. He is also currently one of the principle investigators on a USAID-funded study of opportunity to learn and school-effectiveness in Ethiopia, Guatemala, Nepal, Honduras, and Mozambique for the EQUIP2. Joe helped lead another EQUIP2 study of community-based, complementary approaches to basic education in ten countries. Joe was born in New York and secured his first teaching job in the Bronx, not far from where he grew up. He also served as a math and physics teacher in the Peace Corps in Zaire. Joe now lives in Cleveland Heights, Ohio, with his wife and two daughters.

Hana Addam El-Ghali received her PhD in 2011 in the program of Social and Comparative Analysis in Education from the University of Pittsburgh. El-Ghali is a Program Coordinator at the Institute for International Studies in Education at the School of Education. Her background is in Education, both teaching and administrative. She earned her Bachelor of Arts in Elementary Education, a diploma in Educational Management and Leadership, and a Master's of Arts in Educational Administration and Policy Studies in Lebanon at the American University of Beirut. Before pursuing her doctoral studies, El-Ghali taught English as a second language at two local schools in Beirut. Her research interests are in Comparative, International, and Developing Education (CIDE), particularly in higher education in developing countries. Currently, El-Ghali is working on several research projects looking at higher education and youth unemployment in Lebanon and the Middle East.

Amber K. Gove is Senior Education Researcher at RTI International. Much of her recent work has centered on the development of the Early Grade Reading Assessment, a diagnostic tool for understanding students' foundation skills in reading. To date, EGRA has been used in more than 50 countries and languages to inform policy and improve instruction. Gove has more than a dozen years of experience collaborating with government counterparts in Africa and Latin America in project design, evaluation, and policy dialogue. Her research interests include measurement and improvement of student learning; education finance; conditional cash transfer programs; and factors affecting achievement, enrollment, and attendance. As a Fulbright Scholar, she conducted a study of more than 1,000 families to assess the impact of Brazil's conditional cash transfer program (*Bolsa Escola*) on student attendance and achievement. Gove obtained her PhD in Education and Master's degree in Economics from Stanford University and will complete a Certificate in Literacy Instruction at George Washington University in 2011.

John N. Hawkins is Professor Emeritus and former Chair of the Social Science and Comparative Education Division of the Graduate School of Education and Information Studies at the University of California, Los Angeles (UCLA). He is also Director of the Center for International and Development Studies, an organized research center focusing on global trends in higher education. He served for 12 years as UCLA's Dean of International Studies. He is an author of several books and research articles on education and development in Asia. He has conducted research throughout Asia since 1966 when he first visited the People's Republic of China.

W. James Jacob is Director of the Institute for International Studies in Education at the University of Pittsburgh's School of Education and is the former Assistant Director of the Center for International and Development Education at UCLA. His research focuses on program design, implementation, and evaluation; HIV/AIDS multisectoral capacity building and prevention; and higher education organizational analysis in developing countries with geographic emphases in Africa, East and Southeast Asia, and the Pacific Islands. He has authored a number of articles and books and serves as Coeditor of Palgrave Macmillan's *International and Development Education* Book Series, Sense Publishers' *Pittsburgh Studies in Comparative and International Education* Book Series, and as Associate Editor of the journal *Excellence in Higher Education*.

Xuehong Liao is a doctoral student in Comparative and International Education at UCLA. During her tenure at UCLA she has served as a Teaching Assistant and as a Coadministrative Director of the Center for International and Development Education. She is presently writing her dissertation, which deals with general education reform in two Chinese universities.

Ka-Ho Mok is Associate Vice President (External Relations) and Dean of Faculty of Arts and Sciences of the Hong Kong Institute of Education (HKIED). Before joining HKIED, he was Associate Dean and Professor of Social Policy, Faculty of Social Sciences, University of Hong Kong. He is now Visiting Professor of the Graduate Education and Centre for East Asian Studies, University of Bristol, UK. He also served as Associate Dean of Faculty of Humanities and Social Science at City University of Hong Kong before taking up the position at the University of Bristol. Mok obtained his doctorate degree from the London School of Economics and Political Science, University of London. He has published extensively in the fields of comparative education policy, policy studies, and governance and social development in contemporary China and East Asia. He has also worked with UNICEF and the World Bank as an international consultant.

Audrey-Marie Schuh Moore is Deputy Director of AED's EQUIP2, sharing responsibility for all project activities, including management and technical leadership. She is responsible for research, evaluation, project development, design, and implementation activities on a $350 million portfolio. Moore has more than 12 years of experience in educational development, particularly in the areas of evaluation, economic analysis, micro finance, secondary education and school to career in Latin America, Africa, the Middle East, Asia, and the United States. She has led research work on quantifying the secondary education teacher gap and coled the research efforts under EQUIP2 that looked at opportunities to learn, school-effectiveness, and community-based approaches to organizing primary schools. She is also an Adjunct Faculty member at Georgetown University and has taught at the primary school levels. She received her PhD in Educational Policy and Administration from the University of Minnesota. Moore resides in Northern Virginia with her husband and twin sons.

Christopher B. Mugimu obtained his BSc (1985) and PGDE (1988) from Makerere University in Uganda, and his MEd (2001) and PhD in Education (2004) from Brigham Young University. He is currently a Senior Lecturer in the Department of Curriculum, Teaching, and Media at the School of Education, Makerere University. His research interests are on international development education, higher education, contemporary curricula issues, and entrepreneurship.

Deane Neubauer is Senior Consultant to the Education Program at the University of Hawai'i, Manoa's East-West Center. Educated at the University of California, Riverside (BA) and Yale University (MA, PhD), Neubauer has taught at the University of California (Berkeley and Irvine), Waikato University (NZ), and served as a distinguished external faculty affiliate to the School of Health Science, University of Sydney. From 1970 to 2004 he taught in the Department of Political Science, University of Hawai'i, Manoa. His research interests lie in health policy, political economy, education, and globalization. His work explores globalization phenomena as a major vector of social change throughout the world. In 1980, he became the founding Dean of the College of Social Sciences at the University of Hawai'i, a position he held through August 1988. In 1999 he served as the founding Director of the Globalization Research Center at the University of Hawai'i, Manoa (UHM), and subsequently as founding Executive Director of the Globalization Research Network, a four-university collaboration. He served as Interim Chancellor of UHM from July 2001 to August 2002 and as Interim Vice President for Academic Affairs for the University of Hawai'i System from September 2001 to July 2004. In August 2004 he became Professor Emeritus of Political Science at UHM. Neubauer has also been active in the field of higher education accreditation for over 20 years.

Mikiko Nishimura was an Associate Professor at the Graduate School of International Cooperation Studies, Kobe University, until March 2009 and is currently an Associate Professor at the International Christian University in Tokyo. She has worked extensively in education planning and research in Sub-Saharan Africa (SSA) and lived in Kenya and Uganda as an Associate Specialist of Japan International Cooperation Agency (JICA). As a researcher and freelance consultant, she was involved in project formulation, implementation, and evaluation in education and poverty alleviation in various countries in Asia, Africa, and Latin America. Her research interest lies in empirical studies on education reforms and issues of institutionalized disparities and stratification in education. She has recently led a research team to conduct a study on UPE policy in SSA, endowed by the Ministry of Education, Culture, Sports, Science and Technology of Japan. She obtained her MPhil (Development Studies) from the University of Sussex and an EdD (International Educational Development) from Columbia University.

Maureen K. Porter, an anthropologist of education, holds a PhD from Stanford University and has studied at the University of Wisconsin-Madison and the University of Freiburg im Breisgau (Germany). She does research on the social construction of identity and situated learning within communities of practice. Her engaged scholarship in schools and neighborhoods takes place in five contexts: expanding feminist critiques of gender and culturally-responsive leadership, developing place-based and culturally-inclusive pedagogy, designing meaningful community rituals and events involving youth, sponsoring collaborative, intercultural service-learning exchanges, and cultivating best practices in aesthetic education and arts-based research design. She is an Associate Professor at the University of Pittsburgh, where she served for many years as the coordinator of the graduate program in Social and Comparative Analysis of Education. She teaches sets of courses in anthropology and education and qualitative research methods. She anchors the Gender Studies Certificate, offering graduate seminars in both Gender and Education as well as Gender, Education, and International Development.

Val D. Rust is Professor of Education at UCLA. He was recently the Director of the UCLA International Education Office, the head of the Social Sciences and Comparative Education Division in the Department of Education, and the Associate Director of the Center for International and Development Education. He has served as the President of the Comparative and International Education Society.

Connie Ssebbunga-Masembe is Dean of the College of Education at Makerere University. He is a specialist in Applied Linguistics and Teaching English as a Second Language, and he holds an MPhil and PhD. He has spent 25 years teaching English Language and Literature in English at the primary school, high school, undergraduate, and postgraduate levels in

Uganda. He has also taught and trained teachers of English at both undergraduate and postgraduate levels. His major teaching-research areas are Text Linguistics, Reading Education, and Mediums of Instruction.

E. Doyle Stevick is Assistant Professor of Educational Leadership and Policies at the University of South Carolina, where he serves as Director of the Office of International and Comparative Education. His scholarly interests include issues of democracy and citizenship in educational leadership and policy. Current research projects involve Holocaust education policies and the use of international teachers in the United States. His books are *Reimagining Civic Education: How Diverse Societies form Democratic Citizens*, and *Advancing Democracy through Education? US Influence Abroad and Domestic Practices*, both with Bradley A. U. Levinson. He is currently completing a book, with Deborah Michaels, on education about the Holocaust in the post-Soviet bloc countries where it primarily occurred.

Xiaozhou Xu is Dean and Professor, College of Education, Zhejiang University. He is also Director of the Institute of Innovation Education and Entrepreneurship, the national innovative research base of "Innovation Management and Sustainable Competitiveness." His research focuses on Comparative Education, Education Policy, Higher Education, and Educational Innovation and Entrepreneurship Education. His many books include *Idea and Reality in Higher Education* (China Ocean University Press, 2009); "When China Opens to the World: A Study of Transnational Higher Education in Zhejiang, China" (coauthored with Ka Ho Mok and Xu Xiaozhou) *Asia Pacific Education Review* (2008); *Autonomy and Restriction: Comparative Studies on Policies of Universities* (Zhejiang Education Press, 2007); *Excellence and Efficiency: Studies on Prior Development Strategies of University* (Zhejiang Education Press, 2007); *Changes in Higher Education Policy Series* (which includes six books, ed. with Xu Hui, Zhejiang Education Press, 2007); *Modern Korean Higher Education* (Zhejiang University Press, 2007); *Educational innovation: Perspectives of internationalization* (ed., with Roberto Giannatelli. Zhejiang University Press, 2006); *History of Foreign Educational Thought* (7) (Hunan Education Press, 2002); and *Studies in the Recent Reforms of Higher Education Structure in the Europe and the United States* (Neimenggu University Press, 1997).

John L. Yeager is Associate Professor in the Administrative and Policy Studies Program in the School of Education at the University of Pittsburgh. In addition, he is serving as Director of the Institute for Higher Education Management. He has held several senior university administrative posts, such as Vice Chancellor for Administration and Vice Chancellor for Planning and Budget as well department positions. He has consulted and conducted in-service programs on a number of management subjects and in the development of strategic plans both in the United States and internationally. He currently teaches courses on institutional strategic planning, university finance, human resource management, and program quality. Internationally, he has worked in Mongolia, Kenya, China, Thailand, and South Africa. Currently his major interests are focused on international strategic planning and quality assurance practices. Dr. Yeager has published numerous papers, made professional presentations, and conducted workshops.

Zeinab F. Zein received a Bachelor of Arts degree and a teaching diploma in elementary mathematics and science education from the American University of Beirut (AUB). She continued her education by pursing a graduate degree of Master's of Arts in mathematics education at AUB. The thesis study focused on what ninth-grade students in Lebanon find interesting and useful in mathematics and how their views are connected to the current mathematics curriculum. She worked based in AUB for four years on a nationwide educational research project to improve the quality of elementary mathematics teaching and learning in Lebanon (MARAL-Math Reform for All in Lebanon). She has worked with field activities such as observing classes, examining teachers' actions, teaching in accordance with mathematical reasoning, and higher level thinking and communication. Other duties performed include data analysis and management, organizing conferences, and dealing with teacher development and reform issues in mathematics and science education.

Index